Praise for *The Green Scorecard*
and for Patricia Pulliam Phillips and Jack J. Phillips
of the ROI Institute

"Return on Investment is both the holy grail and the bogeyman of sustainability projects. Misunderstood, ROI can stop worthy projects or green-light terrible ones. Meanwhile, if narrowly defined ROI is the only criteria for determining project worth, we can probably kiss the planet goodbye. And yet ignoring ROI would be equally devastating. That's why a deep dive on this subject is crucial, and that's what Patti and Jack Phillips have done, in a way that will be useful and applicable."

—**Auden Schendler, Executive Director, Sustainability, Aspen Skiing Company**

"Sustainability initiatives have to create value in excess of their costs. *The Green Scorecard* provides a framework to do so. It will help executives move away from 'sustainability voodoo'—assuming projects create value—towards 'sustainability science'—demonstrating value through measurement."

—**Gregory C. Unruh, PhD, professor and Director, The Lincoln Center for Ethics, Thunderbird School of Global Management**

"Written in an easy-to-understand format, this book shows how to measure the success of sustainability projects with a balanced set of data including ROI. This is necessary for the integration of social and environmental impacts into management decision making and the inclusion of metrics for sustainability into ROI calculations."

—**Marc J. Epstein, Distinguished Research Professor of Management at Rice University and author of *Making Sustainability Work: Best Practices in Managing and Measuring Corporate Social, Environmental, and Economic Impacts***

"Jack and Patti Phillips unravel the mystery of measurement by presenting a balanced set of measures that show the full impact of programs, including bottom-line measures such as business impact and ROI."

—**Stephen R. Covey, author of *The 7 Habits of Highly Effective People***

"Return on Investment is an answer to what executives are asking for—Patti and Jack summarize everything a practitioner needs to know and do."

—**William C. Byham, President and CEO, Development Dimensions International, author of *Zapp! The Lightning of Empowerment* and *Heroz***

"Green is the business world's new gold, and the author ... ROI Institute, capitalize on that by adapting their Retu ... methodology to green initiatives. [The book] is well org ... divided into easily accessible segments....The subject n ...

The Green Scorecard

MEASURING THE RETURN
ON INVESTMENT IN
SUSTAINABILITY INITIATIVES

Patricia Pulliam Phillips
and Jack J. Phillips

ROI INSTITUTE™

NICHOLAS BREALEY
PUBLISHING

BOSTON · LONDON

First published by Nicholas Brealey Publishing in 2011.

20 Park Plaza, Suite 1115A
Boston, MA 02116, USA
Tel: + 617-523-3801
Fax: + 617-523-3708

3-5 Spafield Street, Clerkenwell
London, EC1R 4QB, UK
Tel: +44-(0)-207-239-0360
Fax: +44-(0)-207-239-0370

www.nicholasbrealey.com

© 2011 by Patricia Pulliam Phillips and Jack J. Phillips

Printed in the United States of America

15 14 13 12 11   1 2 3 4 5

ISBN: 978-1-85788-554-5

Library of Congress Cataloging-in-Publication Data

Phillips, Patricia Pulliam.
    Green scorecard : measuring the return on investment in sustainability
initiatives / Patricia Pulliam Phillips and Jack J. Phillips.
        p. cm.
    Includes bibliographical references and index.
    ISBN 978-1-85788-554-5 (alk. paper)
  1. Business enterprises—Environmental aspects. 2. Rate of return. 3. Social
responsibility of business. I. Phillips, Jack J., 1945– II. Title.
    HD30.255.P48 2010
    658.4'083—dc22

                                        2010032686

Contents

Introduction

Is Sustainability Sustainable?

Green Is Everywhere

In early 2010, we made a trip to the World Food Programme (WFP) in Rome to provide consulting services on our approach to program accountability, the ROI Methodology. The trip underscored the proliferation of green issues. As we waited in the Atlanta airport to fly directly to Rome, an announcement describing their waste and recycling initiatives declared their plans to become the greenest airport in the world. Aboard the plane, Delta's *Sky* magazine highlighted its efforts to save the environment. As we read *Forbes* magazine en route to Rome, we noticed that the editors announced Monsanto as the company of the year—based on their economic progress as well as their sustainability efforts. The *International Herald Tribune* had a story about the debate on the causes of climate change. The passenger to the right of us was reading a book by Ray Anderson titled *Confessions of a Radical Industrialist,* which highlights the company he founded, Interface, Inc., and its efforts to cut green house gases, fossil fuel consumption, waste, and water. (Incidentally, Ray Anderson was named one of *Time*'s "Heroes of the Environment" and one of MSNBC.com's "Top 15 Green Leaders.")

In Rome, we noticed displays in the hotel lobby that showed the hotel's commitment to the environment. In our room, informational flyers notified us that the housekeeping staff uses environmentally neutral cleaning supplies. We were given the option of not having linens changed or our towels washed each night to help conserve water and energy.

When we arrived at WFP headquarters, we noticed similar displays and announcements about WFP's efforts to engage employees in environmental initiatives. There were booklets about the environment and how its condition affects the food supply. A description of employee learning programs included information about courses on the environment.

That evening, we decided against a cab and walked to the hotel to avoid contributing to the pollution caused by automobiles. We discovered that even the restaurant offered an "environmentally friendly" dinner menu.

Needless to say, we are living in a world where green and sustainability rule—at least on paper—but how many of these efforts are paying off? And if it is so important, why aren't more organizations doing something about it? There is a need for accountability, often up front, to ensure that investments are made in the projects with the greatest potential of working—for the environment and the organization. That is where *The Green Scorecard* comes in.

The Focus on Sustainability

This everyday focus on sustainability is a relatively recent phenomenon. When the issue of global warming first surfaced in the 1980s, it stirred up much public debate and concern throughout the world. However, business leaders resisted the issue of global warming, expecting they would have to pay a lot of money to address the problems causing it. For example, when the United Nations (UN) formed the Intergovernmental Panel on Climate Change (IPCC) in 1989, business groups formed their own organizations— the Global Climate Coalition and the Competitive Enterprise Institute—to counter the issues and the debate about the causes of climate change. While most agreed that climate change was occurring, views differed regarding its origins, and finding solutions was not a priority to the business world at large.

Today, most (if not all) businesses recognize that climate change is a problem. The Global Climate Coalition was disbanded in 2002, and some businesses are making attempts to solve the problem of climate change, resulting in a wave of sustainability, climate change, and environmental projects.

From an organizational perspective, going green offers employees, contractors, volunteers, and other members the opportunity to influence the green movement through involvement and contribution. The challenge is to create the correct approach to involve these people—one that includes teaching, convincing, communicating, enabling, supporting, and encouraging participation in the green process. Mandating change is rarely a recipe for success (Stringer, 2009). Organizations must engage their people and position processes for successful green implementation.

The sheer number of green projects and initiatives, and the fact that not everyone is buying into the issues, brings into focus the need for this book. Many individuals do not see the need for action because they do not understand the issues or know what they can do to help. Some people do not understand green projects and sustainability efforts, feel inconvenienced by them, believe they are negatively affected in one way or another by project outcomes, or perceive projects to require unrealistic investment.

As we suggest in Chapter 2, too many organizations are currently caught in what may be called a green slump, struggling to engage in green projects and making far less progress than is actually required. A reliable measurement and evaluation system will help organizations manage green and sustainability projects so that they improve and thrive. In addition, the measurement approach should provide credible data for decision makers. Organizations must adopt a results-based, return on investment (ROI) focus that helps them identify, develop, and implement green projects that add value from an economic, environmental, and societal perspective. They need a green scorecard.

History of the ROI Methodology

The ROI Methodology described in this book was originally developed by Dr. Jack Phillips in the early 1970s. Its application in the training, development, education, and human resources fields is unmatched. Dr. Patti Phillips, his partner and wife, used her interest in the application of the ROI Methodology in economic, community, and international development to expand its use in government, nonprofit, and non-governmental organizations as well as in private sector organizations. Together, they have applied this approach to accountability in more than twenty fields, in more than fifty countries. To date, the application of the ROI Methodology includes the following areas of focus:

- Human Resources/Human Capital
- Training/Learning/Development
- Leadership/Coaching/Mentoring
- Knowledge Management
- Organization Consulting/Development
- Policies/Procedures/Processes
- Recognition/Incentives/Engagement
- Change Management
- Technology/Systems/IT
- Green Projects/Sustainability Projects
- Safety and Health Programs
- Talent Retention Solutions
- Project Management Solutions
- Quality/Six Sigma/Lean Engineering

- Meetings/Events
- Marketing/Advertising
- Communications/Public Relations
- Public Policy/Social Programs
- Risk Management/Ethics/Compliance
- Ethics/Compliance
- Healthcare Initiatives
- Wellness and Fitness Programs

The ROI Methodology offers a common approach to measure and evaluate project success, so organizations can compare results across functions and channels. More important, it allows organizations to develop information that can guide them to improve and reposition projects as they expand across areas of the organization. By addressing green measures (i.e. Kilowatt-hour usage; tons of solid waste), not only do projects drive improvement at the organizational level, but also with waste eroding our environment.

Motivation for Green

To date, the number one motivator for organizations to implement green projects is the image it presents to the public. Organizations want their constituents, consumers, employees, stakeholders, and any other observers to view them as environmentally friendly.

To examine this issue in detail, MIT conducted a year-long inquiry that involved in-depth interviews with fifty global leaders, followed by a survey of more than 1,500 executives and managers worldwide (Berns et al., 2009). The survey respondents cited the impact on a company's image and brand as its paramount reasons for addressing sustainability. The interview results also emphasized a broad continuum of rewards grounded in value creation. Here are the drivers for addressing sustainability, listed in order of importance:

1. Company or brand image
2. Cost savings
3. Competitive advantage
4. Employee satisfaction, morale, or retention
5. Product, service, or market innovation
6. Business or process innovation
7. New sources of revenue or cash flow
8. Effective risk management
9. Shareholder relations

In terms of importance, the image issue was rated two and a half times ahead of cost savings. This clearly shows the power of image as the principle driver. But this way of thinking is flawed if it ignores the value the project brings given the required investment. For example, if a green initiative is launched to reduce electricity usage and it does reduce electrical consumption, one might assume that the initiative was successful. But if the initiative cost is more than the consumption reduction is worth, has value been added to the organization? Could a less expensive initiative yield similar or even better results, possibly reaping a positive ROI? Questions like these are, or should be, asked on a routine basis. No longer will activity suffice as a measure of successful project implementation. A new generation of decision makers is defining value in a new way. Chapter 2 presents these new definitions of value.

Of course, green projects that improve operational measures valued at an amount that exceeds the investment will still enhance organization image, brand awareness, and reputation. A results-based focus to green projects and initiatives that includes ROI measurement will add value economically, environmentally, and socially.

Purpose of this Book

Throughout this book, our goal is to underscore the importance of and opportunity for measurement and evaluation, including ROI, of green projects. Specifically, *The Green Scorecard* offers the following:

- A proven methodology to evaluate the success of all types of projects and programs
- A balanced profile of success that represents the viewpoints of many stakeholders
- A results-based methodology to ensure that the projects are successful
- A process improvement technique that shifts the focus from evaluating the performance of those involved to improving the process to make the projects more successful
- A set of standards for a CEO- and CFO-friendly evaluation process

This book provides many examples of how to use this methodology, including projects and programs aimed at all types of environmental, climate change, and sustainability issues. The types of projects covered in this book include:

- Energy savings
- Green energy projects

- Water conservation projects
- Green technology projects
- Green meetings and events
- Air pollution projects
- Waste management solutions
- Green training programs
- Sustainable food projects
- Deforestation projects
- Green innovations projects
- Green marketing projects

Useful for every team member who works on a green project—but particularly executives charged with financial planning and accountability—*The Green Scorecard* presents examples in each of these areas. It shows how green projects can be successful with use of the ROI Methodology and underscores why the ROI Methodology is needed to ensure that such projects are effective and long lasting.

Patricia Pulliam Phillips
Jack J. Phillips
of the ROI Institute, Inc.
September, 2010

Part I

Going Green

From Kyoto to Copenhagen

Chapter 1

Green Is Everywhere

The Proliferation of Green Projects

As we discovered on our trip to Rome, which we've described in the Introduction, green is everywhere. This chapter focuses on the variety of green initiatives that permeate the landscape where we live, work, and play; highlights the forces that are driving green initiatives throughout organizations and communities; and addresses issues about managing this change.

The Green Revolution

A green revolution is occurring throughout the world. This effort toward fundamental change is particularly pervasive in the United States. Perhaps Thomas Friedman (2008) captures this revolution best in his bestselling book *Hot, Flat, and Crowded,* in which he makes the case for a green revolution that should sweep through organizations, cities, communities, and governments to create what he describes as the Energy Climate Era. Here are a few examples of green initiatives.

GREEN METROPOLIS

Discussions about environmental issues often dwell on cities, focusing on their congestion, inefficiencies, and unmanageable challenges. Tall buildings, consuming enormous amounts of energy, and heavy traffic, inundating the environment with carbon emissions, are obvious environmental hazards. The cities themselves have taken the brunt of many of the social ills that stem from poverty, illness, crime, pollution, open sewers, and exhaust fumes.

Despite these burdens, however, cities, with their great density, offer perhaps the best opportunities for environmentally friendly places to live and work. For example, the population in Manhattan is 67,000 people per square mile, more than 800 times the nation as a whole and roughly 30 times the city of Los Angeles (Owen, 2009). In every city, residents often swap the convenience of an automobile for proximity to their communities. Working near home allows people to live without the ecological disasters of cars, in contrast to workers who live in rural areas and have to use an automobile for every trip. In a city, people engage in environmentally friendly habits such as bicycling, mass transit, and walking while supporting each other as a community. Some cities are working hard to increase their residential appeal, which reduces the environmental burden caused by the mass exodus of the work force at the end of the day. Some cities, airports, and ports are striving to be the greenest in the world, with much progress. Here are three of the main ways that cities encourage residents to act as major contributors to sustainability efforts.

Driving Less

Perhaps the greatest impact on the environment comes from helping citizens drive less through the use of mass transit. Cities are investing large sums of money, including a large portion from The American Recovery and Reinvestment Act of 2009 stimulus package, in mass transit systems. Not only does this help the environment, but it reduces citizens' travel time and costs. Cities also promote carpooling and vanpooling through a variety of services and regulations of auto use, including high-occupancy vehicle (HOV) lanes. Some large cities, particularly outside the USA, are already restricting the use of automobiles in the center city for certain hours or days. For example, Bogotá, Columbia, is proposing a Car-Free Bogotá, which encourages the use of mass transit and reduces the number of vehicles in the city. Road-space rationing based upon the last digits of the license plate on pre-established days is used in cities like México City, Mexico; Santiago, Chile; and São Paulo, Brazil. Most cities promote walking, jogging, and bicycling as well, providing trails, special biking lanes, and pedestrian plazas. Collectively, these activities have an important impact on the environment.

Living Closer

One of the problems with cities in the past was that more people moved to the suburbs, depending on mass transit to transfer them to the city center. Large, multifamily dwellings, situated close to centers of employment, are now becoming common fixtures in major cities. During the past two decades, many cities have initiated downtown redevelopment projects, particularly in building loft apartments, in an attempt to bring the population back to the inner city. These buildings place people in compact areas conveniently located where mass transit may not be needed. Some city planners cluster businesses in the suburbs near neighborhood communities, which also makes the commute distances shorter.

Living Smarter

Cities are doing a great job of making people aware of how to live smarter, healthier, and more environmentally friendly lives. Recycling programs are often initiated and supported. Cities sometimes require or encourage sustainable products and services. Cities offer all types of networking opportunities to bring people together to discuss, promote, and implement green initiatives. Building codes often require construction to be environmentally friendly. Cities promote and sometimes require energy-efficient utilities. All types of educational opportunities are offered to bring the green movement to citizens.

Because more people now live in urban areas than non-urban areas, these projects hold much promise. For example, the opportunity to influence more than half of the people in the United States—city dwellers—is impressive. However, the success of these projects is often uncertain. With millions of dollars spent on renovating old retail buildings or warehouses to create chic, livable flats, one must wonder, "Does it really work?" Are these cities, which offer so much promise, seeing a return on their investment? Are the benefits of spending taxpayer dollars on these projects paying off for the taxpayers? Considering the return on investment, often from the outset, helps ensure money is spent on the projects that have the greatest potential for success for all stakeholders.

GREEN ORGANIZATIONS

In 1994, Interface founder and chairman Ray Anderson set a daring goal for his commercial carpet company: to take nothing from the earth that cannot be replaced by the earth. At the time, carpet manufacturing was a toxic, petroleum-based process that released immense amounts of air and water pollution and created tons of waste. Fifteen years later, Anderson's call for change at Interface has:

- Cut green house gas emissions by 82 percent
- Cut fossil fuel consumption by 60 percent
- Cut waste by 66 percent
- Cut water use by 75 percent

- Invented and patented new machines, materials, and manufacturing processes
- Increased sales by 66 percent, doubled earnings, and raised profit margins (Anderson and White, 2009)

Ray Anderson and Interface have been featured in three documentary films, including *The Corporation* and *So Right, So Smart*. In 1997, Anderson was named co-chair of the President's Council on Sustainable Development and in 2006 he served on the National Advisory Committee that helped guide the Presidential Climate Action Project, a two-year, $2 million project administered by the Wirth Chair School of Public Affairs at the University of Colorado. He and Interface have been featured in *The New York Times, Fortune, Fast Company,* and other publications. Unfortunately, there are not enough Ray Andersons and organizations like Interface. Still, here are a few ways green organizations like Interface are making a difference.

Organizing for Green

The starting point for most organizations is to organize properly for green initiatives. This process begins with a mission statement, a vision statement, and a value statement that all incorporate green issues and sustainability efforts. This also involves the assignment of specific responsibilities to individuals involved in green projects. Role definition for all organizational stakeholders is a must if involvement, support, encouragement, and accomplishment of green objectives is the goal.

Promoting Green

Employees must understand the necessity for green projects and be aware of important environmental issues. Formal and informal meetings and communications using the plethora of social media tools can help. Training and learning programs make employees aware of the issues and the necessity to make improvements and adjustments. Brochures, guides, fact sheets, program descriptions, and progress reports help to promote and encourage green project participation.

Practicing Green

Organizational leaders must "practice what they preach" through visible and substantial green projects. These projects should be communicated to the organization, and their successes should be clearly documented. An example of a highly visible project is one that has been undertaken by Hewlett-Packard. A problem exists with the mountains of consumer electronics being disposed of in landfills. To set the example in this important area, HP has collected more than a billion pounds of e-waste, the weight of 1,200 jumbo jets, since

1987. HP is on track to recover, refurbish, and recycle two billion pounds of e-waste by the end of 2010 (*www.hp.com/go/reuse-recycle*).

Enabling Green

Organizations and communities are enabling stakeholders to be involved in green projects in their communities and in their personal lives. Organizations assist employees with recycling programs and support employees in a variety of ways to understand, promote, and be involved in green initiatives. For example, eight communities in the Silicon Valley area joined to create Climate Prosperity Project, Inc., a nonprofit organization to pursue climate change and an economic development opportunity. The communities, Silicon Valley/San Jose, CA; Portland, OR; St. Louis, MO/IL; Denver, CO; Seattle, WA; Southwest FL; Montgomery County, MD; and the State of Delaware are convinced that not only does climate change represent an environmental imperative, but it represents an extraordinary economic opportunity.

Rewarding Green

Progressive companies are rewarding stakeholders, for being involved in green efforts. For example, in 2008, Southern Company launched EarthCents programs, which include new and existing programs and educational efforts to help reduce residential and commercial energy consumption. According to Susan Story, CEO of Gulf Power, a subsidiary of Southern Company, the benefits of EarthCents include not only wise use of energy, but also reduction of costs that hit the pocket of their customers. In addition, shareholders are rewarded because corporate costs are reduced and capital expenditures are avoided (Alliance to Save Energy, 2009). Through EarthCents education programs, employees have an opportunity to engage in stewardship that is highly valued and recognized by the organization. Some organizations provide quarterly or annual awards for green efforts by employees or groups of employees. Others provide bonuses for green ideas. SunRidge Farms, a grower of organic and natural foods, offers their employees a $5 per day incentive for riding their bikes back and forth to work as part of the SunRidge bike-to-work program. Rewards are effective in motivating individuals to do more.

Measuring Green

It is important for green project success to be monitored and adjustments to be made along the way. Results must be communicated to stakeholders even if they show processes are not working so well. The lobby of the International Fund for Agriculture Development (IFAD) boasts a large chart showing the progress of green projects. Measurement is a critical part of accountability, and making adjustments as measures are taken is a great way to keep projects on track.

Buying Green

Green organizations purchase green materials and supplies through the procurement function by specifying and requiring green products. This is important with cleaning materials, for example, which are toxic and hazardous to the environment. Purchasing green paper products is a highly visible way to contribute to the green movement, because it touches so many employees and stakeholders.

Selling Green

Progressive green organizations ensure that their products and services are sensitive to environmental issues and help support sustainability efforts. This may mean that new products are developed to support the green movement. For example, Office Depot researched how to transform their market based on creating a green office. These offerings include a green book catalog as well as a green office website (*www.officedepot.com/yourgreeneroffice*). This site provides customers with definitions of terms and certifications, such as post-consumer recycle content. Through its effort, Office Depot reinforces to businesses that there are real cost-saving opportunities with green products.

Collectively, these efforts are appearing and getting repeated in thousands of organizations. If implemented properly, they can make significant progress with sustainability efforts. The important point is to make sure the value and success of these projects are known to stakeholders responsible for design, implementation, and funding of projects. Measurement systems must be put in place not only to measure progress, but also to ensure that each green project is successful. In addition, the right measurement system will provide data that can show how a project can be even more successful in balancing economic, environmental, and societal needs.

GREEN BUILDINGS

Green organizations are housed in green buildings—or at least they should be. Green buildings represent another important opportunity and challenge. The opportunity exists because there are more than thirty million buildings in the United States, most of which are anything but green. These buildings consume about one quarter of the global wood harvest, one-sixth of its fresh water, and two-fifths of the material and energy flows. They account for about 65 percent of electricity consumption and 30 percent of primary energy use. A typical house in the United States produces 26,000 pounds of green house gases each year, enough to fill up a Goodyear blimp (Schendler, 2009). The challenge is that becoming a green building is not easy.

Building Projects

The good news is that major building projects across the country are now largely adhering to new benchmarks with environmentally sustainable construction standards, focusing not only on recycled building materials but on energy efficiency as well. At the center of this movement is a certification program offered by U.S. Green Building Council (USGBC). This program, known as LEED certification (Leadership in Energy and Environmental Design), is a third-party verification system to show that a building was designed and built using true environmental standards, including energy savings, water efficiency, and CO_2 emissions reduction. Almost all of the large-scale commercial projects in the US are now LEED projects, and given that more than half of the green house gases come from buildings (compared to 9 percent for passenger vehicles), this is a huge step in the right direction. One example of a green project is the University of South Carolina's new "Green Dorm." The dorm, housing 500 students, will reduce water consumption by over 20 percent and energy consumption by 30 percent as compared to traditional residence halls. They project an annual savings in water and energy costs of $50,000. To top it off, the new dorm is being built at the same cost as earlier traditional residences (Going Green Saves Green).

While there is some progress being made, considering that there are more than 30 million buildings already in existence, the current success rate is not impressive. To date there have been about 2,000 buildings LEED certified, with less than 20,000 registered but not certified.

Problems and Opportunities

Unfortunately, the greening of buildings has not necessarily entered into the home market. It is difficult to find a green home in any major subdivision in the United States. Builders claim that people are not necessarily interested in green; they are more interested in design, location, landscape, and decoration. Also, even when the LEED certification is achieved, it does not necessarily mean that the building is a well-built, well-designed facility, or that it is healthy. In their report, LEED Certification: Where Energy Efficiency Collides with Human Health, EHHI Report, non-profit organization Environment and Human Health, Inc. suggests that LEED standards are insufficient to protect human health (Wargo, 2010). An LEED certification means that the building achieved 26 of the 69 possible points. Unfortunately, builders are using the LEED certification as a test to pass at a minimum grade, not as a guide to building excellent green buildings.

Imagine a builder's challenge when attempting to build a green home. Doing so can add 10 percent to the cost. Yes, the payback for the owner will probably take less than ten years, but the builder usually has a fixed budget, the housing market is price sensitive, and the consumer is not necessarily willing to pay a 10 percent premium, even though the utility bills will be much less. Homes in the United States consume about 21 percent of the energy or 36 percent of total electricity used in this country.

The construction industry thus has an opportunity to influence the public's understanding, awareness, and perceptions. Consumers' attitudes must shift so that they will opt for paying more for a green building. They will, if convinced to do so.

GREEN WORKPLACE

When people are not at home they are usually at work, so the workplace represents another important area of focus for green initiatives. The workplace provides an opportunity for people to function in a green environment, learn about green issues, experiment with green projects, and observe cost savings at the same time. With regard to the green workplace, there are many areas of focus currently being addressed (Stringer, 2009).

Time and Place for Work

Perhaps the greatest opportunity to save money and have an impact on the environment is to take advantage of the many possible options that let people work at home. Some organizations allow two or more employees to use a single assigned workplace and rotate schedules. Sometimes several people share office space close to their home at a reduced cost. Of course, the greatest environmental benefit comes from working at home full-time. Telecommuting includes many other benefits besides green ones. Government agencies in the United States, such as the Internal Revenue Service (IRS), have been using telecommuting practices for years. They find that not only does the practice contribute to the environmental good, but many find that allowing employees to work at home has such significant savings in real estate costs, they are able to give up office space when leases expire. They also find that productivity increases, because the employees working at home are able to maintain larger work loads. Other benefits include retention, job satisfaction, and talent recruitment.

The benefits of telecommuting are huge, which leaves many to question why this practice is not more commonplace. Barriers often inhibit organizations in supporting a telecommuting strategy. Obviously, some work must be done onsite and, therefore, cannot be done at home. Manufacturing and service processes need to be managed with frontline employees at a particular location. Proprietary and classified information must remain onsite. Also, some employees have difficulty functioning in the home environment due to a variety of distractions and they often like the collegiality of the office environment. The greatest impediment can be managers who are unwilling to let go of the control of employees. Still, working from home represents a major opportunity to impact the environment as well as the organization's bottom line.

Green Office Products

Since the 1980s, businesses have been exploring ways to maintain a green workplace, from paper and toner cartridges to almost every office product category. Unfortunately, the traditional perception of making an office green is that costs will increase. This is not necessarily true. Even when items cost more initially, there is often a payback in the long run. Improvements have been made in the production of green office products. Businesses need to recognize that there is a green cost continuum. Some products, such as remanufactured ink or toner cartridges, are greener and less expensive. Also, investments in durable items rather than disposable ones, as well as in reusable and energy efficient items for the office, can mean dollars to the company's bottom line due to decreased operating costs and repurchase costs.

Brand and Image

Maintaining a green work environment creates an important image for consumers, employees, and others who know about and care about the green movement. Consumers are attracted to companies that are environmentally responsible, and employees often want to work for companies that put the environment first. This can be an attractive recruiting tool, particularly for younger employees who want to work in this type of environment.

Utilities

Another important savings at the workplace is the reduced use of water, electricity, and natural gas. Although technology, design, and control mechanisms can make a difference, behavior change in the workforce can have the greatest impact. Many cost-saving processes can lower the utility bills and help the environment. Simply shutting down computers at the end of the day and using motion-detection lighting can have a big impact on energy usage and operating costs. The University of South Carolina green initiative found that by replacing 250 CRT computer monitors with LCD flat screen monitors has the potential of reducing electricity consumption by $8,000 annually. They project that if all computer monitors are changed from CRT to LCD, the annual savings would be $325,466 to $976,500, depending on daily usage.

Employee Health

Indoor air quality is a critical issue for employee health and well-being. Mold in the workplace—along with exposure to laser toner, cleaning agents, carbon monoxide, aerosols, and other items—can lead to a variety of ailments for employees, such as asthma and nasal irritations. The strict use of cleaning products and proper use of heating, ventilation, and air conditioner system maintenance will make a difference.

The workplace is a fertile ground for many initiatives. It represents a major opportunity to shape employees' behavior. To do so will require a systematic approach to show the value, importance, and success of a variety of green initiatives.

GREEN MEETINGS

One of the top offenders to the environment is the meetings and events field, rated only second to the construction industry. Each year, tens of thousands of meetings are organized globally where people convene to discuss all types of issues. Substantial travel, large meeting places, and many hotel rooms have a huge impact on the environment. For example, the annual conference of the Society for Human Resource Management (SHRM), the world's largest association of human resource professionals, with about 250,000 members, attracts HR specialists, managers, and executives from around the world. A recent meeting in San Diego attracted some 12,000 participants, about a fourth of them from outside the United States. Everyone travels to the meeting; most of the travel is by air and many flights involve long distances. The conference accommodates nearly 2,000 exhibitors, and some exhibits are so large they need to be trucked in prior to the conference. Attendees take up thousands of hotel rooms, consume a tremendous amount of local transportation, and then travel back to their points of origin. The effect this one meeting has on the environment is significant. Multiply this by all types of professional associations, trade shows, and special events, and it becomes clear why this industry is destroying the environment.

Private companies are huge contributors to this industry. For example, a recent annual business development conference for CISCO Systems attracted more than 5,000 participants. The conference is so large that they had to meet in the Moscone Center in San Francisco. Sales teams from all over the world converged to discuss new sales and business development strategies. Starbucks, a company known for its efforts with the environment, recently brought its 10,000 plus store managers, district managers, and field leadership to New Orleans for the Starbucks Mega Leadership Show. The group used the Morial Convention Center and the New Orleans Arena for four full days. Imagine the impact that all the travel, hotel rooms, and activities had on the environment.

Obviously this industry needs attention because of its impact on the environment. At the same time, the organizers of these events claim that conferences are necessary, as do many of the participants.

A few experts in the green and environmental movements suggest that, for the most part, these large-scale meetings should go away. The conferences add little to knowledge and understanding, they destroy the environment, and much of what they do can be accomplished in other ways. While this is a harsh position, the industry is facing challenges on several fronts. Technology has enabled people to meet more conveniently and without the cost of travel. Also, many executives are questioning the value of this expenditure. The most recent global recession has put many events in the crosshairs of cost-cutting CEOs.

Obviously this industry is not going away, nor should it. The industry is important, and it serves a purpose. People need to experience events in person, they need to have face-to-face contact, and some situations require discussions that are not always possible through technology. Also, for some cities, such as Las Vegas, the meetings and events industry is the primary economic driver. Here are some strategies to help reduce the carbon footprint of these meetings.

1. The most extreme strategy is to eliminate all the meetings and events that are not successful. This is difficult because the industry has a history of not measuring the outcomes, but focusing entirely on the input to the process. Using their best guesswork, many executives and association leaders are trimming the meetings and events that appear to be less successful, based on whatever data they can accumulate.

2. Another extreme move is to suggest that most meetings can be completely accomplished with technology through webcasts, webinars, live meetings, social media, and other tools available for interaction and learning.

3. A more sensible approach perhaps is a blended approach, in which some meetings can be replaced with technology and other meetings can be enhanced with technology. For example, a portion of the meeting might occur online, followed by live meetings, thereby, reducing hotel stays.

4. Changing the structure of meetings is another option. Instead of holding large meetings that attract people from all over the country, smaller regional meetings can be scheduled. At least this would reduce some of the travel and, when combined with a blended approach, this option can be more productive. Many companies are taking this approach with corporate meetings.

5. The fifth option involves making the meeting green. Recognizing that sometimes we need to meet face-to-face, some organizers are focusing on ways in which to make meetings environmentally friendly through the choice of location, hotels, and facilities. They also attempt to keep printed materials to a minimum.

When considering these options, the best approach is perhaps to combine a little of each. At a minimum, meetings need to be as green as possible, perhaps eliminating unsuccessful ones, using technology in a way that enables—not necessarily eliminates—the process, and organizing regional meetings whenever possible. The meetings and events industry, through various trade associations such as Meeting Professionals International (MPI) and Professional Convention Management Association (PCMA), is determined to become more environmentally friendly.

GREEN ENERGY

Many observers see green energy as the key to solving the climate change problem. They posit that clean energy is the solution to all environmental ills. The topic of clean energy generates much attention, focus, and money, although some projections are bleak as energy demand increases. There are many projects and programs in place to tackle the issue.

Energy Efficiency

Suppliers of energy realize that the best way to work out of the crisis is to save energy. This is why electrical power companies and other energy providers are advising consumers on ways to save electricity. To them, this may be the only way to meet the demand. This involves saving energy through efficiency light bulbs, pumps and motors, good building design, and refined processes (Schendler, 2009).

Green Power

A variety of new green power sources are being developed from solar wind, small hydro, biomass, and geothermal sources. These are being funded in part by business energy users as they purchase renewable energy certificates (REC). With REC, businesses are buying power that is purchased from the new power sources and placed on the grid. It is impossible to hook a business up to a wind farm, but the business can purchase the equivalent of the power they need to be generated by the wind farm. It is like trading commodities in the commodity market. This is providing significant funding for new sources of green power. According to an article in the *Harvard Business Review*, six sources of limitless energy are under development (Morse, 2009). They are:

1. *High winds.* Conventional wind turbines stop when the wind dies. Turbine-bearing balloons or rotors could intercept powerful reliable winds 1,000 to 15,000 feet up.
2. *Green crude.* Biofuels made from plant oils require multistep harvesting and processing. Genetically engineered algae can streamline production by continuously secreting oil to be refined into transport fuel.
3. *Next wave.* Wave motion energy from the ocean can be captured to run electrical generators.
4. *Star power.* Nuclear fusion—the atomic reaction that powers stars—can be used to generate clean energy.
5. *Deep heat.* Conventional geothermal plants can detect heat only near the earth's surface. Enhanced geothermal systems (EGS), which inject cool water two miles or deeper into the earth for superheating, can work nearly anywhere.
6. *External sunshine.* Terrestrial solar cells are hampered by clouds, dust, and nightfall. Orbiting cells capture the sun's energy twenty-four hours a day nearly every day of the year, and then beam it in radio waves to earth.

These and other projects are currently under development with both private and public funding. They hold great promise to address the critical issue of clean energy.

GREEN TECHNOLOGY

A bright spot in the green revolution is the advent of technologies that support the movement and are in some cases central to green projects and sustainability efforts. Some advocates describe green technology as a huge growth opportunity in the next decade. Just as information technology exploded in the 1990s, green technology is set to be the next major growth sector. Renewable energy, sustainable agriculture, green building design, environmentally friendly construction and retrofits, greater efficiencies in lighting and appliances and smart grids, clean energy transportation—all are markets of promise to generate jobs and profits globally (Clinton, 2009).

Green technology does not have to represent huge projects; small devices can make a difference. Consider, for example, power adaptors, the boxes that sit between the plug and the mobile phone (some are integrated with the plug). There are about five billion power adaptor devices in use worldwide. The function of the power adapter is to convert high voltage alternating current into low voltage direct current that is used for mobile phones, iPods, and other electronic games. Until recently, the conversion was made using copper wire, and as much as 80 percent of the power was lost in the conversion.

Now, conversion can be made more efficiently with an integrated circuit, with as little as 20 percent of the power being lost. It took some time for the manufacturers, utilities, and state and federal authorities to work together to adopt them, but for consumers, the switches meant lower power bills and smaller and lighter power adapters. Although they cost a little more, the savings are tremendous. For the world as a whole, this has meant a drop in global power consumption that is worth about two billion dollars per year and saves thirteen million tons of carbon monoxide annually. This is equivalent to closing down eight coal-fired power stations ("Getting Warmer," 2009).

Technology projects are fast growing and almost limitless. Green technology patents are on a growth path, and the U.S. government is expediting the patent process, reducing the traditional time it takes for a patent to be processed from forty months to one year. Faster patent reviews mean that firms can arrange financing more easily. This action should generate additional research and development from private firms (large and small) and universities as well. New products will likely emerge, including patents for hardware, software, and communication devices to monitor commercial and home energy use. All types of technologies are being developed to cut carbon monoxide emissions.

Managing the Change to Green

The landscape is covered with all types of green initiatives and projects. Green is everywhere. But sustainability must be integrated, managed, and properly implemented to reap the greatest rewards. There are several factors that help drive the changes that are taking place in the green revolution.

GREEN IMAGE

As we noted in the introduction, the number one driver for implementing green projects is the image it presents of an organization. Green is in vogue in all types of organizations. Organizations recognize that it is in their best interests for their constituents, consumers, employees, stakeholders, and the general public to view them as environmentally friendly.

GREEN STRATEGY

In 2009, when Mike Duke took over as CEO of Walmart, the world's largest retailer, which uses more electricity than any other private organization in the world and has the second largest trucking company, his message to employees in a time of recession covered the expected topics about providing good service, keeping costs low, and beating the competition. However, he also talked about sustainability. Specifically, he described many of the environmental projects that Walmart has undertaken to reduce transportation and energy costs. He emphasized that these sustainability efforts must be accelerated and broadened in the future, regardless of the recession.

Why would the world's largest retailer, with approximately $405 billion in net sales during fiscal year 2010, (Walmart, 2010) focus so much on the green issue? Walmart sees this as a way to provide low prices as they manage and control costs, which enables them to stay profitable, drive innovation, and help many of their customers through difficult times.

Sustainability, which includes sustaining the life of an organization, the profits of the organization, and society at large, is a part of Walmart's strategy (Werbach, 2009). A green strategy often focuses on protecting and restoring the ecosystem, and it involves actions and conditions that affect the earth's ecology, including climate change, preservation of natural resources, and prevention of toxic waste.

During the last two decades, organizations have begun to incorporate strategies for sustainability with tremendous focus on green elements. Like all strategies, these plans must evolve from a clear understanding of where the organization is or where it can go, and they require the input and buy-in of all of the stakeholders. Plans should show how the strategies can be implemented and achieved with effort, determination, and deliberation. Organizations must review these strategies occasionally to see how they are working, and apply great leadership throughout the process to make sure that each strategy is challenging, feasible, workable, and successful.

GREEN TO GOLD

In 2008, DuPont launched a new bold energy plan to increase sales and lower energy costs. This goal identified 245 new projects that cost fifty million dollars to implement, but the initiative saves fifty million dollars every year, a short twelve-month payback. This comes from a company that has cut its green house gases by an astonishing 72 percent over the last two decades and set an aggressive goal to hold energy use flat. Today, DuPont uses 6 percent less energy than in 1990, despite growing 40 percent. There are two big lessons here. In tough times even the leanest companies can find new ways to slice costs, and they can add green initiatives and other resources that save the company serious money that falls quickly to the bottom line (Winston, 2009).

There is often a perception that a clean environment is going to cost everyone—that green initiatives come with a premium. This is not always the case. In fact, there are more opportunities for positive ROI values with green projects than negative ROI values (Esty and Winston, 2006). Progressive and smart companies use their environmental strategy to innovate, create value, and build competitive advantage, and the opportunities and products are endless. However, to convince a group of money-conscious executives to undertake green projects, a method must exist that shows there is value in these projects that will ensure continued funding and growth.

In our work at the ROI Institute, we have the opportunity to see hundreds of impact and ROI evaluation studies each year in a variety of different applications. For those that focus on sustainability, the rate of failure (i.e., a project delivering a negative ROI) is about the same across all functions, and it is typically low, usually ranging in the area of 20 to 30 percent. By using the data from an impact evaluation, project teams will adjust most projects to ensure they deliver value in the future. Only about 10 percent of projects are discontinued. A project is discontinued only if it cannot show business value when the principal reason for implementation is to drive business value.

The MIT Business of Sustainability survey of more than 1,500 worldwide executives and managers (Berns et al., 2009) underscores how value is created in green projects and sustainability initiatives. Figure 1.1 shows the different avenues for value creation, all leading to profits, cash flow, and total shareholder return.

According to Andrew Winston (2009), green projects may represent the best way to stimulate the economy to keep companies prosperous. He suggests four strategies to turn green into gold.

- *Get lean.* Generate immediate bottom-line savings by reducing energy use and waste.
- *Get smart.* Use value-chain data to cut costs, reduce risks, and focus innovation efforts.
- *Get creative.* Pose theoretical questions that force you to find solutions to tomorrow's challenges today.
- *Get engaged.* Give employees ownership of environmental goals and the tools to act on them.

As we continue to work to manage the change to green, one of the main challenges is to convince a variety of stakeholders about the value that green projects deliver, up to and including the financial ROI.

GREEN-COLLAR ECONOMY

Another important element of managing change involves taking advantage of the green-collar economy. This concept essentially addresses two of the biggest problems facing most countries: the economy and the environment. According to venture capitalist and 2006 Democratic candidate for governor of California, Phil Angelides, a green job is defined as "pay decent wages and benefits that can support a family. It has to be part of a real career path, with

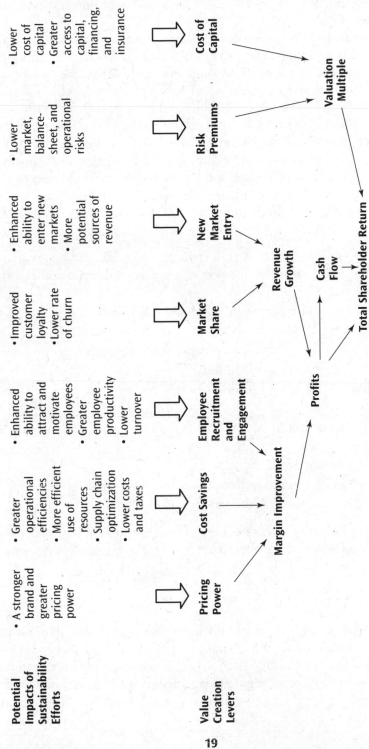

Potential Impacts of Sustainability Efforts

- A stronger brand and greater pricing power

- Greater operational efficiencies
- More efficient use of resources
- Supply chain optimization
- Lower costs and taxes

- Enhanced ability to attract and motivate employees
- Greater employee productivity
- Lower turnover

- Improved customer loyalty
- Lower rate of churn

- Enhanced ability to enter new markets
- More potential sources of revenue

- Lower market, balance-sheet, and operational risks

- Lower cost of capital
- Greater access to capital, financing, and insurance

Value Creation Levers

Pricing Power

Cost Savings

Employee Recruitment and Engagement

Market Share

New Market Entry

Risk Premiums

Cost of Capital

Margin Improvement

Profits

Revenue Growth

Cash Flow

Total Shareholder Return

Valuation Multiple

FIGURE 1.1 How Sustainability Affects Value Creation (Adapted from Berns et. al., 2009)

19

upward mobility. And it needs to reduce waste and pollution and benefit the environment" (Walsh, 2008).

Development of new green products and services, such as new sources of energy and new technologies, lead to new jobs. These jobs are significant in number and the investments are large enough to drive the economy. In addition to the bottom-line contribution both to those who obtain the new jobs and the economy at large, green jobs ultimately have a positive environmental impact (Jones, 2008). In the United States, the best example of perpetuating a green-collar economy is the American Recovery and Reinvestment Act, which included more than sixty billion dollars in clean energy investment intended to help jumpstart the economy and build clean energy jobs for tomorrow. This sixty-billion-dollar investment is expected to easily generate more than five hundred billion dollars in new jobs, business start-ups, expansion, and energy savings in the following areas:

- $11 billion for a bigger, better, and smarter electrical grid that will move renewable energy from rural places where it is produced to cities were it is mostly used
- $4 billion for smart meters to be deployed in homes throughout the United States
- $5 billion for low-income home weatherization projects
- $4.5 billion to green federal buildings
- $6.3 billion for state and local renewable energy and energy efficiency efforts
- $2 billion in competitive grants to develop the next generation of batteries to store energy
- $600 million in green training programs
- $500 million for green workforce training
- $100 million to expand line worker training programs

Collectively these types of efforts, plus the R&D functions driven by companies, entrepreneurs, and governments, can create a huge opportunity for green-collar jobs in the future.

GREEN BEHAVIOR

The fifty interviews conducted by MIT in the Business of Sustainability project revealed significant behavior changes that have taken place and must continue to take place. As organizations work to address environmental sustainability projects, there are eight management behaviors for leaders to keep in mind:

1. Sustainability projects will find you; it is hard to escape it. It is best to plan for it now.
2. Do not be surprised if you see unexpected productivity gains from green projects.
3. Your reputation is at stake; not addressing the green issues could seriously tarnish your efforts.
4. Strategy is needed and must be executed to see the system as a whole and to connect the dots.
5. Sustainability challenges demand innovation that is more iterative, more patient, and more diverse.
6. There must be collaboration across all boundaries to be successful.
7. The fear of risks has skyrocketed, creating a need for any practice or behavior that would assess risk and reduce it.
8. The first adaptors with particular processes will be the winners. (Hopkins, 2009)

With this push and need for sustainability, there must be a focus on changing the behavior of people involved in this process. Attitudes, perceptions, awareness, and the barriers to action must be addressed. As illustrated in the next chapter, there are many obstacles that can kill a project before it has a chance to add the value. The measurement process described in this book can be used to assess a project's success and allow leaders to make adjustments to drive results.

Final Thoughts

This opening chapter underscores the vast scope and opportunity that has arrived with the green movement that permeates all phases of our lives at home, at work, and at play. Green projects are being implemented for buildings, in the workplace, in organizations, and in cities. There is great opportunity and promise for these projects. Unfortunately, some of these efforts are not working so well. The next chapter focuses on some of the issues and problems, and it underscores why the ROI Methodology is needed to ensure that green projects are successful and long lasting.

Chapter 2

Is It Worth It?

The Value of Green Projects

"Is it worth it?" When asked this question about new or proposed green projects and sustainability initiatives, many executives, government officials, community leaders, and others involved with the environmental movement will answer with a resounding, "Yes!" Others, however, respond with hesitancy. Some need convincing that there is value in going green.

This chapter discusses the concept of value as it applies to green projects and sustainability initiatives. First, the chapter addresses the notion that we are in a green slump, making less progress than we need, and the reasons for it. Next, we define different types of value and how definitions are changing based on stakeholder perspectives. The chapter emphasizes the importance of addressing the value of green projects now. It also explains how a comprehensive approach to measurement and evaluation is necessary to measure value and to reposition projects to ensure success and improve results. Finally, the chapter addresses challenges with current measurement approaches and shows how the process described in this book addresses those challenges.

The Green Slump

The ultimate payoff of green projects and sustainability efforts is to address climate change, deforestation, food and hunger, and many other issues we face. Unfortunately, as we noted in the introduction, progress is lacking. Even at the micro-level, as hundreds of green projects are initiated every day, progress is minimal.

When we consider the problems facing the planet and its future state, the need for healing is evident. Unfortunately, there are some people who do not support sustainability efforts. While many individuals stand in the way of progress, much of their inertia is based on misunderstandings of the need to make improvements. The sad truth is that people struggle to change. Elected officials and business leaders are not highly respected these days, and so when they tell us, "Trust me, this is good for all of us, just go and do it," people tend to tune them out.

Table 2.1 shows some of the questions and issues that often arise when people are first introduced to green projects and sustainability efforts. They represent less than supportive attitudes toward such initiatives. These "green killers" inhibit progress and success. They are categorized along a five-level results framework that is fundamental to the ROI Methodology, which is the basis for this book and described in more detail in Chapter 4. The following sections explore each of the components of that framework in more detail.

REACTION AND PERCEIVED VALUE

As the "Reaction/Perceived Value" section of Table 2.1 shows, many people are still apathetic or believe their actions can make no real difference. They seem to think that sustainability is someone else's problem or that the only way to change it is through regulations and laws tackling the energy companies and the big polluters. In the book *Green to Gold* (Esty and Winston, 2006) the authors suggest several reasons why many green projects fail, including:

1. Visions that see the trees but not the forest
2. Misunderstandings about green issues
3. Expectations that green will always cost more
4. Subtle thinking
5. Claims outpacing actions

Because of these initial reactions to green projects, organizations must position them so employees and potential participants do perceive them as relevant and valuable.

LEARNING AND AWARENESS

Try this experiment. Take five of the important elements that describe climate change, such as change in average weather over time, increase in CO_2 in atmosphere, local species extinction due to global loss of biodiversity, variations in solar radiation, or abrupt climate change and ask your friends if they understand their meaning. Chances are, out of ten people, only one

TABLE 2.1 The Green Killers

Reaction/Perceived Value	**Learning/Awareness**
I cannot make a difference.	Why is this important?
This is not a critical issue.	What are the issues?
This is unnecessary.	I do not understand the
It is up to the government.	environmental problems.
It is not important to me.	How does this relate to me?
	What is my role in the green project?

Application/Implementation	**Impact**
This is inconvenient for me.	How will this help me?
I do not want to change.	How will this affect my work?
I cannot do this.	How will this impact my employer?
This does not fit my schedule.	How will this affect the environment?
This takes too much time.	
This will never work.	

ROI
This costs too much.
There is no money here.
This will be a negative ROI.
This is not worth it.

will be able to describe all five. There has not been enough specific information offered about climate change, particularly for the population born prior to 1970. Sustainability issues are now a part of most academic course curricula, but for the majority of the world's population, there has been limited education.

Consider the simple issue of changing to an alternative type of light bulb. In January 2007, Swedish power utility, Vattenfall, along with the help of McKinsey Consulting, Shell Oil, Volvo, and other collaborators developed a detailed study, including an abatement curve describing what methods would be useful for cutting carbons and by how much. In 2009, McKinsey updated the study with a new abatement cost curve (McKinsey, 2009). Some of these methods are more expensive than others, and some of them actually have a double advantage. One method with a double advantage—environmental impact and low cost to implement—is to change traditional light bulbs to more energy-efficient ones. In the United States, for example, lighting represents about 20 percent of all electricity usage. A standard incandescent light bulb costs around two dollars and uses about twenty dollars of electricity per year. In contrast, a low-energy bulb cost about eight to ten dollars but only uses about four dollars of electricity per year. With a cost reduction of $16 per year and an investment of $10, the benefits clearly exceed the costs.

While it makes sense financially as well as environmentally, for people to change their bulbs, changing to energy-efficient lighting is a behavior many consumers cannot conceive. Manufacturers of energy efficient bulbs suggest that the sales are not near where they should be, and they blame this on public apathy or lack of awareness. In this case, the public needs to be aware not only of how a particular green project can work (e.g., changing light bulbs) but also of its benefits to the climate as well as the pocketbook. The learning that must take place is substantial. The more people know, the less resistant they will become. Even with government interventions such as that of the European Union (EU), phasing out the less efficient incandescent bulbs and offering only energy efficient bulbs, educating the public is essential (Phasing Out Conventional Incandescent Bulbs, 2008).

APPLICATION AND IMPLEMENTATION

Perhaps the greatest problem with green projects is the inability to change current habits. Essentially, there is often limited application or implementation of processes focusing on green outcomes or at least at the level that may be needed to achieve desired results. This includes behavior representative of green consciousness. Sometimes people do not do what is needed because it is inconvenient, it requires a change of habit, or they think they cannot do it. Others think that it may take too much time and see many barriers to the actual success of the project. Still others see that they can do it but need support. In the book *Getting Green Done* (Schendler, 2009), the author tells a true story about the difficulty of getting a person to do what is needed and sustain that behavior:

> *After much political wrangling, you manage to install energy-efficient lighting in a high-end hotel restaurant. The project will save thousands of dollars in electricity costs while preventing tons of carbon emissions from entering the atmosphere. It is the "rubber meets the road" of the sustainability movement, the blue-collar work of the climate battle. The restaurant opens, and the manager is put off by the sight of compact fluorescent bulbs. He removes the bulbs, throws them out, and replaces them with inefficient halogens. Not*

because he is ignorant or because he does not care, but because he has a business to run and he is doing it the best way he knows how. His perspective is: You do not put energy-efficient fluorescent bulbs in a fancy restaurant any more than you would put Cool Whip on an éclair.

Nonetheless, this is what your sustainability efforts have brought you: a wasted design and installation fee; inefficient lighting; the manager's loss of faith in green technology; hundreds of expensive compact fluorescent bulbs that, instead of being reused (at the very least), are now leeching costs for new bulbs and installation. This true story happened a decade ago at Aspen Skiing Company. And there has been no improvement in that restaurant's lighting since (12–13).

There must be bottom-line consequences for many people to change their behaviors, particularly toward an outcome they believe is still somewhat elusive.

IMPACT

Most individuals sponsoring green projects want to know the impact a project is going to have and the specific measures it will drive. Those involved want to know how it will affect them personally. Employees want to know how it will affect their work or maybe even the employer. Others want to know the impact on a community group or city where they live. Some want to know what affect it has on the environment or how it helps the sustainability effort. Unfortunately, this evidence is often needed before the decision to begin is made. If the project involves savings in electricity usage, for example, some want to know *before investing* how much savings will occur. While there may be enough credible data to make a reliable forecast, the convincing needs to be strong.

When Auden Schendler first arrived at Aspen Skiing Company, he suggested retrofitting all the lights in the luxurious Little Nell Hotel (Schendler, 2009). Aesthetics and the availability of capital posed a problem to this simple cost-saving and environment-friendly move. Senior managers did not believe that retrofitting lights would save money. Schendler argued that every Fortune 500 company in the world was doing it, but senior managers remained skeptical and told him to prove it. At the next meeting of the company's senior managers, he took a watt-meter and showed the energy usage of the different light bulbs. When he tested incandescent light bulbs, the meter moved rapidly. When he tested the compact fluorescent bulbs, the meter slowed to a near standstill. Still, senior managers remained reluctant to spend the money. Only after additional discussion and analysis did the senior managers agree to invest (55-56). When this level of difficulty occurs with every project, some change proponents may give up, finding it easier to avoid the issue altogether.

From our work at the ROI Institute, we recognize that impact data are the most critical data executives want to see. Yes, the ROI is important but executives are often willing to invest in green projects if there are intangible benefits that do not figure into the ROI calculation. So, it is the impact data that are critical and they must be developed for many executives to invest.

ROI

Some people believe that green projects will result in a negative payoff. In fact, there is often an impression that a premium price is paid for anything that is green in nature. Perhaps this is based on history when, years ago, recycled paper was so expensive. (At the time, it was much less expensive to purchase the bright white new paper stock.) In reality, most green products can actually save money in the long term, but the perception still exists that the cost of green outweighs the benefits, resulting in a negative ROI. As such, people conclude that green is not worth it. More examples are needed to show the costs versus benefits for a variety of projects.

Green Washing

In addition to the perceived value and lack of results that inhibit forward motion with green initiatives, some organizations resort to green washing, which includes a bit of trickery and deception, much of which is purposeful. According to Lori Lake, President of GreenTV.com, green washing is the act of misleading consumers and other stakeholders regarding the environmental practices of a company or the environmental benefits of a product or service. Here are Lake's seven sins of green washing:

1. *Sin of the hidden trade-off.* A claim suggesting that a product is green based on a narrow set of attributes without attention to other important environmental issues. Paper, for example, is not necessarily environmentally preferable just because it comes from a sustainability-harvested forest.

2. *Sin of no proof.* An environmental claim that cannot be substantiated by easily accessible supporting information or by a reliable third-party certification. Common examples are facial tissues or toilet tissue products that claim various percentages of post-consumer recycled content without providing evidence.

3. *Sin of vagueness.* A claim that is so poorly defined that its real meaning is likely to be misunderstood by the consumer. The term *all-natural* is an example. Arsenic, uranium, mercury, and formaldehyde are all naturally occurring elements—and poisonous.

4. *Sin of worshipping false labels.* A product that, through either words or images, gives the impression of third-party endorsement where no such endorsement exists.

5. *Sin of irrelevance.* An environmental claim that may be truthful but is unimportant or not helpful for consumers seeking environmentally preferable products. The term *CFC-free* is a common example, since it is a frequent claim despite the fact that CFCs are illegal and cannot be used anyway.

6. *Sin of lesser of two evils.* A claim that may be true within the product category, but those risks distract the consumer from the greater environmental impacts of the category as a whole. Organic cigarettes could be an example of this sin, as might the fuel-efficient sport-utility vehicle.

7. *Sin of fibbing.* Environmental claims that are simply false. The most common examples are products falsely claiming to be Energy Star certified or registered. (Brewer, 2009)

Change Toward Green

Actions such as green washing represent a lack of buy-in and awareness. These gaps lead to inaction or inappropriate action affecting outcomes associated with green projects. While it is disappointing that attitudes, perceptions, lack of interest, and purposeful (or not) green washing seem to get in the way of making progress with sustainability efforts, these barriers exist with almost any type of change. For change to occur, even when it comes to green, people must have a favorable reaction, understand the issues, and take appropriate action. The good news is that most people have a genuine interest in sustaining and developing our world. Research conducted at Walmart and reported in the book *Strategy for Sustainability* (Werbach, 2009) describes some interesting findings. The author interviewed Walmart associates, exploring the basic concepts of sustainability and discussing what mattered to most of them. Here are some of the findings:

1. *They believe the environment is in crisis.* Once you remove the politics from the equation, people were ready to believe in global warming.

2. *They want to learn more about it.* Walmart associates value learning, and any time they had the chance to learn something new that they could share, they were excited.

3. *They want to do something about it.* They lead busy lives with complex demands from family, work, religion, and hobbies. But if they could do something to help the environment that would also help them achieve their other goals, they were all for it.

4. *They have not made sustainability their top priority.* Sustainability does not work as another "thing" to care or worry about. But when the author presented sustainability as a framework that could help manage the other priorities in their lives, from personal health to finances, they were able to conceive it as a matter of common sense.

Just as sustainability does not work for businesses unless it serves business needs first, sustainability does not engage individuals unless it first and foremost solves problems they experience in their lives (Werbach, 2009).

Value Redefined

Everyone has an opinion about value, and these opinions vary considerably. A person's reaction to involvement in a green project is representative of that person's perceived value. People may see it as important, necessary, and valuable, or they may see it as unnecessary, irrelevant, and a waste of time. As they become involved, they gain awareness of issues, principles, trends, terms, and concerns about environmental and sustainability issues. This new awareness also represents value.

"Show me the money" represents the newest value statement toward green projects. Many initiatives are measured by activity, such as the number of people involved, the number of actions taken, and the time to complete. Less consideration is given to the benefits derived from these activities. Today the value definition has shifted: value is defined by results more than activity. More frequently, value is defined as monetary benefits compared with costs.

The ROI Methodology described in this book can "show the money" in a credible way. The process had its beginnings in the 1970s and has since expanded in recent years to become the most comprehensive and broadreaching approach to demonstrating the value of investing in projects.

TYPES OF VALUES

Value is determined by stakeholders' perspectives, which may include organizational, spiritual, personal, and social values. Value is defined by consumers, employees, taxpayers, and shareholders. Capitalism defines value as the economic contribution to shareholders. The Global Reporting Initiative (GRI), established in 1997, defines value from three perspectives: environmental, economic, and societal.

Even as projects, processes, and programs are implemented to improve the social, environmental, and economic climates, monetary value is often sought to ensure that resources are allocated appropriately and that investments reap a return. No longer is it enough to report the number of projects initiated, the number of participants or volunteers involved, or the awareness generated through a green project. Stakeholders at all levels—including executives, shareholders, managers and supervisors, taxpayers, project designers, and participants—are looking for outcomes, and in many cases, the monetary values of those outcomes.

THE IMPORTANCE OF MONETARY VALUES

Some critics are concerned that too much focus is placed on economic value. But it is economics, or money, that allows organizations and individuals to contribute to the greater good. Monetary resources are limited, and they can be put to best use—or underused or overused. Organizations and individuals have choices about where they invest these resources. To ensure that monetary resources are put to best use, they must be allocated to programs, processes, and projects that yield the greatest return. The good news is that most green projects can create a positive return for their investors.

As an example, the ROI Institute was involved in a green project with a large non-governmental organization (NGO) based outside the United States. The organization had not focused much on green issues, and they wanted to pursue several green projects. We discussed measuring the impact and monetary value to demonstrate the success of the project. They dismissed this suggestion as unnecessary; they simply wanted the public and their donors to view the agency as a green organization.

However, while this type of thinking is typical at the onset of many green projects, it only works for those projects that are inexpensive, easy to implement, and consume only a limited amount of resources. Comprehensive projects involving large numbers of people and high costs require a different type of accountability, one that shows the impact and ROI. Activity will no longer suffice as a measure of results. As we noted in the introduction, a new generation of decision makers is defining value in a new way.

THE "SHOW ME" GENERATION

Figure 2.1 illustrates the requirements of the "show me" generation. "Show me" implies that stakeholders want to see actual data (i.e., numbers and measures). This request is the initial attempt to see value in projects. This request has evolved into "show me the money," a direct call for financial results. But this alone does not provide the monetary evidence needed to ensure that projects add value. The assumed connection between projects and value must give way to the need to show the *amount* of connection. Hence, "show me the real money" is an attempt at establishing credibility. This phase, though critical, still leaves stakeholders with an unanswered question: "Do the monetary benefits linked to the project outweigh the costs?" This final question

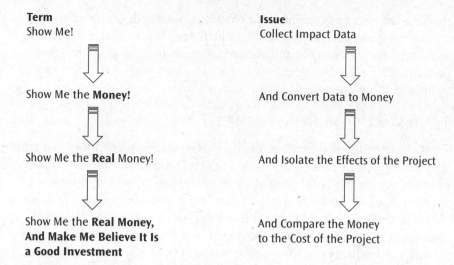

Term
Show Me!

Issue
Collect Impact Data

Show Me the **Money!**

And Convert Data to Money

Show Me the **Real** Money!

And Isolate the Effects of the Project

Show Me the **Real Money,
And Make Me Believe It Is
a Good Investment**

And Compare the Money
to the Cost of the Project

FIGURE 2.1   The "Show Me" Evolution

is the mantra for the new "show me" generation: "Show me the real money, and make me believe it is a good investment." But this new generation of green project sponsors also recognizes that value is more than just a single number. Value is what makes the entire organization system tick—hence the need to report value based on people's various definitions.

THE NEW DEFINITION OF VALUE

The changing perspectives of value and the shifts that are occurring in organizations have all led to a new definition of value. Value is not defined as a single number. Rather, its definition is composed of a variety of data points. Value must be balanced with quantitative and qualitative data, as well as financial and nonfinancial perspectives. The data sometimes reflect tactical issues, such as activity, as well as strategic issues, such as ROI. Value must be derived at different time frames, and it does not necessarily represent a single point in time. It must reflect the value systems that are important to all stakeholders. Data composing value must be collected from credible sources, using cost-effective methods, and value must be action oriented, compelling individuals to change habits and make adjustments in their processes. And yes, value may be intangible, not converted to money.

The processes used to calculate value must be consistent from one project to another. Standards must be in place so that results can be compared. These standards must support conservative outcomes, leaving assumptions to decision makers. The ROI Methodology presented in this book meets all these criteria. It captures six types of data that reflect the issues contained in the new definition of value: reaction and perceived value, learning and awareness, application and implementation, impact, return on investment, and intangible benefits (those impact measures not converted to money, but still important to outcomes).

Why Now?

In the past decade, a variety of forces have driven additional focus on measuring the impact of green projects, including financial contribution and ROI. These forces have challenged the ways of defining green success.

PROJECT FAILURES

Almost every organization encounters unsuccessful projects—including green projects that go astray, costing far too much and failing to deliver on promises. Project disasters occur in business organizations as well as in government and nonprofit organizations. Some project disasters are legendary. Some are swept into closets and covered up, but they exist, and the numbers are far too large to tolerate. They are rarely reported in the literature or media. These failures have generated increased concerns about measuring project and program success—before, during, and after implementation. Many critics of these projects suggest that the failure can be avoided if:

1. The project is based on a legitimate need from the beginning.
2. Adequate planning is in place at the outset.
3. Data are collected throughout the project to confirm that the implementation is on track and adjustments are made accordingly.
4. An impact study is conducted to detail the project's contribution.

Unfortunately, these steps are sometimes unintentionally omitted, not fully understood, or purposely ignored; hence, greater emphasis is being placed on the processes of accountability.

PROJECT COSTS

The costs of projects and programs continue to grow. As costs rise, the budgets for these projects become targets for others who would like to have the money for their own projects. What was once considered a mere cost of doing business is now considered an investment, to be wisely allocated. These days, the annual direct costs of these projects are hundreds of billions of dollars in the United States. Some large organizations spend as much as one billion dollars every year on green initiatives. With numbers like these, green is no longer considered a frivolous expense (as it was twenty years ago); rather, it is regarded as an investment, and many executives expect a return, both environmentally and economically. Take for instance, recycling. It is seemingly a simple enough effort to contribute to environmental sustainability; however, it is one in which many organizations and municipalities are unwilling to invest due to the cost versus benefit. In 2002, New York City temporarily halted its glass and paper recycling due to the cost. According to Mayor Michael Bloomberg, the benefits of recycling plastic and glass were outweighed by the cost, citing that recycling cost twice as much as disposal (Earth Talk, n.d.). In 2005, the city of Baltimore faced a similar decision. Curbside pickup was placed on the chopping block and was only removed when taxes were increased (Evitts, 2004). Project cost is a key cause for the interest in measuring the return on green investments.

ACCOUNTABILITY TREND

A consistent and persistent trend in accountability is evident in organizations across the globe: today almost every function, process, project, or initiative is judged based on higher standards than in the past. Various functions in organizations are attempting to show their worth by capturing and demonstrating the value they add to the organization. They compete for funds; therefore, they have to show value. For example, the research and development function must show its value in monetary terms to compete with mainstream processes, such as sales and production, which for more than a century have shown their value in direct monetary terms. The green movement is not exempt from this trend. Because it is relatively new, sometimes mysterious, a little uncertain, and often expensive, accountability is surrounding green projects.

BUSINESS FOCUS OF GREEN MANAGERS

In the past, managers of support functions (such as environmental and sustainability departments) in government, nonprofit, and private organizations had little business experience. Today things have changed. Many of these managers have a business background, a formal business education, or a business focus. These enlightened managers are more aware of bottom-line issues in the organization and are more knowledgeable of operational and financial concerns. They have studied the use of ROI in their academic preparation, where the ROI Methodology was used to evaluate purchasing equipment, building new facilities, or buying a new company. Consequently, they understand and appreciate ROI and are eager to apply it in the area of green management.

THE GROWTH OF PROJECT MANAGEMENT

Green initiatives and sustainability efforts represent projects in organizations—projects that must be managed with a schedule and budget. Few processes in organizations have grown as much as the use of project management. Just two decades ago it was considered a lone process, attempting to bring organizational and management structure to project implementation. In contrast, today, for example, the Project Management Institute (PMI), which offers three levels of certification for professional project managers, has more than two hundred thousand members in 125 countries. Jobs are being restructured and designed to focus on projects. The growing use of project management solutions, tools, and processes requires a heavy investment for organizations. With this growth and visibility come requests for accountability. Critics want to know if they are producing results—and this includes the management of green projects.

EVIDENCE-BASED OR FACT-BASED MANAGEMENT

Recently, an important trend in the use of fact-based or evidence-based management has worked its way into green projects. Although many key decisions have been made using instinctive input and gut feeling, more managers are now using sophisticated and detailed processes to show value. Important decisions must be based on more than gut feeling or the blink of an eye. With a comprehensive set of measures, including financial ROI, better organizational decisions regarding people, products, projects, and processes are possible.

When taken seriously, evidence-based management can change how every manager thinks and acts. It is a way of seeing the world and thinking about the craft of management. Evidence-based management proceeds from the premise that using better, deeper logic and facts to the extent possible helps leaders do their jobs better. It is based on the belief that facing the hard facts about what works and what does not work, and understanding and rejecting the total nonsense that often passes for sound advice, will help organizations perform better. This move to fact-based management sometimes expands measurement to include ROI.

REDUCTION IN SUPPORT STAFF

Green initiatives and projects usually reside in support functions in organizations, although the issues cut across all functions, including operations and sales. Sometimes the function reports to environmental affairs, engineering, operations, marketing, public relations, or human resources.

Support functions are often regarded as overhead, a burden on the organization, and an unnecessary expense. The approach of some top executives is to outsource, automate, or eliminate overhead. Great strides have been made in all three approaches. These days, staff support departments must show value to exist as viable support functions or administrative processes. Since green projects and sustainability efforts are usually administered as a support (or staff) function, they must show value to continue to be funded at appropriate levels.

BENCHMARKING LIMITATIONS

For years, executives have been obsessed with benchmarking, using benchmarking studies to compare every type of process, function, and activity. Unfortunately, benchmarking has its limitations. First, the concept of best practices is sometimes an elusive issue, particularly with green projects. Not all participants in a benchmarking project or report necessarily represent the best practices. In fact, they may represent just the opposite. Benchmarking studies are developed from organizations willing to pay to participate. So, while these organizations may be doing well, they do not represent the many others who are investing their resources in getting the job done. Second, what is needed by one organization is not always needed by another. An organization new to green projects will have needs (business, environmental, and otherwise) that are different from an experienced organization with a twenty-year history of sustainability efforts. A specific benchmarked measure or process may be limited in its use by some. Finally, the benchmarking data are often lacking measurement data, reflecting few if any measures of the success and financial contributions with ROI values. Because of this, executives have asked for more specific internal processes that can show these important measures.

THE EXECUTIVE APPETITE FOR MONETARY VALUE

For years, managers and department heads in public relations, public affairs, corporate communications, and human resources convinced executives that their processes could not be measured and that the value of their activities should be taken on faith. Unfortunately, many green projects were implemented as "faith-based" initiatives as well. Today, executives no longer buy that argument; they demand the same accountability from these functions as they do from the sales and production areas of the organization. "Show me the money" is more than a line from a Tom Cruise movie. Top executives are requiring organizations to shift their measurement and evaluation processes to include financial impact and ROI.

The Chain of Impact for Green Projects

Sometimes it is helpful to think about the success of a green project in terms of a chain of impact that must occur if the project is going to be successful in terms of business contribution. After all, if there is no business contribution, it is unlikely the project will be implemented. The chain of impact includes the five categories of data discussed in general terms previously. These categories, also referred to as levels, are Reaction and Perceived Value (Level 1), Learning and Awareness (Level 2), Application and Implementation (Level 3), Impact (Level 4), and ROI (Level 5). Together, these five levels form a chain of impact that occurs as projects are implemented. But this chain of impact begins with the inputs to the process. Inputs, referred to as Level 0, define the people involved in the project, how long it will take it to work, and the cost, resources, and efficiencies. Obviously, these data are essential to move forward with a project, but they do not speak to the success of the project. It is through reaction, learning, and application of knowledge, skill, and information that a positive impact on business measures is attained. Stakeholders realize how much impact is due to the project because a step occurs that will isolate the effects of the project from other influences. Impact measures are converted to money and compared to the cost to determine the ROI. In addition, to these outcomes, intangible benefits are reported. Though they are not a new level of data, intangibles represent impact measures purposefully not converted to money and are always reported in addition to the monetary contribution of a project. Figure 2.2 represents this chain of impact that occurs through the implementation of green projects and key questions asked at each level.

Reaction is the first level of outcome. Participants in the project must see the value in green projects. They must perceive the project is important, necessary, useful, and practical. If the reaction is adverse, the project is dead.

Next, there must be learning (Level 2). With green projects, there is a tremendous amount of learning and awareness that must occur for projects to be successful. As this chapter has already explored, there is much to be learned about climate change, environmental issues, and sustainability and green projects as they are implemented. Learning involves several issues. Participants involved must understand the issue itself, they must understand what they need to do and what is involved in the project, and they must be aware of the project's potential success. If no learning occurs, the project is dead. For example, when the city of New York stopped their recycling program a research study found that the city failed to educate its citizens about the recycling program. Many residents did not know what they could put out on the curb, and many could not identify eight out of twelve household items

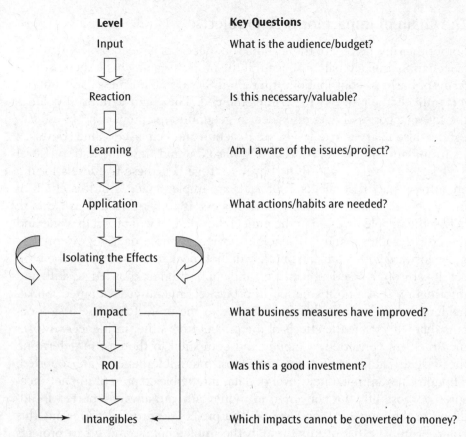

Level	Key Questions
Input	What is the audience/budget?
Reaction	Is this necessary/valuable?
Learning	Am I aware of the issues/project?
Application	What actions/habits are needed?
Isolating the Effects	
Impact	What business measures have improved?
ROI	Was this a good investment?
Intangibles	Which impacts cannot be converted to money?

FIGURE 2.2   The Chain of Impact for Green Projects

as either recyclable or not (Evitts, 2004). Positive results at the learning level are essential if successful implementation is to occur.

Level 3 is Application, which represents action on the part of the participants involved in the project. They must change their habits, take action, take new steps, or change procedures. This is activity (i.e., action, behavior), which is essential for the project to be successful. Unfortunately, it is at this level that projects usually break down. People often do not do what they need to do. There are many barriers to success with application; these barriers have to be identified and either removed, minimized, or circumvented. In addition to barriers, enablers exist to support successful application. These must be identified and enhanced to allow people to fully engage in projects and have success with them.

Level 4 is Impact. What participants know and what they do with what they know leads to a consequence, or impact, on key measures. When people

are involved in green projects, they want to know why they should participate. This answers the question, "So what?" What will be the impact? Will
there be a cost savings? Will there be a reduction in waste? Will there be improvement? As project implementation succeeds, efficiencies result, meaning we use less electricity, fuel, or paper. In addition, long-term impacts, such
as reduction in carbon emissions, occur. These impact measures, which are
available in organizational record systems, represent the most important data
set for top executives, leaders, and administrators.

Finally, Level 5 is ROI. Still, for some, the ultimate evaluation is a comparison of the costs and benefits. If the monetary benefits exceed the costs
of the project it is perceived as a good investment, economically. Positive
economic returns are critical to the continuation of any initiative.

Another data set, not level, that is critical in this chain of impact is the
intangibles. Again, not a new level of outcome measures, intangibles are the
impact measures that cannot be converted to money credibly with minimum
resources. These are important and often provide the rationale for many of
the early projects an organization selects. Image, reputation, and brand are
powerful measures, even without the monetary value tied to them. These
measures are often reported as intangible. Positive results at each level of the
chain of impact are critical to achieving a positive ROI.

The Problem with Current Measurement and Evaluation Systems—and How to Improve Them

For the most part, the current systems of measuring and evaluating green
projects and sustainability efforts fall short of providing the proper system for
accountability, process improvement, and results generation. As we examine
the ways in which projects are evaluated, we see ten areas for improvement.
Table 2.2 lists each problem or issue and presents what is needed for improvement. It also shows how the ROI Methodology meets all ten of these areas.

FOCUS OF USE

Sometimes evaluation looks like auditing. Someone checks to see if the project is working as planned, and a report is generated to indicate if there is a
problem. Many capital expenditures, for example, are often implemented
this way. The project is approved by the board, and after it is completed, a
board-mandated follow-up report is produced by internal auditors and presented to the board. This report points out how things are working and/or
not working, often at a point that is too late to make any changes. Even in
government, social sciences, and education, the evaluations are often struc-

TABLE 2.2 Problems and Opportunities with Current Measurement Systems

Topic	Problem or Issue	What Is Needed	ROI Methodology
Focus of use	Audit focus—punitive slant	Process improvement focus	This is the number one use for the ROI Methodology
Standards	Few, if any, standards exist	Standards needed for consistency and comparison	Twelve standards accepted by users
Types of data	Only one or two data types	Need a balanced set of data	Six types of data representing quantitative, qualitative, financial, and non-financial data
Dynamic adjustments	Not dynamic—does not allow for adjustments early in the project cycle	A dynamic process is needed so that adjustments are made—early and often	Adjusts for improvement at four levels and at different time frames
Connectivity	Not respectful of the chain of impact that must exist to achieve a positive impact	Data must be collected at each stage of the chain	Every stage has data collection and includes a method to isolate the project's contribution
Approach	Activity based	Results based	Twelve areas for results-based processes
Conservative nature	Analysis not very conservative	A conservative approach is needed for buy in	Very conservative: CFO and CEO friendly
Simplicity	Not user friendly—too complex	User friendly, simple steps	Ten logical steps
Theoretical foundation	Not based on sound principles	Should be based on theoretical framework	Endorsed by hundreds of professors and researchers; grounded in research and practice
Acceptance	Not adopted by many organizations	Should be used by many	More than 5,000 organizations using the ROI Methodology

tured in a similar way. For example, our friends in the British government tell us that when new projects are approved and implemented, there are always funds set aside for evaluation. When the project is completed, an evaluation is conducted and a detailed report is sent to appropriate government authorities. Unfortunately, these reports reveal that many of the programs are not working, and it is too late to do anything about it. Even worse, the people who implemented the project are either no longer there or no longer care. When there is accountability, often the evaluation reports serve as punitive information to blame the usual suspects or serve as the basis for a performance review of those involved.

It is no surprise that auditing with a punitive twist does not work with green projects. These project evaluations must be approached with a sense of process improvement. If the project is not working, then changes must take place for it to be successful in the future. Process improvement is the focus of the ROI Methodology.

STANDARDS

Unfortunately, many of the approaches to evaluate green projects lack standards unless the project is a capital expenditure, in which case the evaluation process is covered by Generally Accepted Accounting Principles (GAAP). However, many green projects are not capital expenditures. In these instances, standards must be employed to ensure consistent application and reliable results.

Overall, the standards provided by the ROI Methodology as described in Chapter 4 provide consistency, conservatism, and cost savings as the project is implemented. This enables the results of one project to be compared to those of another, and the project results to be perceived as credible.

TYPES OF DATA

The types of data that must be collected vary. Unfortunately, many projects focus on impact measures alone, showing cost savings, less waste, improved productivity, or less energy consumption. These are the measures that will change if this project is implemented. At most, there are a couple of types of measures, including intangibles.

What is needed is a balanced set of data that contains financial and nonfinancial measures as well as qualitative and quantitative data. Multiple types of data not only show results of investing in green projects, but help explain how the results evolved and how to improve them over time. As shown in Figure 2.2, the ROI Methodology develops six types of data including reaction, learning, application, impact, ROI, and intangible benefits.

DYNAMIC ADJUSTMENTS

As mentioned earlier, a comprehensive measurement system must allow opportunities to collect data throughout the project implementation rather than waiting until it has been implemented (perhaps only to find out it never worked from the beginning). Reaction and learning data must be captured early. Application data are captured when project participants are applying knowledge skills and information routinely. All of these data are used to make adjustments in the project to ensure success, not just to report post-program outcomes at a point that is too late to make a difference. Impact data are collected after routine application has occurred and represent the consequences of implementation. These data may not be connected to the project and must be monitored and reviewed in conjunction with the other levels of data. Once the connection is made between impact and the project, a credible ROI is calculated. The ROI Methodology allows data to be collected early and often, using the information gathered to make adjustments throughout project implementation.

CONNECTIVITY

For many measurement schemes, it is difficult to see the connection between the project and the results. It is often a mystery as to how much of the reported improvement is connected to the project, or even if there is a connection.

Data need to be collected through the process so that the chain of impact is validated. In addition, when the business measure improves, there must be a method to isolate the effects of the project on the data to validate the connection to the measure. The ROI Methodology described in this book provides both methods.

APPROACH

Too often, the measurement schemes are focused on activities. People are busy. They are involved. Things are happening. Activity is everywhere. However, activities sometimes are not connected to impact. The ROI Methodology is based on results. Not only does the process track monetary results, but also its steps and processes along the way focus on results. It is a measurement process with the inherent ability to drive improvement. By having a measurement process in place, the likelihood of positive results increases. A complete focus on results versus activity improves the chances that people will react positively, change their attitudes, and apply necessary actions, which leads to a positive impact on immediate and long-term outcomes.

CONSERVATIVE NATURE

Many assumptions must be made in the collection and analysis of data. If these assumptions are not conservative, then the numbers are overstated and unbelievable, which decreases the likelihood of accuracy and buy-in. The ROI Methodology has conservative assumptions known as guiding principles that are CFO and CEO friendly.

SIMPLICITY

Too often, measurement systems are complex and confusing for practical use, which leaves users skeptical and reluctant to embrace them. The process must be user-friendly, with simple, logical, and sequential steps. It must be void of sophisticated statistical analysis and complicated financial information, at least for the projects that involve participants who lack statistical expertise. The ROI Methodology is a step-by-step, logical process that is user-friendly, even to those who do not have statistical or financial backgrounds.

THEORETICAL FOUNDATION

Sometimes measurement systems are not based on sound principles. They use catchy terms and inconvenient processes that make certain researchers and professors skeptical. A measurement system must be based on sound principles and theoretical frameworks. Ideally, it must use accepted processes as it is implemented. The ROI Methodology has been endorsed by hundreds of professors and researchers who have participated in our certification process with a goal of making it better. The books written by the ROI Institute's top executives have been adopted by more than one hundred universities.

ACCEPTANCE

A measurement system must be used by practitioners in all types of organizations. Too often, the measurement scheme is presented as theoretical and lacks evidence of widespread use. The ROI Methodology, first described in publications in the 1970s and 1980s (with an entire book devoted to it in 1997 (Phillips, 1997), now enjoys 5,000 users. It is used in all types of projects and programs including technology, quality, marketing, and human resources. In recent years it has been adopted for green projects and sustainability efforts.

The success of the ROI Methodology will be underscored in detail throughout this book with examples of applications. It is a comprehensive process that meets the important needs and challenges of those striving for successful green projects.

Green Leadership: Getting Results

Strong leadership is necessary for projects to work. Leaders must ensure that green projects and sustainability efforts are designed to achieve results rather than just to improve image. These projects and efforts must deliver the value that is needed by all stakeholders. Table 2.3 shows the twelve actions that must be taken to provide effective, results-based green leadership, which is critical to delivering results at the ultimate level, ROI. However, only one of the items involves data collection and evaluation (number 11). The remaining leadership areas represent steps and processes that must be addressed throughout a green project's cycle. We developed these actions after observing, studying, conducting, and reviewing literally thousands of ROI studies. At the ROI Institute, we know what keeps projects working and what makes

TABLE 2.3 Green Leadership for Results
1. Allocate appropriate resources for green projects and sustainability efforts.
2. Assign responsibilities for green projects and programs.
3. Link green projects and programs to specific business needs.
4. Address performance issues involving the key stakeholders in the project, identifying the behavior that must change.
5. Understand what individuals must know in order to make projects successful, addressing the specific learning needs.
6. Develop objectives for the projects at multiple levels, including reaction, learning, application, impact, and, yes, ROI.
7. Create expectations for the projects' success with all stakeholders involved, detailing their role and responsibilities.
8. Address the barriers to a successful project early, so that the barriers can be removed, minimized, or circumvented.
9. Establish the level of evaluation needed for each project at the beginning so that participants will understand the focus.
10. Develop partnerships with key administrators, managers, and other principle participants who can make the project successful.
11. Ensure that measures are taken and the evaluation is complete with collection and analysis of various types of data.
12. Communicate project results to the appropriate stakeholders as often as necessary to focus on process improvement.

them successful. Following these twelve leadership roles can ensure green success.

Challenges Along the Way

The journey to increased accountability and the quest to show monetary value for benefits, including ROI, are not going unchallenged. This movement represents a cultural shift for many individuals, a systemic change in processes, and often a complete rethinking of the initiation, delivery, and maintenance of green projects and sustainability processes in organizations.

THE COMMITMENT DILEMMA

Commitment is key to successful implementation of the ROI Methodology. Without it, the project is dead. Some users hope to obtain an immediate ROI value using the ROI Methodology, but, there is more to it than a simple calculation. To achieve success, a commitment is needed to make changes when the data reveal that the change needed is imperative. Also, commitment is needed to properly use the information provided by the process. Finally, there must be a commitment to have the discipline and determination to make it work—to implement it successfully.

LACK OF PREPARATION AND SKILLS

Although the interest in proving the value of green projects and measuring ROI is heightened and much progress has been made, these are still issues that challenge even the most sophisticated and progressive functions. One problem is the lack of preparation and skills needed to conduct these types of analyses. The preparation for green project leaders often omits the necessary skill building for measurement and evaluation. Rarely do the curricula in degree programs or professional development courses include processes and techniques to show accountability at this level. Consequently, these skills must be developed by the organization or individual, using a variety of resources, so that they are in place for successful implementation. More information on skill building is available at *www.roiinstitute.net*.

FEAR OF ROI

Few business topics stir up emotions to the degree that ROI does. For a few executives, the conclusion behind the ROI value is simple: if it is negative, they kill the project; if it is extremely positive, they do not believe it. Although those extreme responses are rare, the potential for this response from executives causes some professionals to avoid the issue altogether. A familiar reaction emerges: "If my sustainability initiative is not delivering impact and

ROI values, the last thing I want to do is publish a report for my sponsor." Unfortunately, if the project is not delivering value, the sponsor probably already knows it, or at least someone in the organization does. In this case, the best thing to do is to show the value (or lack thereof) using a systematic, credible process, and make adjustments accordingly.

Then there is the fear of how the data will be used. Will the data be used to punish people, reward individuals, or improve processes? Some green project owners feel that disappointing results will reflect unfavorably on their performance evaluation. Ideally, results should be used to improve processes—to make them more successful. The challenge is to ensure that data are not misused or abused.

The process improvement perspective must be understood and agreed to by all parties. The fear of ROI can be minimized when the individuals involved understand the process, how it is designed and delivered, and the value that it can bring from a positive perspective.

LACK OF TIME TO RESPOND

Thorough analysis takes time. Some green project leaders and some sponsors are restless and do not want to take the time to do the appropriate analyses. In a fast-paced work environment where decisions are often made quickly and with little input or data, some executives question the time and the effort involved in this type of analysis. What must be shown, however, is that this effort is necessary and appropriate and will ultimately pay off. When the process is implemented, the individuals involved usually see that the value of the increased effort far outweighs the cost of the time to do it.

PROCRASTINATION

Too often individuals wait to measure projects and evaluate sustainability efforts until the requests come, essentially waiting for a top administrator to say, "Show me the money. Show me the value." Often this request is followed by "immediately," and the implementation team is left unprepared to show the results. This can be disastrous for the project and the team. It is best to anticipate accountability throughout the process. This means starting the evaluation process early, building capability, putting systems in place, and making things work before senior executives request an evaluation.

FAILURE TO SEE THE POWER OF CREDIBLE DATA

Having appropriate data represents power to many individuals. If used for constructive purposes or to improve processes, data are perceived as valuable. If data are used for destructive or political purposes, they may be seen as less valuable. If the information is based on credible facts, then it generates power. If it is based on opinions or gut feelings, then the person who provides those opinions is more influential than the opinions themselves. Essentially, facts create a level playing field for decision making. As one executive from a technology company said, "If a decision is based on facts, then anyone's facts are equal as long as they are relevant; however, if it must be based on opinions, then my opinion counts a lot more." This underscores the power of having credible data for making decisions.

MISLEADING HYPE

Claims of success abound. But when the facts are examined, they often reveal something completely different. Impressive claims, ads, and success stories are presented to promote a concept or an idea. Exaggerated statements in marketing campaigns add to the confusion and the green sector is not without its share of misleading hype.

Green projects are evaluated in a variety of ways, and few accepted standards, rules, and processes exist to validate those assumptions and claims. Books, articles, and research reports present hundreds of successful case studies of green projects and sustainability efforts, many with amazing results. Critics, however, may suggest that at least some of them represent greenwashing. For example, as reported in 2007 by Environmental Leader: Energy and Environmental News for Business, TerraChoice Environmental Marketing found that of 1,018 consumer products they surveyed, 99 percent were guilty of greenwashing. Even with this study, however, it is rare to find published reports on green failures. A systematic process with conservative, accepted standards can create a credible, believable story of project success that deters the critics and naysayers.

FAILURE TO SUSTAIN THE USE OF ROI

The final challenge is sustaining this shift in accountability. The implementation of the ROI Methodology must consist of more than just conducting one or two studies to show the value of a green project. It must represent a change in processes so that future projects focus on results. This change requires building capability, developing consistent and compelling communication, involving stakeholders, building measurement process into projects, creating expectations, and using data for process improvements. This is the only way to sustain any change for the long-term; otherwise, it becomes a one-shot or short-term project opportunity.

Final Thoughts

So what does all of this mean? This chapter makes the case for having a more comprehensive, credible process to show the value of green projects and sustainability efforts. Many stakeholders, particularly those who are funding initiatives, are demanding, requiring, or suggesting more accountability, up to and including impact and ROI. "Show me the money" has become a common request—and it is being made now more than ever. At the same time, there is a green slump, which suggests that many green projects are not working. When we consider the debate about the need for green projects and then throw in politics and campaign rhetoric, the need for more accountability intensifies.

A variety of forces have created this current focus on results, leaving green project planners with only one recourse: to step up to the accountability challenge, create a process that can make a difference, develop data that please a variety of important stakeholders, and use a process that makes projects and initiatives better in the future. That is the intent of the process described in this book. The next chapter introduces strategies for investing in green projects, of which one is the use of the ROI Methodology.

Chapter 3

Investment Strategies

How Companies Approach
the Green Investment

Most organizations, communities, and cities start green projects slowly. This initial investment is usually small but often evolves into a large amount, and leaders must reflect on how much they should spend. Ultimately, top executives set the investment level for green projects and sustainability initiatives. Some rely only on benchmarking; others adopt more well-defined strategies. Still others opt to avoid the investment altogether. This chapter outlines the five strategies that are often taken to set the investment level in green projects, either intentionally or unintentionally:

1. Avoid the investment.
2. Invest the minimum.
3. Invest with the rest.
4. Invest until it hurts.
5. Invest when there is a payoff.

Some of these strategies are unproductive and will not produce the desired results from green initiatives. Even overinvesting (investing until it hurts) can often unintentionally be harmful. This chapter analyzes each of these investment options in some detail and offers specific recommendations provided at the end of each section and at the end of the chapter. Although an investment level may be set initially, by using one or more of the five strategies or some other process, addressing the level of spending on green initiatives is an issue that should be reviewed periodically.

Strategy 1: Avoid the Investment

Some executives prefer to take a passive role with sustainability efforts, attempting to avoid the investment altogether. After all, no one is making them do it. While appearing somewhat dysfunctional, this approach has proven effective for some organizations, depending on the strategic focus, resource accountability, and perception of the green movement. There are a variety of factors driving this strategy, some of which may be familiar to you.

FORCES DRIVING THIS STRATEGY

Several factors motivate an executive to approach investing in green and sustainability initiatives using this strategy. First, when the organization has little contact with the public; the situation is "out of sight, out of mind." Organizational leaders feel no compelling reason to invest in green. Second, when the organization is small. Some small businesses feel they cannot make a difference; they view themselves as only a small part of the picture, and investing in the green movement is not a concern. The third driving force is when organizations have chosen to outsource most of what they do: production, marketing, advertising, distribution, logistics, and sales. With only a few employees, green is not an issue for them. Fourth, when survival is the focus of concern. Some industries and organizations are struggling to survive, and when this is the case, spending money to protect the environment is not at the top of the list.

Out of Sight, Out of Mind

Many organizations do not need to deal directly with the public. They do not have direct consumers. They do not make products that are sold directly to consumers or provide services that are delivered directly to them. Instead, they sell to other business organizations (B2B). With no consumer contact, there is little pressure from consumers to go green.

Others produce obscure products that are used only as a small part of another product. For the most part, these are small, privately held organizations that serve a specific niche. For example, Buntrock Industries, based in Williamsburg, Virginia, serves only the investment casting industry. A small business, Buntrock serves others who apply their equipment and materials to the process of investment casting. They do not necessarily invest in green initiatives.

Another example is American Plastics Company (APC), a small manufacturer of plastic mugs for the specialty advertising industry. These mugs always feature someone else's brand or logo, making the company "out of mind" in terms of the ultimate consumer and the public. The plant, which

employs about 200 people, is privately held, and the owners are always concerned about making a profit. This type of business has a huge impact on
the environment, yet they invest essentially nothing in the green movement.
The strategy is to avoid it. The owners of the company are convinced that
investing in green projects is not necessarily a wise investment, because there
is no immediate payoff. They are not convinced that cost savings are forth-
coming to this sort of change, and they have not taken the time to explore
and understand the green issue. Their only requirements are meeting health
and safety standards, adhering to requirements for hazardous chemicals, and
following environmental regulations for disposing of the materials and waste
for the plant.

Too Small for Green

While large organizations attract the most attention, most of the businesses
in the United States are small. Small businesses represent both a challenge
and an opportunity when it comes to going green. Because of the total numbers of small businesses, getting them to embrace the green movement will
make a significant impact in many different areas. However, the challenge is
convincing them to do it. Because they are small (and inconsequential from
their perspective), they see no reason to invest in green; they see no value.

Some small companies are more willing to change because they sell
directly to the customer. For example, patrons of Southside Cleaners, a small
dry cleaning business, would not necessarily require their dry cleaners to
be involved in the green movement. However, because the cleaning materials used may include harmful chemicals, consumers might be interested to
know that the company is also taking care of the environment. Customers
of a small print and copy shop, such as Pete's Print and Copy, might also be
interested in knowing that the print shop is environmentally sensitive, using
recycled paper and sustainable products

For small companies as these, if customer interest in sustainability is
strong enough, owners may be compelled to rethink their green investment
strategy.

Outsourced Products and Services

Some organizations outsource most of what they do, which leaves only a
small central group of employees. They outsource production, marketing,
and distribution. Because other people are doing most of the work and driving the business, they are less likely to focus on green initiatives. For example, one of our publishers outsources printing, editing, design, marketing,
book inventory, and distribution. The books are sold in book stores; there is
no sales force. Because the publisher has a small staff, why should they be

concerned about the green movement? Customers and authors do not visit their offices. There are no external shareholders. There is no pressure for them to pursue green projects.

Survival Is an Issue

Some organizations, particularly those in declining industries and those that must deal with a particular economic crisis because of industry issues or external environment, face the prospect that they may not survive much longer. They may consider investing in green to be similar to rearranging the chairs on the Titanic. It is not a priority issue for them so they avoid it altogether. For example, for ten years a well-known self-help company that is traded on the New York Stock Exchange struggled to survive, making no profit. The stock fell from thirty-five dollars a share to fifty-five cents. During this period, there was almost no focus on green projects or sustainability initiatives. Although they were in the public eye, survival was the issue. When will we make a profit? Can we make it? Which strategy is going to work? These are the critical issues. In these circumstances, green initiatives just do not make the top of the list.

Some entire industries are facing these kinds of problems. For example, although newspapers have a tremendous impact on the environment, many are going out of business—not because of the economic decline, but because of growth of and demand for digital media. Expectations are that print news will be extinct in the future. If you are trying to survive in an industry that many are predicting will disappear, spending on green initiatives is not at the top of the list of investment concerns.

TECHNIQUES TO PERSUADE THESE ORGANIZATIONS TO CHANGE THEIR INVESTMENT STRATEGY

Changing the attitude and behavior of this "no investment" group is problematic, but it represents a great opportunity because of the numbers of people in this category. Essentially, the goal is for them to move from this strategy of deliberately avoiding the investment to investing more. This fundamental switch requires several actions.

Educate Leaders and Staff

Educational and awareness sessions are needed to show this particular group that by investing in green they can make a difference and reduce costs or increase profit as a result. One person can make a little difference and many of them can make a huge difference. They must see that there is not only a reason to invest in green projects and sustainability initiatives, but that there is some value in doing it. They must realize that most green projects will result in cost savings, but only if they are implemented properly, if the projects are measured systematically, and if the results are used to drive improvement.

Engage Industry Associations

Almost every type of organization in this category is part of an industry or trade association. By informing their members about the green movement and emphasizing what is available, what is possible, and what is essential, industry associations can influence these organizations. They can demonstrate the economic opportunity to invest and how they can achieve a positive return on that investment. Educational sessions, workshops, webinars, conferences, and newsletters can help. Producing case studies, booklets, pamphlets, and other materials will let the members know about green issues and what they should do about them. In industries that have a tremendous impact on the environment, this is absolutely critical. Otherwise they will be forced into actions through legislation, which is never the desired position.

Engage the Business Groups

Just as a trade association may help to persuade reluctant organizations to embrace the green movement, business groups such as the Chamber of Commerce, National Association of Manufacturers, and others can push the green agenda. These support organizations can provide information, educate, inform, and show value in the same way as trade associations.

Engage Cities and Communities

Local communities can reach reluctant organizations through citizen communications, community groups, and networks that bring the green message to all of the constituents and business owners. Involving, educating, showing, helping, and enabling reluctant businesses are all possible approaches. As mentioned in Chapter 1, cities that work through their citizens represent a great opportunity to have a positive impact on the environment.

Regulate Processes and Practices

The least desired approach is to regulate industry with new laws. This approach is undertaken when nothing else works. For example, regulations now exist that involve cleaning materials, chemical waste, land fill deposits, and pollution. Sometimes, this last resort may be the only way to influence non-investors to change their strategy.

Strategy 2: Invest the Minimum

While the previous strategy avoids investing in green initiatives, this strategy leads to investing only what is necessary to avoid any problems. A few organizations adopt this strategy as a preferred choice; others do it out of economic necessity. Either way, this is a viable investment strategy for some organizations.

BASIC APPROACH

This strategy involves investing the minimum in green projects and initiatives, providing only the level of investment that meets the minimum expectations and regulations. Executives adopting this philosophy operate in a culture that is sometimes reflective of a particular industry and the competitive forces within the industry. These organizations experience low profit margins and usually adjust processes and systems to take into account the constant churning of customers and employees.

This strategy should not be confused with efficient resource allocation. Obviously, efficiency is gained by keeping costs at a minimum, and many green projects will lower costs. The strategy is a deliberate effort to allocate only the minimum investment in green projects. Forces are at play; this is a decision to invest as little as possible in this issue.

FORCES DRIVING THE STRATEGY

The primary forces driving this strategy can be put into four words: image, cost, value, and survival. These organizations are often managed by executives who see little value in green initiatives and view the minimum investment as the only option. They consider the initiatives to be necessary but not substantial.

Image

As mentioned in Chapter 1, the principle driver for most organizations to invest in green projects is image. Almost all research supports this conclusion. Leaders want to be seen as promoting green, with high visibility to consumers, stakeholders, employees, associates, volunteers, and a list of other stakeholders. They want to be perceived as being environmentally sensitive. Too often these efforts may be high profile (and highly visible), but they are not meaningful because the leaders have deliberately set a strategy to invest only enough to look acceptable. For example, it appears that some hotels are investing the minimum for image only. Although they have green announcements about changing the linens only when necessary and only washing towels as needed, which protects the environment and results in significant cost savings, it is unclear how much deeper they are going with the green commitment. They do not appear to be moving beyond the obvious things that are easy to do and are primarily for the cost savings.

This strategy to invest with image-only in mind often causes leaders to practice green washing, the process of making it appear that the organization is doing more than it is. The practice focuses on creating a false image only, exaggerating the progress, and even presenting bogus data to present a favorable impression. As mentioned in Chapter 2, green washing is alive and well and can be a serious problem.

Cost

Some organizations are in low-margin industries and cannot afford to invest in green beyond the minimum, due to the cost. Yes, they want to do enough to have a positive image and reap the obvious cost savings. However, they cannot afford to go deeper than that, because it will affect profits too much. Sometimes this is the case with retail stores, restaurants (particularly fast food restaurants), and even airlines. They are unable to invest heavily because they have such low profits or sometimes no profits. However, there are many good examples in this area where leaders have stepped up to this challenge. For example, Walmart, the world's largest retailer, is obviously a low-margin industry. Yet Walmart is probably having a greater impact on the environment than any other organization, because they are forcing their suppliers to go green, eliminating or reducing packaging, saving paper (saving trees), and reducing transportation costs (reducing carbon emissions).

Walmart's size clearly ensures that it has a lot of clout, but more actions can be taken in smaller retail organizations as well. While many fast food, quick stop restaurants often ignore this issue, investing only the minimum for the obvious image reasons, others like Starbucks have invested heavily in the environment beyond the obvious signs in the store. For example, they are in the process of developing a comprehensive recycling cup solution where they are working with local governments, cup manufactures, recyclers, and other stakeholders to jointly identify the steps required to make their cups recyclable in form and in practice; in 2009 they increased the number of beverages served in reusable serveware or tumblers by 4.4 million over 2008; in 2009 their electricity usage decreased by 1.7 percent in company-owned stores; in 2009 they increased renewable energy purchases to the equivalent of 25 percent of the electricity used in company-owned stores; and in 2009 they decreased water consumption by 4.1 percent. (For a copy of Starbuck's 2009 Global Responsibility Scorecard go to http://assets.starbucks.com/assets/ssp-g-p-scorecard.pdf)

Even in the airline industry, where profits are constantly squeezed, airlines such as Continental are investing in biofuels to replace traditional jet fuel. In 2009, Continental became the first U.S. carrier to perform a flight demonstration with a two-engine aircraft using sustainable biofuels, which could reduce airplane carbon emissions. Continental partnered with Boeing, GE Aviation/CFM International, and Honeywell's UOP to select algae and jatropha—sources that do not compete with food crops or water resources or contribute to deforestation—as sustainable biofuel sources for the demonstration flight.

Value

Many organizations invest the minimum because they are not convinced that there is value in green projects. They perceive green as a cost—not as an opportunity. They are unaware of what investing in green can achieve for their bottom line as well as the environment. Yes, it is true that not every green project will have a quick monetary return, but the right ones will. Even the projects that have a negative ROI will have a positive payoff in intangibles. The projects that do have a positive payoff can help fund those that do not.

Survival

As in the case of investment strategy number one, some organizations invest the minimum due to their need to focus on survival. While they value the idea of investing in green, their bottom line takes priority over their desire to contribute to a greater good. Survival is the key, so they invest only the minimum in green and remain focused on their core business.

TECHNIQUES TO PERSUADE THESE ORGANIZATIONS TO CHANGE THEIR STRATEGY

Attempting to influence leaders to change their strategy and invest more than the minimum requires several coordinated efforts. Changes here fall in line with the recommendations for addressing the previous strategy of avoiding the investment altogether. The difference is that this second group is already investing; they see a need to invest, but they can do much more.

This group needs examples of what others are doing. They need to see the payoff. Positive examples in their type of business or industry can help. Fortunately, there are hundreds of examples where investing in green and sustainability projects are paying off such as Nestle, BASF, Dow, SC Johnson, Shell, DuPont, Cargill, and Adidas. They must see and understand the value of investing more in this area.

As with the previous strategy, trade associations can be helpful. These groups must encourage organizations to invest more by showing benchmarking data, presenting real case studies, and by showing the economic value of investing more in these projects in a convincing, credible way.

Strategy 3: Invest with the Rest

Many executives prefer to invest in green projects and sustainability efforts at the same level that others invest. This approach involves collecting data from a variety of comparable organizations, often perceived as implementing best practices, to determine the extent to which those organizations invest in the green movement. The benchmarking data are used to drive improvement or changes, if necessary, to achieve the benchmark level. In essence, this strategy aligns the organization to a level of investment that other organizations achieve.

FORCES DRIVING THE STRATEGY

There has been phenomenal growth in benchmarking in the last two decades. Virtually every function in an organization has been involved in some type of benchmarking to evaluate activities, practices, structure, and results. Because of its popularity and effectiveness, many environmental and sustainability leaders use benchmarking to show the value of, and investment level for, green initiatives. In some situations, the benchmarking process develops standards of excellence from "best practice" organizations. The cost of connecting to existing benchmarking projects is often low, especially when considering the available data. However, when a customized benchmarking project is needed, the costs are higher. Organizations such as the Triple Bottom Line Alliance have benchmarking data. Other helpful benchmarks come from the U.S. Green Building Council, The Carbon Consultancy, Ltd., European Wind Energy Association, and the World Business Summit on Climate Change. These sources provide opportunities to understand and validate investments in green initiatives.

An important force driving the invest-with-the-rest strategy is that it is a safe approach. Benchmarking has been accepted as a standard management tool, often required and suggested by top executives. It is a low-risk strategy. The decisions made as a result of benchmarking, when proven to be ineffective, can easily be blamed on the faulty sources or faulty processes, not the individuals who initiated or secured the data.

Benchmarking is a strategy that should be used in conjunction with other approaches. With its low-cost approach, benchmarking provides another view of the sustainability function and the investment required for it.

BENCHMARK MEASURES

Investment benchmarks are captured in a variety of benchmarking studies focused on a few measures. For example, it may be helpful to understand how much is invested annually or quarterly for a particular employee, category, or group with data showing the investment per employee. This is particularly helpful when green projects involve many employees. Similar data can be captured for customers or suppliers. How much should a company invest to educate and assist customers with green issues? How much should be invested in suppliers, encouraging, assisting, or requiring them to practice green? Benchmark data may provide insight.

Another potential measure is the investment in green projects as a percent of total employee payroll. The numbers typically range from 1.5 percent to 3.5 percent. Best practice is on the high side. A similar measure is the total investment in green projects as a percent of revenue. This is particularly helpful in the manufacturing and process industries, where the cost of going green is so expensive and a portion of the revenue is allocated to this issue. Another measure that is helpful in most situations is to consider green initiatives as a percent of operating costs. This measure recognizes that most green projects come from, and support, the operational issues in an organization, and it is helpful to compare the costs with other operational expenditures.

The total investment in green initiatives can be divided into different job groups, categorized by department, division, regions, or units. Still other ways to analyze the investment is by functional categories in the life cycle of a green project, such as analysis, design and development, implementation and delivery, coordination and management, and measurement and evaluation. This type of breakdown can be helpful. The investments in analysis and measurement and evaluation are usually too low.

For cities and community groups, a similar set of benchmark measures are sometimes available. The investment per citizen, the investment as a percent of budget, and the investment as a per-cost of tax revenue are examples.

In short, the investment number must represent a meaningful value for the organization, particularly when it comes from organizations representing a best practice.

CONCERNS WITH THIS STRATEGY

Several issues that often inhibit the benchmarking process should be addressed. Benchmarking involves three challenges. The first challenge is to understand the sources that currently exist for benchmarking studies. Respected organizations are needed for benchmarking studies because having credible data is important. It is even more difficult to benchmark at the international level. A replication process is necessary for benchmarking in each country.

The second concern is the organizations participating in the benchmark study. Data must come from organizations regarded as best practice and similar to other organizations. Not all benchmarking sources represent best practices. Often, they involve organizations willing to pay the price to participate.

A third concern is the benchmarked measures. The measures must be meaningful, respected, and comparable. Some benchmark reports contain data that are not easily replicated or easily obtained in organizations. Businesses use "competitive intelligence" to drive business decisions based on comparative and competitive data. It is important for sustainability executives to determine the right measures for their own organization and management. Once shared, the measure should be used routinely in order to make comparisons. Measures should be replicable and easily obtained.

CUSTOMIZED BENCHMARKING

The concerns about benchmarking may leave executives with little choice but to develop a customized benchmarking project to address their organization's interests and needs. If more organizations developed their own benchmarking studies, there would be more available data from the various partners. Figure 3.1 shows a seven-phase benchmarking process that can be used to develop the custom-designed benchmarking project.

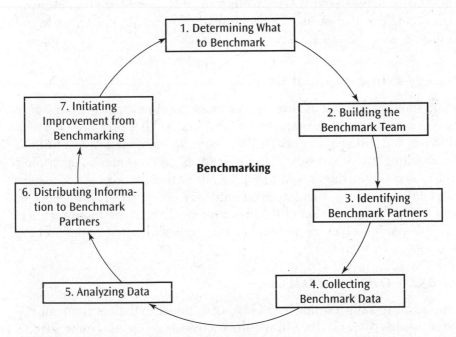

FIGURE 3.1 Phases of the Benchmarking Process

ADVANTAGES AND DISADVANTAGES OF THIS STRATEGY

Benchmarking satisfies a variety of needs and is used in several important applications. It is helpful in the strategic planning for the sustainability function and in decision-making processes used to determine the desired investment level. Information and measures derived from the benchmarking process can enable executives to meet strategic objectives. Benchmarking is also useful in identifying trends and critical issues for green project management. Measures from benchmarking can become the standard of excellence for an activity, function, system, practice, program, or specific initiative. It has become an important measurement tool for senior executives.

The benchmarking process is not without its share of problems, consequences, and issues, however. Benchmarking must be viewed as a learning process, not necessarily a process to replicate what others have accomplished. Each organization is different; what is needed in one organization may not be the same as in another. Also, developing a custom-designed benchmarking project is time-consuming. It requires discipline to keep the project on schedule, within budget, and on track to drive continuous process improvement. Determining what the best practices are is an elusive goal; benchmarking can create the illusion that average data, taken from a group willing to participate in a study, represent best practices. National and international data are a difficult issue that often limits benchmarking as a global tool. Finally, benchmarking is not a quick fix; it is a long-term improvement process, and one that needs to be continually replicated to be valuable and accurate.

Strategy 4: Invest Until It Hurts

While some organizations invest at the same level of other organizations, many operate under the premise that more is better. They overinvest in green initiatives and sustainability efforts. The results of this approach can be both disappointing and disastrous. A few executives do this intentionally; most do it unknowingly. Either way, this is a strategy that deserves serious attention, because the investment in green initiatives is beyond what is needed to meet the goals and mission of the organization. Executives approve almost every green project they see and explore every green idea that comes over the horizon.

RATIONALE FOR THE STRATEGY

Some advocates suggest that overinvesting in green initiatives is not an important issue—after all, they think, the more you invest, the more success with green projects. Also, they suggest that this issue is too important for overinvestment to even be possible: you cannot spend too much on protecting the environment. However, others will argue that overinvesting occurs regularly and is unnecessarily burdening organizations with excessive operating costs. Overinvesting puts pressure on others to follow suit, thus creating an artificial new benchmark. As noted, this is often not a deliberate strategy. Rather, executives are usually unaware that the increase in spending is not adding value.

SIGNS OF OVERINVESTING

Many signs indicate that companies are overinvesting in green projects. For example, consider the comments of the CEO of a major retail company, who had to announce a disappointing financial performance. In an interview, the CEO indicated that the company's poor performance was due, in part, to the excessive amount of sustainability investment. In this case, employees enjoyed participating in green projects, and store managers supported these efforts to the extreme. The result: employees were away from work and there was not enough staff to serve the customers, causing customer dissatisfaction and ultimately loss in revenue. There were no data to show the value of these green projects.

Here's another example. An automotive supplier, once the shining star for environmental work, had a commitment that 15 percent of revenue would be invested each year in green projects. Manager bonuses were attached to this goal and were trimmed significantly if targets were not met. As expected, all types of projects were initiated. Some employees and managers complained that they were taking on too many projects—often unrelated to their work— simply to meet this goal. What was once designed to show a commitment to sustainability turned into an expensive practice and, in some cases, a major turnoff in the eyes of employees. Some employees suggested that the money gained from these projects be distributed to them as a special bonus. The company had little data about the success of these projects. When the economy dipped, the funding stopped. No data were available to show the results of the projects.

FORCES DRIVING THIS STRATEGY

Several forces cause excessive spending. Some of these are realistic challenges; others are mythical. Either way, they cause firms to overinvest. Around the year 2000, green became a battle cry of many organization leaders. A few executives were willing to do almost anything to focus on the issue. This often led to investing excessively in sustainability, well beyond what would be necessary or acceptable in many situations. The conventional wisdom was that offering all types of green initiatives would fix the problem and was necessary for business survival. However, many organizations—even industries—were able to do well without having to resort to this strategy.

Some executives spend excessively to remain competitive in the market. They must attract and maintain highly capable employees and have a perfect image with consumers. Consequently, they are willing to invest heavily in green projects. They sometimes offer all types of projects, which can cost the company in operating profits. They want certain capabilities and are willing to invest to keep the talent. The green image becomes an important competitive recruiting strategy.

Some executives have an appetite for new fads. They have never met one they did not like, so they adopt new fads at every turn, adding additional costs. The landscape is littered with green projects and dozens of sustainability solutions. Once a fad is in place, it is hard to remove; this adds layers of projects and goes beyond what is necessary or economically viable. Some of these executives become the leaders in this movement, with much recognition and praise. This creates more projects.

Spending too much on green initiatives can occur because executives are unwilling or are unable to conduct the proper initial analysis to see if a project is needed. A proper analysis will indicate if the specific green project is the right solution to a particular problem or concern. Without the proper analysis, green projects are implemented when they are not needed, possibly wasting money.

Some executives spend an excessive amount on green issues because they can afford to do so. Their organizations are profitable, enjoying high margins and ample growth, and the executives want to share the wealth to save the planet. However, there are little data to show the value of these expenditures. Furthermore, when the economy turns sour, a new CEO is appointed, or the company is sold, the company may not be able to sustain these projects.

CONCERNS WITH THIS STRATEGY

Obviously, spending excessively is not a recommended strategy. There are many potential problems with this approach, not only to the company but also for the industry. The most significant disadvantage of overinvestment is the less-than-optimal financial performance. By definition, this strategy involves investing more than necessary to meet the objectives of the organization. While some increases in green investment yield additional financial results, for many green projects there is evidence of a point of diminishing return, where the added benefits peak and then drop as investments continue. This relationship between performance and investment in green initiatives is depicted in Figure 3.2. Excessive investing can eventually deteriorate performance in the organization, particularly in industries where the green and

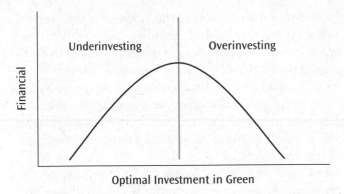

Underinvesting   Overinvesting

Financial

Optimal Investment in Green

FIGURE 3.2   The Relationship Between Investing in Green Projects and Financial Performance

sustainability expense is an extraordinarily high percentage of the total operating cost.

Strategy 5: Invest as Long as There Is a Payoff

Some executives prefer to invest in green projects when there is evidence that the investment is providing benefits. They often compare the monetary benefits of supporting green projects with the costs of green. This strategy is becoming more popular following the increased interest in accountability, particularly with the use of return on investment (ROI) as a project evaluation tool. With this strategy, all green initiatives are evaluated, and a few key projects are measured at the ROI level. The ROI in these projects is calculated the same way as the ROI is calculated for investments in buildings or equipment.

THE STRATEGY

This strategy focuses on implementing a comprehensive measurement and evaluation process for expenditures in an organization. This involves the possibility of capturing the types of data in the chain of impact, as shown in Chapter 2. These data include reaction, learning, application, impact, ROI, and intangible benefits. Using this philosophy, only a small number of projects are evaluated at the ROI level, whereas every project is evaluated at the reaction level. Also, when business impact and ROI are developed for green projects, one or more techniques are used to isolate the impact of the projects on the business data.

FORCES DRIVING CHANGE

Although the trend toward additional accountability has been increasing over the last decade, there are several reasons why this strategy is critical at this time. In the last few years, the demonstration of the value of green projects to the organization has been at the forefront of executive agendas. With this mandate, sustainability team members have had to develop the skill to communicate to other managers the contribution to the financial bottom line in the language of business. In a world where financial results are measured, a failure to measure the success of green initiatives destines the project team to risk oversight, neglect, and potential failure. The leader responsible for green initiatives needs to be able to evaluate, in financial terms, the costs and benefits of selected projects and practices. ·

The increasing cost of sustainability is another driving force. As we discuss throughout this book, investment in green initiatives is quite large and growing. As these budgets continue to grow—often at a growth rate outpacing other functions of the organization—the costs alone are requiring some executives to question the value of the investment. Some executives are requesting that the impact of green projects be forecasted before they are implemented. In some cases, the ROI is required at budget review time.

Let's say that a production manager proposes investing in new technology to help speed up production and decrease unit production cost. To ensure the benefits of this investment are clear, the production manager compares the resulting cost savings to the cost of implementing the new technology, providing a forecast ROI. Because of this effort, decision makers can clearly see how investment in the technology compares to other proposed investments. Sustainability professionals must compete for scarce organizational resources in this same vein. While requesting funds on the basis of environmental impact can be effective, it is more effective when environmental impact is associated with organization cost savings (or profit increases) and how they match up to the amount of the requested funds.

Another driving force is the role of the Chief Financial Officer (CFO). *The Economist* magazine labeled 2009 the year of the CFO, based on the importance of this executive role. The CFO views sustainability as an unavoidable cost of business. When considered as a collection of smaller investments, though, there are clearly choices to be made. Which green projects are worth the investment? If managers can gain some sense of the return on these different options, then they can ensure that money is being put to the best use. This may not always mean putting a dollar value on the different choices, but perhaps understanding their effect on key nonfinancial indicators, such as customer retention.

A final driving force is that more sustainability leaders are managing the function as a business. These executives have operational experience and, in some cases, financial experience. They recognize that green projects should add value to the organization and, consequently, these executives are implementing a variety of measurement tools, even in the hard-to-measure areas.

These tools have gradually become more quantitative and less qualitative. ROI is now being applied in green initiatives just as it is in technology, quality, and product development.

THE ROI METHODOLOGY

In keeping with the strategy to invest as long as there is a payoff, many organizations are employing comprehensive accountability processes including ROI. The ROI Methodology, the process described in this book, is one of the most comprehensive and credible approaches to account for and improve upon investments in green and sustainability projects. This process helps decision makers understand which projects are paying off in terms important to all stakeholders. To develop a credible approach for calculating the ROI in green projects, several components must be developed and integrated. This strategy comprises five important elements, which form the basis for this book:

1. An evaluation framework is needed to define the various levels of evaluation and types of data, as well as to determine how data are captured. This framework includes how to connect the project to business needs.
2. A process model must be created to provide a step-by-step procedure for developing the ROI calculation. Part of this process is the isolation of the effects of a project from other factors in order to show its monetary payoff.
3. A set of operating standards with a conservative philosophy is required. These "guiding principles" keep the process on track to ensure successful replication. The operating standards also build credibility with key stakeholders in the organization.
4. Successful applications are critical to show examples of how ROI works with different types of green projects and initiatives.
5. Resources should be devoted to implementation to ensure that the ROI Methodology becomes operational and routine in the organization. Implementation addresses issues such as responsibilities, policies, procedures, guidelines, goals, and internal skill building.

Together, these elements are necessary to develop a comprehensive evaluation system that contains a balanced set of measures, has credibility with the various stakeholders involved, and can be easily replicated.

ADVANTAGES AND DISADVANTAGES OF THIS STRATEGY

Employing the ROI Methodology to help manage this last investment strategy has several important advantages. With it, the sustainability team and the sponsor who requests and authorizes a green project will know the specific contribution of a project in a language that all stakeholders understand. Measuring the ROI is one of the most convincing ways to earn the respect and support of the senior management team—not only for a particular project, but for the sustainability function as well.

Because a variety of feedback data are collected during project implementation, the comprehensive analysis provides data to drive changes in processes and make adjustments during implementation. Throughout the cycle of project design, development, and implementation, the entire team of stakeholders focuses on results. If a project is not effective, and the results are not materializing, the ROI Methodology will prompt modifications. On rare occasions, the project may have to be halted if it is not adding the appropriate business value, but only if it was specifically designed to add business values.

Note that this methodology has some important barriers to success. It is not suitable for every organization and certainly not for every green project. For one thing, the ROI Methodology adds additional costs and time to the green budget, although not a significant amount—typically no more than 3 to 5 percent of the total direct green budget. (The additional investment in ROI should be offset by the results achieved from implementation.) This cost barrier often stops many ROI implementations early in the process.

As well, many sustainability staff members may not have the basic skills necessary to apply the ROI Methodology within their scope of responsibilities. The typical green project does not focus on results, but on qualitative feedback data and occasional cost-savings data. It is necessary to move green initiatives and sustainability projects from an activity-based practice to a results-based practice, which often requires skill-development in the ROI Methodology for the team. In some cases, staff members do not pursue ROI because they perceive an ROI evaluation as an individual performance evaluation instead of a process improvement tool. This misconception can be remedied through education and skill building.

Final Thoughts

As the analysis in this chapter shows, some investment strategies work better than others. Avoiding the investment is a disappointing and perhaps disastrous approach. Investing the minimum is appreciative but not enough; more needs to be done. Investing with the rest is a moderate attempt at making investment decisions, although, following the crowd may not be best for a specific organization and their stakeholders. Overinvesting has its own unique

problems; while more is being accomplished, it can have a negative effect
that may ultimately reduce investments. This leads to the fifth strategy, the
desired approach: invest when there is a payoff.

Figure 3.3 shows the strategies for shifting the investments toward the desired results. For example, the leaders who are avoiding the investment need
to at least move to the minimum. (It may be difficult in any reasonable time
frame to move this group beyond investing the minimum; they will invest
more if they see a reason to do it.)

Leaders in the second strategy are already investing; they just need to
invest more. While they should invest at least to the benchmark levels, ideally they should look beyond that to investing when there is a payoff. So the
third and fifth strategies would be the goals for those stuck at investing the
minimum.

Leaders who are investing with the rest need to continue to work to make
sure that there is a payoff, capturing data to ensure that their investments are
working as desired. This may mean that there should be more investment
(or even less investment); the crucial element is to show the value in some
organized, credible way.

Overinvestors need to ensure that new projects are working. While they
may be overinvesting intentionally or unintentionally, an accountability system requiring evaluation of every project and even some to ROI is a sensible,

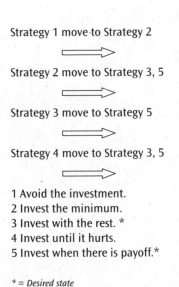

Strategy 1 move to Strategy 2

Strategy 2 move to Strategy 3, 5

Strategy 3 move to Strategy 5

Strategy 4 move to Strategy 3, 5

1 Avoid the investment.
2 Invest the minimum.
3 Invest with the rest. *
4 Invest until it hurts.
5 Invest when there is payoff.*

* = *Desired state*

FIGURE 3.3   Shifting the Investment Strategy Toward the Desired State

rational approach to resource allocation that stakeholders will accept and appreciate.

Finally, investing when there is a payoff is an emerging strategy to show an organization the return on its sustainability investment. The remainder of the book focuses on how to accomplish this in a credible, feasible way.

Chapter 4

The ROI Methodology

A Brief Overview

The process for showing the value of green initiatives, including measuring the ROI, is comprehensive and systematic. It includes five key components: a results framework, a process model, operating standards and philosophy, application and practice, and implementation (Figure 4.1). Together, these five components ensure that a practice of accountability is sustainable. This chapter briefly describes the components of the ROI Methodology that are necessary to achieve the level of accountability demanded in today's environmental, societal, and economic climates. Detailed information on these components is presented throughout the remainder of the book.

Results Framework

The richness of the ROI Methodology is inherent in the results framework. This framework represents a variety of types of data, categorized by levels, which are measured and monitored during a green project's implementation. Each level represents a link in the chain of impact that occurs as projects are launched. People react and acquire the requisite knowledge, skill, and information and apply that knowledge and information. As a consequence, positive impact occurs. Figure 4.2 shows the levels of data and describes their measurement focus. Subsequent chapters provide more detail on each level, including how to collect and analyze the data, and how to report the data so they are meaningful to stakeholders.

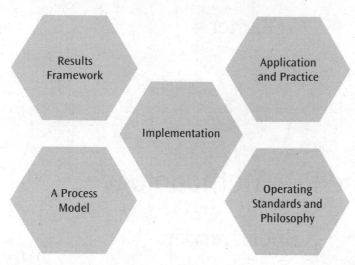

FIGURE 4.1   The Key Components of the ROI Methodology

LEVEL 0: INPUT AND INDICATORS

Level 0 represents the input to a project and includes measures such as the number of people, hours of involvement, focus of the project, cost of the project, project duration, and project resources. These data represent the activity of a project versus the contribution of the project. Level 0 data also represent the scope of the effort, the degree of commitment, and the support for a particular project. For some, this equates to value. However, commitment as defined by expenditures is not evidence that the organization, environment, or society are reaping value.

LEVEL 1: REACTION AND PERCEIVED VALUE

Reaction and perceived value (Level 1) marks the beginning of the project's value stream. Reaction data capture the degree to which stakeholders react favorably or unfavorably to the project. The interest in and passion for a green initiative are essential leading indicators of a project's success. The key is to capture the measures that reflect the content and intent of the project, focusing on issues such as perceived value, relevance, importance, and appropriateness.

An adverse reaction to a green initiative usually means that it will not achieve the desired level of success. At this level, project participants identify their intended next actions, make suggestions to advance success, and identify potential barriers to success. Data at this level provide the first sign of achievable project success. These data also present project leaders with in-

Level	Measurement Focus	Typical Measures
0: Inputs and Indicators	Inputs into the project, including costs, project scope, and duration	Types of projects Number of projects Number of people Hours of involvement Cost of projects
1: Reaction and Perceived Value	Reaction to the project, including the perceived value of the project	Relevance Importance Value Appropriateness Fairness Commitment Motivation
2: Learning and Awareness	Acquisition of knowledge, skill, and/or information to prepare individuals to move the project forward	Skills Knowledge Capacity Competencies Confidence Awareness Attitude
3: Application and Implementation	Use of knowledge, skill, and/or information and system support to implement the project	Extent of use Actions completed Tasks completed Frequency of use Behavior change Success with use Barriers to application Enablers to application
4: Impact	Immediate and long-term consequences of application and implementation expressed as business measures usually contained in the records	Productivity Revenue Quality/Waste Costs Time/Efficiency CO_2 emissions Brand Public image Customer satisfaction Employee satisfaction
5: ROI	Comparison of monetary benefits from project to the project costs	Benefit-cost ratio (BCR) ROI (percentage) Payback period

FIGURE 4.2 Levels and Types of Data

formation they need to make adjustments to project implementation, thereby increasing the chances of positive results.

LEVEL 2: LEARNING AND AWARENESS

The next level involves measuring learning. For every process, program, or project there is a learning component. For some—such as projects for new technology, new systems, new competencies, new processes, and new marketing—this component is substantial. According to Parrs and Weinberg (2009), founders and principals of Mind Over Markets, education is everything: "So moving your communications to educate and inform can do much to grow your green business or initiatives" (95). Even implementation of a new green policy or new procedure includes a learning component to ensure successful execution.

Regardless of the initiative, measurement of learning is essential to success. Measures at this level focus on skills, knowledge, capacity, competencies, confidence, attitude, and awareness.

LEVEL 3: APPLICATION AND IMPLEMENTATION

This level measures the extent to which the project is properly applied and implemented. Effective implementation is a must if economic, environmental, and societal outcomes are the goals. This is one of the most important data categories because it is here, in execution of a project, where breakdowns usually occur. Research has consistently shown that in almost half of all projects, participants and users are not doing their part to make it successful. At this level, measures of success include the extent of use of technology; task completion; change in behavior; frequency of use of knowledge, skills, and information; success with use; and actions completed. Data collection also requires the examination of barriers and enablers to successful implementation of the green project. Application and implementation data provide a picture of how well the organization system supports the successful transfer of knowledge, skills, processes, and information to action that leads to the desired outcomes.

LEVEL 4: IMPACT

Perhaps the most important level of data for understanding the immediate and long-term consequences of the project is collected at Level 4. These data will attract the attention of the sponsor and other executives as well as consumers, suppliers, and distributors. This level shows the energy used, waste reduced, time saved, food produced, efficiencies, customer satisfaction, and employee satisfaction connected to the project. For some, this level reflects the ultimate reason the project exists: to drive economic, environmental, and societal impact. Without this level of data, many stakeholders assert, there is no project success.

When this level of measurement is achieved, it is necessary to isolate the effects of the project on the specific measures. Without this extra step, the link between the project and subsequent outcomes is not evident, diminishing the ability to make decisions about project-specific issues.

LEVEL 5: RETURN ON INVESTMENT

When impact measures are identified, converting them to money and comparing the monetary value to the investment results in the financial return on investment (ROI). This metric places benefits and cost in equal terms: money. Normalizing benefits and costs enables project owners and other stakeholders to see how resource expenditures compare to benefits. This financial metric is typically stated in terms of a benefit-cost ratio (BCR), ROI percentage, and payback period. This level of measurement requires two important steps: first, the impact data (Level 4) must be converted to monetary values; second, the cost of the project must be captured.

While some stakeholders may suggest that calculating the actual ROI on a green initiative diminishes the global value of such a project, two important benefits emerge from this process. First, by knowing the ROI, stakeholders concerned with the economic component of sustainability see that financial resources are allocated appropriately. Appropriate use of financial resources leads to organization viability and longevity. Second, when a green project reaps positive benefits in one building or region, the results may be used to justify implementation in another building or region. Funds from projects with a positive ROI can be used to help fund the not-so-successful projects or those with longer-term outcomes. It is also helpful to remember that when projects are properly developed and implemented, the chances for a positive ROI are high.

INTANGIBLE BENEFITS

Along with the five levels of results and the initial level of activity (Level 0), there is a sixth type of data—not a sixth level—developed through the processes described in this book. This sixth type of data is the intangible benefits: those benefits that are purposefully not converted to money. A decision to not convert benefits to money is made when the conversion consumes too many resources or the process is not credible. Yet intangibles are still important measures of success. For green initiatives, intangibles may include brand awareness, reputation, customer satisfaction, employee satisfaction, engagement, and public image.

Results Framework and Business Alignment

Our research suggests that the number one reason projects fail is lack of alignment with the business. The results framework supports this alignment by connecting the project needs with its objective and the evaluation of its success. The first opportunity to obtain business alignment is in the initial analysis.

INITIAL ANALYSIS

Initial analysis of stakeholder needs sets the stage for deciding on the best projects to pursue given those needs and the available resources. This initial analysis represents the first phase in aligning projects with the business. It begins with the determination of the payoff needs—the potential opportunity or problem that is worth solving.

Payoff Needs

From the start, several steps should be taken to make sure that the project or initiative is necessary. As shown in Figure 4.3, this is the beginning of the complete, sequential model that we often refer to as the V-model. This model is at the heart of the results framework. The first step in this analysis examines the potential payoff of solving a problem or taking advantage of an opportunity. Is this a problem worth solving? Is the project worthy of implementation? For some situations the answer is obviously yes, because of the project's critical nature, its relevance to the issue at hand, or its effectiveness in tackling a major problem that affects the organization. A serious CO_2 emissions problem, for example, is one worth pursuing. Potential payoff opportunities may be short-term or long-term.

Business Needs

The next step is to ensure that the project is connected to one or more key business measures. Key measures that must improve as a reflection of the overall success of the project are defined. Business needs may be long-term, but they often represent more immediate outcomes to the organization, such as cost savings due to more efficient energy use. These measures are in the system now, in operating reports, key performance indicators, performance scorecards, or goals for individuals, departments, functions, or organizations.

Performance Needs

Next, the performance needs are examined. What must change in terms of behaviors, habits, application, or implementation to address the business needs? This step aligns the project with the business and may involve a series

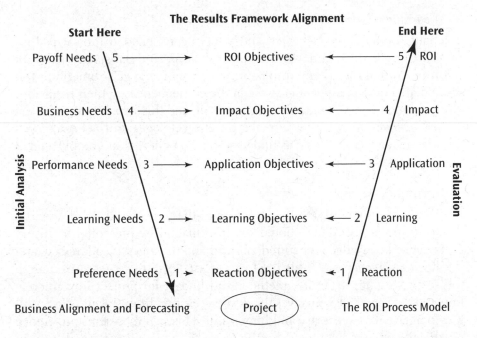

FIGURE 4.3   The V-Model

of analytical tools to determine the cause of the problem or the changes necessary to take advantage of an opportunity. This step appears to be complex, but it is really a simple approach. A series of questions helps:

- What is keeping the business measure from being where it needs to be?
- If it is a problem, what is its cause?
- If it is an opportunity, what is hindering the measure from moving in the right direction?

This step is important because it provides the link to the project or initiative. A simple example may explain. Energy cost, an ongoing business issue, can be reduced with less energy usage. A forward-thinking Chief Information Officer (CIO) of Partners Healthcare examined employee practices for placing their computers in the sleep mode. Choosing not to rely on the habits of people, this CIO set rules for all of the company's 27,000 computers. At one time, the CIO can force idle computers into standby mode, which reduces energy usage by 60 percent. By identifying a simple performance need (placing computers in standby mode), this initiative addressed a business need (energy cost) with a fairly substantial payoff. The result is the elimination of 5.5 million kilowatt-hours of electricity usage and a savings of $1.4 million per year (Winston, 2009).

Learning Needs

To change performance behaviors and habits, people need to know what they must do, how to do it, and when to do it. What specific skills, knowledge, or information must be acquired so performance can change? Sometimes it is just a matter of making people aware of the consequences of their behaviors. Every solution involves a learning component, and this step defines what the people involved must know to make the project successful. The required knowledge may be as simple as understanding a policy, or as complicated as developing a new set of competencies.

Preference Needs

The final step is identifying the structure of the project and the desired re-action to the project. How should the information be presented to ensure that needed knowledge is acquired, performance changes are addressed, and the business needs met? This level of analysis involves issues surrounding the scope, timing, structure, method, and budget for project implementation and delivery. It also involves the desired reaction from stakeholders. Will they perceive it as necessary and important? This step represents preference needs—the preferred approach for the project.

PROJECT OBJECTIVES

Collectively, these steps define the issues that lead to project initiation. But the actual positioning comes with the development of clear, specific objectives or targets that are communicated to all stakeholders. Objectives represent each level of need and define how stakeholders will know that the need has been met. If the criteria of success are not communicated early and often, project participants will simply go through the motions, and there will be little change. Developing detailed objectives with clear measures of success positions each project to achieve its ultimate goal. Objectives provide the connection between organization needs and project accountability.

FORECASTING

Using stakeholder needs and project objectives as the basis, developing a forecast may be useful in making adjustments or choosing alternative solutions. This forecast can be simple, relying on the individuals closest to the situation, or it can involve a more detailed analysis of the situation, expected outcomes, and potential risks. Recently, forecasting has become a critical tool for project sponsors who need evidence that the project will be successful before they are willing to commit to funding.

Benefits of Developing the Chain of Impact

Developing data represented in the results framework—including five-levels of results along with inputs (Level 0) and intangible measures—provides a variety of benefits, including the following:

- Describing the chain of impact that occurs as people become involved in green projects
- Showing project results from multiple perspectives
- Demonstrating how immediate and long-term outcomes are achieved
- Providing information as to why and how outcomes are or are not achieved
- Providing project owners data they can use to make improvements with implementation
- Holding stakeholders accountable for success of all project stages
- Providing stakeholders data they need to make decisions about the project and the organization

At first, the thought of collecting and analyzing such a comprehensive set of data may seem daunting. However, without this set of information, explaining the basis for an ROI calculation will be a challenge. In addition, decisions about projects and their subsequent success require more than an economic metric. By reviewing data that represent the chain of impact, stakeholders can understand how project implementation evolves, what changes are necessary to improve or sustain success, and how the project contributes to the overall good of the organization. Chapter 5 provides more detail.

To simplify the collection and analysis of data in the results framework a step-by-step process model is required. This is presented next.

The ROI Process Model

The second component of the ROI Methodology is the process model. This ten-step process, shown in Figure 4.4, develops the data representing the chain of impact. The process begins with the project objectives and concludes with reporting of data. The model assumes that proper analysis is conducted to define stakeholders' needs prior to project implementation.

PLANNING THE EVALUATION

The first phase of the ROI process model is evaluation planning. This phase involves understanding the purpose of the evaluation, determining the fea-

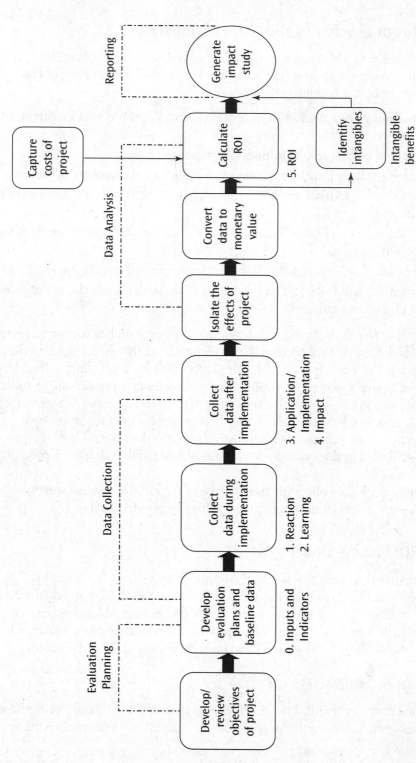

FIGURE 4.4 The ROI Process Model

sibility of the planned approach, planning data collection and analysis, and outlining the details of the project.

Evaluation Purpose

Evaluations are conducted for a variety of reasons:

- To improve the quality of projects and outcomes
- To determine whether a project has accomplished its objectives
- To identify strengths and weaknesses in project implementation
- To enable the cost-benefit analysis
- To assist in the development of future projects or programs
- To determine whether the project was the appropriate solution
- To establish priorities for project funding

Prior to developing the evaluation plan, the purposes of the evaluation should be considered because they will often determine the scope of the evaluation, the types of instruments used, and the type of data collected. As with any project, making the purpose of the evaluation clear will give it focus, and it will help gain support from others.

Feasibility

An important consideration in planning an ROI study is the determination of the levels to which the program will be evaluated. Some project evaluations will stop at Level 2, measuring learning and awareness. Other evaluations will stop at Level 3, application, where analysis will determine the extent to which participants are applying what they learned through a project launch. Other projects will be evaluated at Level 4, business impact, where the consequences of application are monitored and measures directly linked to the project are examined. If the ROI calculation is needed, the evaluation will proceed to Level 5, converting project benefits to money and comparing them to project implementation costs. Evaluation at Level 5 is intended for projects that are expensive, high-profile, and have a direct link to operational and strategic objectives.

Feasibility of a project is determined through the initial analysis and the development of project objectives. The objectives are defined along the same five levels as the needs assessment:

- Reaction objectives (Level 1)
- Learning objectives (Level 2)
- Application and implementation objectives (Level 3)
- Impact objectives (Level 4)
- ROI objectives (Level 5)

Specific objectives take the mystery out of what each project should achieve. They also serve as the basis for comparing results. If application and impact objectives are unavailable, they must be developed using input from a variety of stakeholders.

With clear purpose and project feasibility, evaluation planning continues with the development of the data collection plan, the ROI analysis plan, and the project plan. Appropriate up-front attention to these planning documents will save time later, when data are actually collected.

Data Collection Plan

Table 4.1 shows a completed data collection plan for a project, Better Building Better Business Conference, undertaken to support home builders as they build more efficient homes (Anderson, Bensch, and Pigg, 2007). This technical conference, which was offered to residential builders by the Energy Center of Wisconsin, included:

- Skills-based, hands-on workshops
- Focused training in building science concepts
- Integration of the Wisconsin ENERGY STAR™ programs into curriculum, general sessions, trade shows, and satellite events
- Hands-on technology demonstrations
- Celebration of leadership in energy efficiency

The primary objective of the project was to increase energy efficiency of homes in Wisconsin. Research questions addressed through the evaluation included:

- Did the conference have an impact on job-site practices or product selection?
- Did the recognition and community-building activities create more motivation to maintain builders' commitment to energy efficiency?

The data collection plan shown in Table 4.1 provides a place for the major elements and issues regarding data collection. Broad objectives are appropriate for planning. Specific, detailed objectives are developed later, before the project is designed. Entries in the *measures* column define the specific measure for each objective; entries in the *methods* column describe the technique used to collect the data. In the *sources* column, the source of the data is identified; the *timing* column indicates when the data are collected. Finally, the *responsibilities* column identifies who will collect the data.

TABLE 4.1 Data Collection Plan

Data Collection Plan Project: *Better Building, Better Business Conference* Responsibility: _____ Date: _____

Level	Objectives	Measures/Data	Data-Collection Method	Data Sources	Timing	Responsibilities
1	**Reaction/Satisfaction** • Overall score Customer service Session scores	4.3 on a 5-point scale for overall satisfaction 90 percent or higher on "treated like a valued customer" question Majority sessions ≥ 4.3; less than 10 percent fall below 4.0	Questionnaire	Attendees	Lunch, second day of conference	Conference staff
2	**Learning** • Voluntarily recall a sponsor name	Rating scale	Post-event interview	Attendees in target demographic	10 months following conference	Evaluation staff
3	**Application/Implementation** • Change a building practice or practices such as air sealing, framing technique, insulation changes, or use of ENERGY STAR™ lighting	Checklist	Post-event interview	Attendees in target demographic	10 months following conference	Evaluation staff
4	**Impact** • Energy savings	Energy costs	Monitoring records Questionnaire	Internal records Attendees	10 months following conference Lunch, second day of conference	Evaluation staff Conference staff
5	**ROI** • Achieve a 0 percent (break even) ROI					

TABLE 4.2 ROI Analysis Plan

ROI Analysis Plan Project: *Better Buildings, Better Business Conference*   **Responsibility:** _____

Data Items (Usually Level 4)	Methods for Isolating the Effects of the Project	Methods of Converting Data to Monetary Values	Cost Categories	Intangible Benefits	Communication Targets for Final Report	Other Influences/ Issues During Application	Comments
Energy savings	• Participant estimation • Expert input	• Previous studies • Internal experts • Industry standards	• Conference Planning • Coordination/ speaker time • Marketing • Program materials • Food/ refreshments • Facilities/ travel • Instructor honoria • Evaluation (time and materials)	• Client/ customer satisfaction • Staff motivation • Sponsor satisfaction • ENERGY STAR™ consultant motivation	• Energy Center Board of Directors • Industry program evaluators and designers • Conference organizers • Builders • Sponsors • Exhibitors	• Existing practices	Use results to help establish baseline for future performance comparison.

ROI Analysis Plan

Table 4.2 shows a completed ROI analysis plan for the home builder's conference described in the previous section. This planning document captures information on key items that are necessary to develop the actual ROI calculation. In the first column, impact measures are listed. In some cases this column includes application measures. These items will be used in the ROI analysis.

The method employed to isolate the project's effects is listed next to each data item in the second column. Data conversion methods are included in the third column. Cost categories that will be captured for the project are outlined in the fourth column. Normally, the cost categories will be consistent from one project to another. Intangible benefits expected from the project are outlined in the fifth column. This list is generated from discussions about the project with sponsors and subject-matter experts. Communication targets are outlined in the sixth column. Finally, other issues or events that might influence project implementation and its outputs are highlighted in the seventh column. Typical items include the capability of participants, the degree of access to data sources, the engagement of stakeholders, and unique data analysis issues. The comments column is for notes and issues important to the team and the evaluation project implementation.

The ROI analysis plan, when combined with the data collection plan illustrating how the evaluation will develop from beginning to end, including the calculation of the ROI.

Project Plan

The final planning document is a project plan, as shown in Table 4.3. A project plan consists of a description of the project and brief details, such as duration, target audience, and number of participants. It also shows the timeline of the project, from the planning of the study through the final communication of the results. This plan becomes an operational tool to keep the project on track.

Collectively, the three planning documents provide the direction necessary for the ROI study. Most of the decisions regarding the process are made as these planning tools are developed. When the project team spends time up front to plan an evaluation, the project becomes a methodical, systematic process. Planning is a crucial step in the ROI Methodology, in which valuable time allocated to planning will save precious time later.

COLLECTING DATA

Data collection is central to the ROI Methodology. Both hard data (representing output, quality, cost, and time) and soft data (including job satisfac-

TABLE 4.3 Project Plan

	Month						
	F	M	A	M	J	J	A
Decision to conduct ROI study	■						
Plan evaluation	■						
Design and test instruments		■					
Collect data		■			■		
Tabulate data					■		
Conduct analysis						■	
Write report						■	
Print report						■	
Communicate results							■
Initiate improvements							■
Complete implementation							■

tion, customer satisfaction, and public image) are collected. A variety of data collection methods are employed, including:

- Surveys
- Questionnaires
- Tests
- Observations
- Interviews
- Focus groups
- Action plans
- Performance contracts
- Business performance monitoring

The important challenge in data collection is to select the method or methods appropriate for the setting and the specific project, within the time and budget constraints of the organization. Data collection is covered in more detail in Chapters 6 and 7.

ISOLATING THE EFFECTS OF THE PROJECT

An often overlooked issue in evaluation is the process of isolating the effects of the project. In this step, specific strategies are explored that determine the amount of output performance directly related to the project. This step is essential because many factors influence performance data, and it is often necessary to identify contribution of certain key factors. The specific strategies of this step pinpoint the amount of improvement directly related to the project, which results in increased accuracy and credibility of ROI calculations. The following techniques have been used by organizations to address this important issue:

- Control groups/comparison groups
- Trend-line analysis
- Forecasting and recession models
- Participants' estimates
- Managers' estimates
- Senior manager's estimates
- Experts' input
- Customer input

Collectively, these techniques provide a comprehensive set of tools to handle the important and critical issue of isolating the effects of projects. Chapter 8 addresses this issue in detail.

CONVERTING DATA TO MONETARY VALUES

To calculate the ROI, Level 4 impact data are converted to monetary values and compared with project costs. This requires that a value be placed on each unit of measure connected with the project. Many techniques are available to convert data to monetary values. The specific technique selected depends on the type of data and the situation. The techniques include:

- Use of output data, as standard values
- Cost of quality, usually as a standard value
- Time savings converted to participants' wages and employee benefits
- An analysis of historical costs and records
- Use of internal and external experts
- Search of external databases
- Use of participant estimates
- Use of manager estimates
- Soft measures mathematically linked to other measures

This step in the ROI process model is necessary in developing the numerator of the ROI equation. Converting benefits to money normalizes the benefits so a comparison can be made to the costs. The process is challenging, particularly with soft data, but it can be methodically accomplished using one or more of these strategies. Because of its importance, this step in the ROI Methodology is described in detail in Chapter 9.

IDENTIFYING INTANGIBLE BENEFITS

In addition to tangible, monetary benefits, intangible benefits (those not converted to money) are identified for most projects. Intangible benefits include items such as:

- Increased brand awareness
- Improved reputation
- Enhanced public image
- Increased employee engagement
- Improved customer loyalty
- Enhanced recruiting

During data analysis, every attempt is made to convert all data to monetary values. All hard data—such as output, quality, cost, and time—are converted to monetary values. The conversion of soft data is attempted for each data item. However, if the process used for conversion is too subjective or inaccurate, and the resulting values lose credibility in the process, then the data are listed as an intangible benefit with the appropriate explanation. For some projects, intangible, nonmonetary benefits are extremely valuable, and these often carry as much influence as the hard data items. Chapter 9 describes in more detail the issue of intangible benefits.

TABULATING PROJECT COSTS

An important part of the ROI equation is the calculation of project costs, which make up the denominator of the ROI equation. Tabulating the costs involves monitoring or developing all the related costs of the project targeted for the ROI calculation. Among the cost components to be included are:

- Initial analysis costs
- Cost to design and develop the project
- Cost to acquire equipment and technology
- Cost of all project materials
- Cost of the facilities for the project

- Travel, lodging, and meal costs for the participants and team members
- Participants' salaries (including employee benefits)
- Administrative and overhead costs, allocated in some convenient way
- Operating costs
- Evaluation costs

The conservative approach is to consider the fully loaded costs of a project. Chapter 10 addresses this step in the ROI Methodology.

CALCULATING THE RETURN ON INVESTMENT

Return on investment is reported using a variety of metrics. Standard calculations include the benefit-cost ratio (BCR), ROI percentage, and payback period. The BCR is calculated as the project benefits divided by the project costs. In formula form:

$$BCR = \frac{\text{Project Benefits}}{\text{Project Costs}}$$

The ROI is based on the net project benefits divided by project costs, then multiplied by 100 to develop the percentage. The net benefits are calculated as the project benefits minus the project costs. In formula form, the ROI becomes:

$$ROI\ (\%) = \frac{\text{Net Project Benefits}}{\text{Project Costs}} \times 100$$

This is the same basic formula used in evaluating other investments, in which the ROI is traditionally reported as earnings divided by investment. In addition, it may sometimes be necessary to calculate the payback period. Payback period requires that the project costs be compared to annual project benefits. In equation form, the payback period is calculated as:

$$\text{Payback Period} = \frac{\text{Project Costs}}{\text{Annual Project Benefits}}$$

A simple example of the benefit-cost ratio, ROI, and payback period illustrate the calculations. An energy savings project for a city's municipal buildings involved replacing current bulbs with energy-saving bulbs. A three-year benefits stream was selected at the beginning of the project based on the expected life of the new bulbs. The project benefits for the three years are $570,000 ($190,000 per year), and the fully loaded cost of replacement is $350,000.

$$BCR = \frac{\$570,000}{\$350,000} = 1.63{:}1$$

$$ROI\ (\%) = \frac{\$220,000}{\$350,000} \times 100 = 63\%$$

$$Payback\ Period = \frac{\$350,000}{\$190,000} = 1.84\ years\ or\ 22\ months$$

The ROI calculation of net benefits ($570,000 minus $350,000) divided by total costs brings an ROI of 63 percent. This is what is earned after we get back the $350,000 spent for the project. The ROI calculation accounts for the project costs and shows the resulting net gain.

The BCR calculation uses the total benefits in the numerator. Therefore, the expressed BCR of 1.63:1 does not account for replacing the expended costs. This is why, when using the same values, the BCR will always be 1 greater than the ROI. The BCR of 1.63:1 in this example means that for every dollar spent, $1.63 is gained. One dollar has to pay for the investment, so the net is $0.63 (as expressed in the ROI calculation). The payback period shows that it takes about twenty-two months to pay back the project's investment.

For short-term projects in which an immediate payoff is expected, consider the first-year benefits only. This approach is the most conservative approach to accounting for project costs. With a project investment for which the payoff may not occur for two or three years post-project implementation, consider the time value of the investment and benefits stream. Again, this is a conservative accounting of financial resources. These calculations, along with other issues pertinent to developing the ROI, are described in Chapter 10.

REPORTING

The final step in the ROI process model is reporting, a critical step that often lacks the degree of attention and planning required to ensure its success. The reporting step involves developing appropriate information in impact studies and other brief reports. At the heart of this step are the different techniques used to communicate to a wide variety of target audiences. In most ROI studies, several audiences are interested in and need the information. Careful planning to match the communication method with the audience is essential to ensure that the message is understood and that appropriate actions follow. Chapter 11 is devoted to reporting evaluation results developed through the ROI Methodology. Chapter 11 also describes development of *The Green Scorecard* macro-level reporting of success for all sustainability initiatives.

Operating Standards and Philosophy

An organization's philosophy and standards can have an important influence on how stakeholders perceive the quality of data. This is the third component necessary to create a sustainable evaluation practice. Consistency and replication of studies is the output of evaluation standards. Progress and assumptions inherent in an evaluation process should not vary depending on the individual conducting the evaluation. In addition, instilling a philosophy of conservative assumptions will ensure that results do not overstate the project contribution to outcomes, often positioning decision makers to make unnecessary and inappropriate overinvestments in a project. Table 4.4 shows the twelve guiding principles that serve as standards of use for the ROI Methodology.

TABLE 4.4   Twelve Guiding Principles of the ROI Methodology

Guiding Principles

1. When conducting a higher-level evaluation, collect data at lower levels.
2. When planning a higher-level evaluation, the previous level of evaluation is not required to be comprehensive.
3. When collecting and analyzing data, use only the most credible sources.
4. When analyzing data, select the most conservative alternative for calculations.
5. Use at least one method to isolate the effects of a project.
6. If no improvement data are available for a population or from a specific source, assume that no improvement has occurred.
7. Adjust estimates of improvement for potential errors of estimation.
8. Avoid use of extreme data items and unsupported claims when calculating ROI.
9. Use only the first year of annual benefits in ROI analysis of short-term projects.
10. Fully load all costs of a project when analyzing ROI.
11. Intangible measures are defined as measures that are purposely not converted to monetary values.
12. Communicate the results of ROI Methodology to all key stakeholders.

The guiding principles serve not only to consistently address each step of the evaluation process, but also to provide a conservative approach to the analysis. A conservative approach may lower the actual ROI calculation, but it will build credibility and buy-in with the key stakeholders, especially CEOs, managing directors, top administrators, and CFOs.

Application and Practice

The fourth component necessary for a sustainable measurement practice is application and practice. This component puts theory to practice. While the results framework serves as the basis for the ROI Methodology, and the process model and standards are systematic, it is the practice and use of the process that is important. Application quickly shows the power of this methodology.

Implementation

A variety of environmental issues and events must be addressed early to ensure the successful implementation of the ROI process. Specific topics or actions important to successful implementation include:

- A policy statement concerning results-based green projects
- Procedures and guidelines for different elements and techniques of the evaluation process
- Formal meetings to develop staff skills with the ROI Methodology
- Strategies to improve management commitment to and support for the ROI Methodology
- Mechanisms to provide technical support for data collection, design, data analysis, and evaluation strategy
- Specific techniques to place more attention on results

In addition to implementing and sustaining ROI use, the process must undergo periodic review. An annual review is recommended to determine the extent to which the process is adding value. This final element involves checking satisfaction with the process and determining how well it is understood and applied. Essentially, this review follows the process described in this book to determine the ROI on ROI. Chapter 12 is devoted to this important topic.

Benefits of Applying the ROI Methodology

The approach to evaluating the success of green projects presented in this book has been used consistently and routinely by thousands of organizations in the past decade. It has been more prominent in some fields and industries than in others, such as performance improvement, quality, human resources, meetings and events, and marketing. Much has been learned about the success of this methodology and what it can bring to the organizations using it. Along with the benefits described earlier in the book, specific benefits of applying the ROI Methodology are as follows.

ALIGNING PROJECTS WITH THE BUSINESS

The ROI Methodology ensures alignment with the business, which is enforced in three steps. First, even before the project is initiated, the process ensures that alignment is achieved up front, at the time the green project is validated as the appropriate solution. Second, by requiring specific, clearly defined objectives at the impact level, the project focuses on the ultimate outcomes, in essence driving the business measure by its design, delivery, and implementation. Third, in the follow-up data, when the outcome measures may have changed or improved, a method is used to isolate the effects of the project on those data, consequently proving the connection to that business measure (i.e., showing the amount of improvement directly connected to the project and ensuring there is business alignment).

VALIDATING THE VALUE PROPOSITION

In reality, most projects are undertaken to deliver value, whether value is defined in business, environmental, or societal terms. The definition of value may on occasion be unclear, or may not be what a project's various sponsors, organizers, and stakeholders desire. Consequently, there are often value shifts. When the values are finally determined, the value proposition is detailed. Using the ROI Methodology, organizations can forecast the value in advance, and if the value has been delivered, it verifies the value proposition agreed to by the appropriate parties.

IMPROVING PROCESSES

This is a process improvement tool by design and by practice. It collects data to evaluate how projects are—or are not—working. When green projects are not progressing as they should, data are available to indicate what must be changed to make the projects more effective. When things are working well, data are available to show what else could be done to make them better. Continuous feedback and process improvement are inherent in the ROI Methodology.

ENHANCING IMAGE

Many functions, and even entire professions, are criticized for being unable (or unwilling) to deliver what is expected. For this, their public image suffers. The ROI Methodology is one way to help build the respect a function, organization, or profession needs. By showing value defined by all stakeholders and by using evaluation results, green project owners communicate to stakeholders their successes and their desire to continuously improve. This methodology shows a connection to the bottom line and the greater good.

IMPROVING SUPPORT

Securing support for green projects is critical. Many projects enjoy the support of key stakeholders who allocate the resources to make the projects viable. Unfortunately, some stakeholders may not support certain projects because they do not see the value the projects deliver in terms they appreciate and understand. Having an accountability approach that shows how a project or program is connected to business goals and objectives can change this support level.

JUSTIFYING OR ENHANCING BUDGETS

Some organizations have used the ROI Methodology to support existing proposed budgets. Because the process shows the monetary value expected or achieved with specific projects, the data can often be leveraged into budget requests. When a particular function is budgeted, the amount budgeted is often in direct proportion to the value that the function adds. If little or no credible data support the contribution, the budgets are often trimmed—or at least not enhanced. Bringing accountability to the level achieved through use of the ROI process is one of the best ways to secure future funding.

BUILDING PARTNERSHIPS WITH KEY EXECUTIVES

Almost every function attempts to partner with operating executives and key managers in the organization. Unfortunately, some managers may not want to be partners. They may not want to waste time and effort on a relationship that does not help them succeed. They want to partner only with groups and individuals who can add value and help them in meaningful ways. Showing the projects' results will enhance the likelihood of building these partnerships, by providing the initial impetus for making the partnerships work.

EARNING A SEAT AT THE TABLE

Many functions are attempting to earn a seat at the table, however defined. Typically, this means participating in the strategy- or decision-making process, and in high-level discussions at the top of the organization. Department and project leaders hope to be involved in strategic decision-making, particularly in areas that will affect the projects and programs in which they are involved. Showing the actual contribution and getting others to understand how projects add value can help earn the coveted seat at the table, because most executives want to include those who are genuinely helping the business by providing input that is valuable and constructive. Application of the ROI Methodology may be the most important action toward earning the seat at the table.

Final Thoughts

The ROI Methodology is an accountability process designed to collect and report multiple types of data that are crucial to the development of an organization's green scorecard:

- Inputs and indicators (Level 0)
- Reaction and perceived value (Level 1)
- Learning and awareness (Level 2)
- Application and implementation (Level 3)
- Impact (Level 4)
- ROI (Level 5)
- Intangible benefits

By developing these data and following a step-by-step process grounded in conservative standards, project owners can be confident their results will be perceived as credible. In addition, this process will ensure that projects are aligned with the business from the outset. The remainder of the book will describe how to develop data, attribute results to the project, and develop the ROI for sustainability initiatives.

Chapter 5

Project Positioning

Beginning with Objectives in Mind

Consider the following statements:

1. Most experts agree that organization leaders will fully embrace green projects and sustainability initiatives only when there is a business payoff.
2. The vast majority of green projects and sustainability initiatives result in a significant payoff.
3. Green projects and sustainability initiatives fail primarily because they lack connection to the business need at the onset.

These three conclusions underscore the need for aligning green projects to the business. This chapter describes the first two phases of the alignment process: defining the initial needs and developing the corresponding objectives for a project. Aligning a project's intended outcome with business needs positions the project for success. Business alignment is essential if the investment in a project is to reap a positive return.

Creating Business Alignment

As we've noted, aligning green projects and sustainability initiatives with business needs (as well as environmental and societal needs) serves a variety of purposes. Alignment ensures that an organization not only steps up to the environmental plate, but also serves up a home run pitch to shareholders, taxpayers, employees, and other stakeholders with an interest in the organization's economic vitality.

THE PURPOSE OF ALIGNMENT

According to approximately two thousand published and unpublished case studies, the number one cause of project failure is moving forward without a clearly defined need. The second is misalignment between the project objectives and business needs.

Projects must begin with a clear focus on the desired outcome. The end must be specified in terms of business needs and measures so that the outcome—the actual improvement in the measures—and the corresponding ROI are clear. This establishes expectations throughout the project design, development, delivery, and implementation stages. It ensures that the right projects are put into place at the right time—involving the right people for the right reason.

Beginning with the end in mind requires pinning down all the details to ensure that the project is properly planned and executed according to schedule. But conducting this up-front analysis is not as simple as one may think—it requires a disciplined approach.

DISCIPLINED ANALYSIS

Proper analysis requires discipline and determination to adhere to a structured, systematic process supported by standards. A standardized approach adds credibility and allows for consistent application so that the analysis can be replicated. A disciplined approach maintains process efficiency through the development and use of various tools and templates. This initial phase of project development calls for focus and thoroughness, with little allowance for major shortcuts.

Not every project should be subjected to the type of comprehensive analysis described in this chapter. Some outcomes and processes are obvious and require little analysis in order to implement the project. For example, in-depth analysis is unnecessary to determine the best approach to changing incandescent light bulbs to fluorescent bulbs in a single building. The greatest part of analysis is calculating the monetary payoff. People are not too involved in the process unless the light becomes a distraction or an inconvenience. Another example is purchasing recycled paper that is less expensive than the current paper; this may not require any analysis other than the cost. Of course, if there is a noticeable difference in the quality of the paper, then users will get involved.

The amount of analysis required often depends on the expected opportunity to be gained if the project is appropriate, or the negative consequences anticipated if the project is inappropriate. Usually large-scale and expensive projects need in-depth analysis. When outcomes involve a large number of people whose perceptions, knowledge, and attitudes must change, detailed analysis is a must. In essence, if the project is important, strategic, expensive, and involves a large number of people, comprehensive analysis at the five levels described in this chapter, is appropriate.

Sponsors may react with concern or resistance when analysis is initially proposed. Some indicate concern about the potential for "paralysis by analysis," where requests and directives lead only to additional analyses. These reactions can pose a problem for an organization because analysis is necessary to ensure that a project or an initiative is appropriate for a situation. Unfortunately, the thought of analysis often conjures up images of complex problems, confusing models, and a deluge of data along with complicated statistical techniques in an effort to cover all of the bases. In reality, analysis need not be so complicated. Simple techniques can uncover the cause of a problem or the need for a particular project.

Organizations often avoid analysis because:

1. *The specific need appears to point to a particular solution.* Sometimes the information gained from asking individuals what they need appears to point to a legitimate solution, but in fact the solution is inadequate or inappropriate. For example, when employees are asked what they need to improve the environment, they may identify specific tools, suppliers, materials, or equipment. In reality, the solution may be learning to conserve and recycle. Implementing a solution in response entirely to individual input can prove shortsighted and costly.

2. *The solution appears to be obvious.* In the process of examining a problem or identifying a potential opportunity, some seemingly obvious solutions will arise. For example, if at a professional development conference print costs are too high, the immediate conclusion may be to eliminate the automatic distribution of handouts and require participants to print only what they want. However, although this solution appears obvious, deeper analysis may reveal that another approach may be appropriate— such as the use of online learning, webinars, or other technology. These larger solutions reduce not only print costs to the conference provider, but also travel costs to participants. Costs go down and the environment wins twice as much.

3. *Everyone has an opinion about the cause of a problem.* The person requesting a particular project may think that he or she has the best solution. Choosing the solution championed by the highest-ranking or most senior executive is often tempting. Unfortunately, this person may not be close enough to the situation to offer a solution that will have a lasting effect on the problem.

4. *Analysis takes too much time.* Yes, analysis takes time and consumes resources. However, the consequences of no analysis can be more expen-

sive. If the implemented solutions do not appropriately address the needs, time and money are wasted and the problem is left unsolved. Ill-advised solutions based on no analysis can have devastating consequences. When designed properly and conducted professionally, an analysis can be completed within the budgetary and time constraints of most organizations. The secret is to focus on the right tools for the situation.

5. *Analysis sounds confusing.* Determining a problem's causes may seem complex and puzzling. However, analyses can be simple and straightforward and achieve excellent results. The challenge is to select the level of analysis that will yield the best solution with minimal effort and the simplest techniques.

In the face of these misconceptions, the difficulty of promoting additional analysis is apparent. But this step is critical and should not be omitted, or else the process will be flawed from the outset.

The remainder of the chapter delves into the components of analysis that are necessary for a solid alignment between a project and the business. First, however, reviewing the model introduced in the previous chapter, Figure 4.3, may be helpful.

Determining the Potential Payoff

The first step in the alignment process is to determine the potential payoff of solving a problem or seizing an opportunity. This step begins with answers to a few crucial questions:

- Is the problem or opportunity worth pursuing?
- Is the investment in a project or solution feasible?
- What is the likelihood of a positive ROI as well as the environmental contribution?

For projects addressing problems or opportunities with high potential rewards, the answers are obvious. The questions may take longer to answer for opportunities where the expected payoff is less apparent.

Essentially, from an economic perspective, a project will pay off in profit increases and cost savings. Profit increases are generated by projects that drive revenue (e.g., projects that improve sales, drive market share, introduce new green products, open new markets, enhance customer service, or increase customer loyalty). Other revenue-generating measures such as increasing memberships or donations show an increase in profit after subtracting the cost of doing business.

However, most green projects drive cost savings. Cost savings come through cost reduction or cost avoidance. Improved quality, reduced cycle time, lowered downtime, reduced energy use, reduced consumption, and minimized delays are all examples of cost-saving measures.

Cost-avoidance projects are implemented to reduce risks, avoid problems, or prevent unwanted events. Some finance and accounting professionals may view cost avoidance as an inappropriate measure used to determine monetary benefits and calculate ROI. However, if the assumptions prove correct, accomplishing an avoided cost (e.g., compliance fines) can be more rewarding than reducing an actual cost. Preventing a problem is more cost-effective than waiting to solve it.

Determining the potential payoff is the first step in the needs analysis process. This step closely relates to the next one, determining the business need, since the potential payoff is often based on a consideration of the business. The payoff depends on two factors: the monetary value derived from the business measure's improvement, and the approximate cost of the project. Identifying monetary values in detail usually yields a more credible forecast of what to expect from the chosen project. However, this step may be omitted in situations where the problem (business need) must be resolved regardless of the cost, or if it becomes obvious that this is a high-payoff activity. For example, if the problem involves a safety concern involving toxic materials, a regulatory environmental compliance issue, or a competitive matter, a detailed analysis is not needed.

The target level of detail may also hinge on the need to secure project funding. If the potential funding source does not recognize the value of the project compared with the potential costs, more detail may be necessary to provide a convincing case for funding.

OBVIOUS VERSUS NOT-SO-OBVIOUS PAYOFF

The potential payoff is obvious for some projects and not so obvious for others. Examples of opportunities with obvious payoffs include:

- Operating costs are 47 percent higher than industry average
- Environmentally friendly rating of 3.89 on a 10-point scale
- A cost to the city of $12,000 annually per person for landfill operation
- Noncompliance environmental fines totaling $1.2 million, up 82 percent from last year
- Energy costs are 35 percent above benchmark figure
- Carbon emissions are 58 percent above industry average

Each item appears to reflect a serious problem that needs to be addressed by executives, administrators, or politicians.

For other projects, issues are sometimes unclear and may arise from political motives or bias. These potential opportunities are associated with payoffs that may not be so obvious. Examples of such opportunities may include:

- Becoming an environmental leader
- Becoming a green company
- Improving sustainability competencies for all managers
- Improving branding for all products
- Creating a great place to work
- Implementing green recruiting

With each of these opportunities, there is a need for more specific detail regarding the measure. For example, if the opportunity is to become a green company, one might ask: What is a green company? What are the advantages of becoming a green company? How is green defined? Projects with not-so-obvious payoffs require greater analysis than those with clearly defined outcomes.

THE COST OF A PROBLEM

The potential payoff establishes the fundamental reason for pursuing new or enhanced projects. But the payoff—whether obvious or not—is not the only reason for moving forward with a project. The cost of a problem is another factor. If the cost is excessive, it should be addressed. If not, then a decision must be made as to whether the problem is worth solving.

Problems are expensive and their solution can result in high returns, especially when the solution is inexpensive. Problems may encompass time, quality, productivity, and team or customer issues. All of these factors must be converted to monetary values if the cost of the problem is to be determined. Inventory shortages are often directly associated with the cost of the inventory as well as with the cost of carrying the inventory. Time can easily be translated into money by calculating the fully-loaded cost of an individual's time spent on unproductive tasks. Calculating the time for completing a project, task, or cycle involves measures that can be converted to money. Errors, mistakes, waste, delays, and bottlenecks can often be converted to money because of their consequences. Productivity problems and inefficiencies, equipment damage, and equipment underuse are other items for which conversion to monetary value is straightforward.

In examining costs, considering *all* the costs and their implications is crucial. For example, the full cost of disposing of computers includes not only the disposal fee but transportation, record keeping, time required for investigations, damage to image, and time spent by all involved employees who are addressing the issue. The cost of an environmental complaint includes not only the cost of the time spent resolving the complaint, but also the cost of the penalty or adjustment because of the complaint. The costliest consequence of the complaint is the lost future business and goodwill from the negative image and from potential customers who learn of the complaint. Placing a monetary value on a problem helps in determining if the problem's resolution is economically feasible.

THE VALUE OF AN OPPORTUNITY

Just as the cost of a problem can be easily tabulated in most situations, the value of an opportunity can also be calculated. Examples of opportunities include implementing green cost-saving projects, exploring new technology, increasing research and development efforts, and upgrading the workforce to create a more environmentally friendly company. In these situations a problem may not exist, but an opportunity to get ahead of the competition or to prevent a problem's occurrence by taking immediate action does. Assigning a proper value to this opportunity requires considering what may happen if the project is not pursued or acknowledging the potential windfall if the opportunity is seized. The value of an opportunity is determined by following the different possible scenarios to convert business impact measures to money. The difficulty in this process is conducting a credible analysis. Forecasting the value of an opportunity entails many assumptions compared with calculating the value of a known outcome.

TO FORECAST OR NOT TO FORECAST?

The need to seek and assign value to opportunities leads to an important decision: to forecast or not to forecast ROI. If the stakes are high and support for the project is not in place, a detailed forecast may be the only way to gain the needed support and funding for the project or to inform the choice between multiple potential projects. In developing the forecast, the rigor of the analysis is an issue. In some cases, an informal forecast is sufficient, given certain assumptions about alternative outcome scenarios. In other cases, a detailed forecast is needed that uses data collected from a variety of experts, previous studies from another project, or perhaps more sophisticated analysis. Other references provide techniques for developing forecasts (Phillips and Phillips, 2010).

Determining Business Needs

Once the potential payoff, including its financial value, has been determined, the next step is to clarify the business needs. This requires identifying specific measures so that the business situation can be clearly assessed.

The concept of business needs refers to the need for gains in productivity, quality, efficiency, time, and cost. This is true for the private sector as well as in government, nonprofit, non-governmental, and academic organizations.

THE OPPORTUNITY

A business need is represented by a business measure. For example, let's say you have been receiving an extraordinary number of complaints regarding your waste disposal processes. Your need is to reduce complaints. The specific measure is number of complaints regarding waste disposal processes. Any process, item, or perception can be measured, and such measurement is critical to this level of analysis. If the project focuses on solving a problem, preventing a problem, or seizing an opportunity, the measures are usually identifiable. The important point is that the measures are present in the system, ready to be captured for this level of analysis. The challenge is to define the measures and to find them economically and swiftly.

HARD DATA MEASURES

To focus on the desired measures, distinguishing between hard data and soft data may be helpful. Hard data are primary measures of improvement presented in the form of rational, undisputed facts that are usually gathered within functional areas throughout an organization. These are the most desirable type of data because they are easy to quantify and are easily converted to monetary values. The fundamental criteria for gauging the effectiveness of an organization are hard data items such as revenue, productivity, and profitability, as well as measures that quantify such processes as cost, control, and quality assurance.

Hard data are objective and credible measures of an organization's performance. Hard data can usually be grouped in four categories, as shown in Table 5.1. These categories—output, quality, costs, and time—are typical performance measures in any organization.

Hard data from a particular project involve improvements in the output of the work unit, section, department, division, or the entire organization. Every organization, regardless of the type, must have basic measures of output, such as number of pages printed, tons produced, or packages shipped. Since these values are monitored, changes can easily be measured by comparing "before" and "after" outputs.

Quality is another important hard data category. If quality is a major priority for the organization, processes are likely in place to measure and monitor quality. The rising prominence of quality improvement processes (such as Total Quality Management, Continuous Process Improvement, and Six

TABLE 5.1 Examples of Hard Data

Output	Quality	Costs	Time
Energy use	Failure rates	Energy costs	Cycle time
Units produced	Scrap	Supplies costs	Equipment downtime
Carbon emissions	Waste	Fuel costs	Overtime
Recycle volume	Rejects	Budget variances	On-time shipments
Items assembled	Error rates	Unit costs	Time to project completion
Money collected	Rework	Cost by account	Processing time
Items sold	Shortages	Variable costs	Supervisory time
Materials consumed	Product defects	Fixed costs	Time to proficiency
New accounts generated	Deviation from standard	Overhead costs	Adherence to schedules
Forms processed	Product failures	Project cost savings	Repair time
Inventory turnover	Inventory adjustments	Material costs	Efficiency
Applications processed	Incidents	Sales expense	Work stoppages
Tasks completed	Compliance discrepancies		Order response
Output per hour	Agency fines		Late reporting
Productivity			Lost-time days
Work backlog			
Shipments			

Sigma) has contributed to the tremendous recent successes in pinpointing proper quality measures—and assigning monetary values to them.

Another important hard data category is cost. Many projects are designed to lower, control, or eliminate the cost of a specific process or activity. Achieving cost targets has an immediate effect on the bottom line. Some organizations focus narrowly on cost reduction. For example, consider Walmart, whose tagline is "Always low prices. Always." All levels of the organization are dedicated to lowering costs on processes and products and passing the savings along to customers. With this focus on cost savings comes environmental contribution.

Time is another critical measure in any organization. Hundreds of publications, workshops, and seminars focus on saving time. Some organizations gauge their performance almost exclusively in relation to time. When asked what business FedEx is in, company executives say, "We engineer time."

SOFT DATA MEASURES

Soft data are probably the most familiar measures of an organization's effectiveness, yet their collection can present a challenge. Values representing attitude, motivation, and satisfaction are examples of soft data. Soft data are more difficult to gather and analyze, and therefore, they are used when hard data are unavailable or to supplement hard data. Soft data represent qualitative measures, which make them more difficult to convert to monetary values than hard data. They are less objective as performance measurements and are usually behavior related, yet, organizations place great emphasis on them. Improvements in these measures represent important business needs, but many organizations omit them from the ROI equation because of their subjectivity. However, soft data can contribute to economic value to the same extent as hard data measures. Table 5.2 shows typical examples of soft data by category. The key is to avoid focusing too much on the hard versus soft data distinction. A better approach is to consider data as tangible or intangible.

TANGIBLE VERSUS INTANGIBLE BENEFITS

A challenge with regard to soft versus hard data is converting soft measures to monetary values. The key to addressing this challenge is to remember that, ultimately, all roads lead to hard data. Although creativity may be categorized as a form of soft data, a creative workplace can develop new products or new patents, which lead to, for example, greater revenue and reduction in carbon emissions—clearly hard data measures. Although it is possible to convert the measures listed in Table 5.2 to monetary amounts, it is often more realistic and practical to leave them in nonmonetary form. This decision is based on considerations of credibility and the cost of the conversion. According to the standards of the ROI Methodology, an intangible measure is defined as a measure that is intentionally not converted to money. If a soft data measure can be converted to a monetary value credibly using minimal resources, it is considered tangible, reported as a monetary value and incorporated in the ROI calculation. If a data item cannot be converted to money credibly with minimal resources, it is listed as an intangible measure. Therefore, in defin-

TABLE 5.2   Examples of Soft Data

Work Habits	Customer Service	Work Climate/Satisfaction
Excessive socialization	Customer complaints	Grievances
Wasteful activities	Customer satisfaction	Discrimination charges
Visits to the dispensary	Customer dissatisfaction	Employee complaints
Violations of rules	Customer impressions	Job satisfaction
Communication	Customer loyalty	Organization commitment
breakdowns	Customer retention	Employee engagement
Initiative/ Innovation	Lost customers	Employee loyalty
Creativity		Intent to leave
Innovation	**Employee Development/ Advancement**	
New ideas	Promotions	**Image**
Suggestions	Capability	Brand awareness
New products and services	Intellectual capital	Reputation
Trademarks	Requests for transfer	Leadership
Copyrights and patents	Performance appraisal ratings	Social responsibility
Process improvements		Environmental friendliness
Partnerships/alliances	Readiness	Social consciousness
	Networking	External awards

ing business needs, the key difference between measures is not whether they represent hard or soft data, but whether they are tangible or intangible. In either case, they are important contributions toward the desired payoff and important business impact data.

IMPACT DATA SOURCES

Sources of impact data, whether tangible or intangible, are diverse. Data come from routine reporting systems in the organization, city, or community. In many situations, these measures have led to the need for the project; therefore, the source is evident. A vast array of documents, systems, databases, and reports can be used to select the specific measure or measures to be monitored throughout the project. Impact data sources include—but are not limited to—quality reports, service records, suggestion systems, and employee engagement data.

Some project planners and project team members assume that corporate data sources are scarce because the data are not readily available to them. However, data can usually be located by investing a small amount of time. Rarely do new data collection systems or processes need to be developed in order to identify measures representing the business needs of an organization.

In searching for the proper measures to connect to the project and to identify business needs, it is helpful to consider all possible measures that could be influenced. Sometimes, collateral measures move in harmony with the project. For example, efforts to reduce energy costs may also improve quality and increase job satisfaction. Weighing adverse impacts on certain measures may also help. For example, when using recycled materials, quality may suffer; or when delivery schedules are altered to save fuel, customer satisfaction may deteriorate. Finally, project team members must anticipate unintended consequences and capture them as other data items that might be connected to or influenced by the project.

In the process of settling on the precise business measures for the project, it is useful to examine various "what if" scenarios. For example, what if the organization does nothing? The potential consequences of inaction should be made clear. The following questions may help in understanding the consequences of inaction:

- Will the situation deteriorate?
- Will operational problems surface?
- Will budgets be affected?
- Will we lose influence or support?

Answers to these questions can help the organization identify a precise set of measures and can provide a hint of the extent to which the measures may change as a result of the project.

Determining Performance Needs

The next step in the needs analysis is to understand what led to the business need. If the proposed project addresses a problem, this step focuses on the cause of the problem. If the project makes use of an opportunity, this step focuses on what is inhibiting the organization from taking advantage of that opportunity. Answers to the following questions help determine changes in performance necessary to address business needs:

- What is happening or not happening within the organization that is causing the business measure to be at its current level?
- What behaviors or habits need to change in order to improve the business measure?
- What systems or processes need to change in order to support the change in behavior?

- What barriers prevent people from employing behaviors or habits necessary to improve the business measure?

Change in behaviors and habits are often the critical success factor in implementing green projects. People often get stuck in their comfort zones and prefer not to change. Analysis of behavioral aspects of performance ensures the right behaviors are targeted for the business need or opportunity. For example, if your business measure is to reduce landfill costs, analysis may reveal that employees do not recycle. The behavior that needs to change is placing recyclable materials in the appropriate bins.

ANALYSIS TECHNIQUES

Uncovering the causes of the problem or the inhibitors to success with key business measures that can be influenced by green projects requires a variety of analytical techniques. These techniques—such as interviews, focus groups, problem analysis, nominal group technique, force field analysis, and just plain brainstorming—clarify job performance needs. The technique employed depends on the organization or community setting, the apparent depth of the problem, and the funding available for such analysis. Multiple techniques can be used since job performance may be lacking for a number of reasons. Detailed approaches of techniques can be found in many sources (Langdon, Whiteside, and McKenna, 1999).

A SENSIBLE APPROACH

Analysis takes time and adds to a green project's cost. Examining records, researching databases, and observing individuals can provide important data, but a more cost-effective approach may include employing internal or external experts to help analyze the problem. Performance needs can vary considerably and may include ineffective behavior, dysfunctional habits, inadequate processes, a disconnected process flow, improper procedures, a nonsupportive culture, outdated rules and methods, and a non-accommodating environment, to name a few. When needs vary and with many techniques from which to choose, the opportunity exists for overanalysis and excessive costs. Consequently, a sensible approach is needed.

Determining Learning Needs

Changing behaviors, habits, and supporting processes often requires acquiring new knowledge, skills, and information. For example, participants and team members may need to learn about the environment and green solutions, how to perform a task differently, or how to use a process, system, or technology. In some cases learning is the principal solution, as in competency or capability development for green projects and major technology and system installations. For many green projects, however, learning is a minor aspect of an overall solution and may involve simply understanding the process, procedure, or policy. For example, in the implementation of a new recycling project for an organization, the learning component requires understanding why this is necessary, how the project works, and the participant's role in the project. In short, a specific learning solution is not always needed, but all green solutions have a learning component.

A variety of approaches are available for measuring specific learning needs. Often, multiple tasks and jobs are involved in a project and should be addressed separately. One of the most useful ways to determine learning needs is to ask the individuals who understand the process. Subject matter experts can often best determine what skills and knowledge are necessary to address the performance issues. This may be the appropriate time to find out the extent to which the knowledge and skills already exist.

Job and task analyses are effective when a new job is created or when an existing job description changes significantly. As jobs are redesigned and the new tasks must be identified, this type of analysis offers a systematic way of detailing the job and task. Essentially, a job analysis is the collection and evaluation of work-related information. A task analysis identifies the specific knowledge, skills, tools, and conditions necessary to the performance of a particular job.

Perhaps the most effective way to assess learning needs is to conduct informal discussions, surveys, and self-assessments with the planned participants of green projects. Understanding what they know (or do not know) about issues and their roles and responsibilities can provide insight into the best approach to addressing the performance issue.

Sometimes, the demonstration of knowledge surrounding a certain task, process, or procedure provides evidence of what capabilities exist and what is lacking. Such demonstration can be as simple as a skill practice or role play or as complex as an extensive mechanical or electronic simulation. The point is to use demonstrations as a way of determining if employees know how to perform a particular process.

Testing as an assessment process for learning needs is not used as frequently as other methods, but it can be helpful. Employees are tested to reveal what they know about the environment, green solutions, climate change, and sustainability. This information helps guide learning issues.

Input from managers or team leaders may provide a good assessment of knowledge, skill, and information gaps. Input can be solicited through surveys, interviews, or focus groups. It can be a rich source of information about what the users of the project, if it is implemented, will need to know to make it successful.

Where new knowledge, skill, and information are minor components, learning needs are simple. Determining learning needs can be time-consuming for major projects in which new procedures, technologies, and processes must be developed. As in developing performance needs, it is important not to spend excessive time analyzing learning needs but rather to collect as much data as possible with minimal resources.

Determining Preference Needs

The final level of needs analysis determines the preferences that drive the project requirements. Essentially, individuals prefer certain processes, schedules, or activities for the structure of the project. These preferences define how the particular project will be perceived and launched. If the project is a solution to a problem, this step defines how the solution will evolve. If the project takes advantage of an opportunity, this step outlines how the opportunity will be addressed, considering the preferences of those involved in the project.

Perhaps the most important aspect of preference is the desired reaction for the key stakeholders in the project. Stakeholders include participants, their supervisors, managers, and the client funding the project, among others. The green project must be perceived as important, relevant, useful, needed, appropriate, and valuable. Perhaps the most powerful reaction occurs when employees report their intent to do something about the issue. This indicates commitment and has a strong correlation with actual action.

Preference needs typically define the parameters of the project in terms of scope, timing, budget, staffing, location, technology, deliverables, and the degree of allowable disruption. Preference needs are developed from the input of several stakeholders rather than from one individual. For example, participants in the project (those who must make it work) may have a particular preference, but the preference could exhaust resources, time, and budgets. The immediate manager's input may help minimize the amount of disruption and maximize resources.

The urgency of project implementation may introduce a constraint in the preferences. Those who support or own the project often impose preferences on the project in terms of timing, budget, and the use of technology. Because preferences represent a Level 1 need, the project structure and solution will relate directly to the reaction objectives and to the initial reaction to the project.

In determining the preference needs, there can never be too much detail. Projects often go astray and fail to reach their full potential because of misunderstandings and differences in expectations surrounding the project. Preference needs should be addressed before the project begins. Pertinent issues are often outlined in the project proposal or planning documentation.

Developing Objectives for Green Projects and Programs

Green projects are driven by objectives. Objectives position the project or program for success if they represent the needs of the business and include clearly defined measures of achievement. Developing project objectives is the second phase of alignment. A project may be aimed at implementing a solution that addresses a particular need, problem, or opportunity. In other situations, the initial project is designed to develop a range of feasible solutions, with one specific solution selected prior to implementation. Regardless of the project, multiple levels of objectives are necessary. These levels define precisely what will occur as a project is implemented. Project objectives correspond to the levels of evaluation and the levels of needs presented in Figure 5.1.

REACTION OBJECTIVES

For a project to be successful, the stakeholders immediately involved in the process must react favorably—or at least not negatively—to the project. Reaction objectives come from the preference needs. Ideally, those directly involved should be satisfied with the project and see its value. This feedback must be obtained routinely during the project in order to make adjustments, keep the project on track, and redesign certain aspects as necessary. Unfortunately, for many projects, specific objectives and data collection mechanisms are not developed and put in place to allow channels for feedback.

Developing reaction objectives should be straightforward and relatively easy. The objectives reflect the degree of immediate as well as long-term satisfaction and explore issues important to the success of the project. They also form the basis for evaluating the chain of impact, emphasizing planned action, when necessary. Typical issues addressed in the development of reaction objectives are relevance, usefulness, importance, necessity, appropriateness, and motivation. The most important reaction objective is for participants to indicate intent to apply, use, or implement the concepts important to the success of green projects.

LEARNING OBJECTIVES

Every project involves at least one learning objective, and most involve more. With projects entailing major change, the learning component is quite important. In situations narrower in scope, such as the implementation of a new policy, the learning component is minor but still necessary. To ensure that the various stakeholders have learned what they need to know to make the project successful, learning objectives are developed. Here are some examples of learning objectives supporting successful implementation of a green project:

- Identify the six features of the new green policy.
- Demonstrate the use of each new energy-saving procedure within the standard time.
- Score 75 or better on the sustainability quiz.
- Explain the value of the green initiative to a work group.
- Complete the energy-savings simulation with a score of 80 percent or greater within the thirty-minute time limit.
- Report confidence in ability to apply for assistance for weatherization.

Objectives are critical to the measurement of learning because they communicate the expected outcomes from the learning component and define the competency or level of performance necessary to make project implementation successful. They provide a focus to allow participants to clearly identify what it is they must learn and do—sometimes with precision.

APPLICATION AND IMPLEMENTATION OBJECTIVES

The application and implementation objectives clearly define what is expected of the project and often the target level of performance. Application objectives are similar to learning objectives but relate to actual performance. They provide specific milestones indicating when one part or all of the process has been implemented. For example, here are some typical application objectives for when a project or program is implemented:

- At least 99.1 percent of users will know the correct sequences after three weeks of use.
- Within two months, 10 percent of employees will submit documented suggestions for going green.
- Twenty-five percent of employees will participate in community green projects within two years.
- Forty percent of the city's population will routinely recycle two waste products in one year.
- Eighty percent of employees will use one or more of the three environmentally friendly cost-saving projects.
- Fifty percent of green conference attendees will follow up with at least one green exhibitor from the conference.

Application objectives are critical because they describe the expected outcomes in the intermediate area—between the learning of new tasks and procedures and the delivery of the impact of this learning. Application and implementation objectives describe how things should be or the desired state of the workplace once the project solution has been implemented. They provide a basis for evaluating on-the-job changes and performance.

IMPACT OBJECTIVES

Impact objectives indicate key business measures that should improve as the application and implementation objectives are achieved. The following are typical impact objectives:

- Energy costs will be reduced by 30 percent at the tire plant in nine months.
- Operating costs at the foundry should decrease by 20 percent within the next calendar year.
- The average number of fully functioning department-level green projects will reach twelve by year end.
- The company-wide environmentally friendly index should increase by 2 percent during the next calendar year.
- There should be a 40 percent increase in recycling in the city during the next two years.
- Water usage at the headquarters building should decrease by 25 percent within three years.

Impact objectives are critical to measuring business performance because they define the ultimate expected outcome from the project, describing the business unit performance that should result. Above all, impact objectives emphasize achievement of the bottom-line results that key client groups expect and demand.

ROI OBJECTIVES

The fifth level of objectives for projects represents the acceptable ROI—the economic impact. Objectives at this level define the expected payoff from investing in a green project. An ROI objective is typically expressed as an acceptable ROI percentage, which is expressed as annual monetary benefits minus cost, divided by the actual cost, and multiplied by one hundred. A 0 percent ROI indicates a breakeven project. A 50 percent ROI indicates recapture of the project cost and an additional 50 percent "earnings" (fifty cents for every dollar invested).

For some projects, such as the purchase of a new company, a new building, or major equipment, the ROI objective is large relative to the ROI of other expenditures. However, the calculation is the same for both. For many organizations, the ROI objective for a green project is set slightly higher than the ROI expected from other "routine investments" because of the relative newness of applying the ROI concept to green projects. For example, if the expected ROI from the purchase of a new company is 20 percent, the ROI from a new green project might be around 25 percent. The important point is that the ROI objective should be established up front and in discussions with the project sponsor. Excluding the ROI objective leaves stakeholders questioning the economic success of a project. If a project reaps a 25 percent ROI, is that successful? Not if the objective was a 50 percent ROI.

Case Study Examples

The following two case studies may prove helpful in describing the alignment process. One case study involves a medium-sized service organization in the private sector that is focusing on a variety of green initiatives, principally involving employees. The second case study includes a large non-government organization (NGO) that is addressing a different type of issue: the sustainability of food sources.

BLAKE ENGINEERING COMPANY

Blake Engineering Company(BE) is a design and development organization for a variety of industries. BE conducts feasibility studies, provides inspection services, and designs and manages projects, chiefly for the chemical and paper industries. BE uses sustainability principles in environmental studies and projects and ensures that fuel efficiency, savings, and sustainability are always an important part of what they do. However, the headquarters office has done little to focus on green projects and sustainability efforts. To improve their image in the community and to ensure that the customers and other stakeholders are aware of their commitment to the environment, BE decided to implement a variety of green projects at company headquarters.

Approximately 500 people work in two buildings at the headquarters and are, for the most part, professional employees. Executives could see possible opportunities to save costs with energy savings and procurement supplies as a result of the initiatives; these savings would be in addition to the benefit of enhancing the corporate office image. After their needs were clearly defined, the project was positioned around a specific set of objectives. Table 5.3 shows the framework for the project assessment, objectives, and evaluation.

TABLE 5.3 Create a Green Organization: Blake Engineering (BE)

Level	Needs	Objectives	Evaluation	Level
5	• Help protect the environment. • Reduce costs.	• Reach ROI target of 10 percent.	• Compare project benefits to costs.	5
4	• Raise image as a green company. • Reduce high energy costs. • Address rising costs of operations. • Address increasing costs of materials/supplies.	• Improve image. • Reduce energy costs. • Reduce materials/supplies • Reduce operating costs	• Conduct external survey. • Examine organization records.	4
3	• Increase recycling of materials. • Change consumption habits. • Use less materials and supplies. • Start making environmentally friendly choices.	Six months after the project begins, employees will: • recycle in eight categories • alter consumption patterns • reduce usage, increase conservation • use environmentally friendly supplies	• Conduct self-assessment questionnaire. • Check recycle records. • Check records of purchasing eco-friendly products.	3
2	• Need to determine how actions affect the environment. • Need to identify specific green methods. • Need to understand environmental issues.	All employees will learn: • environmental issues • specific green actions they can take • how to make eco-friendly choices	• Conduct self-assessment questionnaire. • Conduct environment quiz.	2
1	• Ensure that employees see project as necessary, important, relevant, and feasible.	Program receives favorable rating of 4 out of 5 on: • necessary to BE • relevant to employees • important to adhering to concepts in support of public good	• Administer reaction questionnaire to all project participants.	1

Level 5 analysis determined the rationale for pursuing the project: Is it needed? Is it necessary? Is it a problem worth solving? Is it an opportunity worth pursuing? Two issues clearly indicated that the opportunities were worth pursuing. First, the potential environmental impact was a valuable opportunity to pursue. BE wants to be seen as an organization supportive of environmental sustainability. In addition, cost-saving opportunities existed in a variety of operational and supply categories. This is important from an organization perspective. Three specific business measures include:

1. Energy costs
2. Operations costs
3. Materials costs

Improvement in these measures led to a reduction in another measure: carbon emissions. A brief Level 3 analysis revealed that employees needed to do more to help the environment and save costs. Specifically the behaviors observed involved not recycling, failing to change consumption habits, and not making enough environmentally friendly choices.

At the learning level (Level 2), several specific needs were identified through brief conversations with employees and with a quiz that was promoted in the company newsletter as a contest, offering an incentive for people to complete it. Executives noticed there was a lack of understanding about green projects, their effects on the environment, and why they are necessary.

With the learning needs defined, the project was defined around preference needs, which covered when projects would be implemented, how they would be implemented, and the specific target audiences. Details about how participants should view these projects was also addressed. Because there is often apathy about green initiatives, the preference needs analysis considered the overall participant perspective of perceived necessity, importance, and relevance to the organization's goals as well as feasibility of pursuing needs at the higher level.

With these needs in mind, the objectives were set at multiple levels and the evaluation system was employed based on these objectives. Aligning green initiatives using this approach is especially valuable when multiple projects are undertaken at the same time.

GLOBAL FOOD NETWORK

Global Food Network (GFN) is a non-governmental organization that distributes food to feed communities in developing countries or regions that are suffering from drought, natural disasters, or even conflicts that have contributed to food shortage and displacement. The GFN purchases food from reputable sources and distributes to those in need. It is funded by donor countries from around the globe. Food purchases follow quality standards to ensure that the food is healthy and will remain fresh until consumption.

Most of the countries that need the food have fertile soil and an appropriate climate for food production for their own country. Unfortunately, it is not being produced in quantities that are sufficient to meet the need or at a quality level to meet GFN standards.

Most of the food is purchased in countries where there is plentiful food production and quality standards are quite high. These countries are often long distances from where the food is required.

A program is needed that will enable farmers in those impoverished countries to increase their food production and quality to be able to supply food in that country. As production and quality improve, GFN will purchase food directly from those farmers to be distributed to hungry people in that country. This process will ensure that farmer production is in appropriate demand.

There are many reasons for the lack of product and poor quality of food. Inadequate equipment, processes, and tools exist, and knowledge about how to produce food at appropriate quantities and quality is needed. Table 5.4 shows the alignment between the needs and the GFN farmer production program. The payoff need is obvious and broad. The country should be producing the food that its citizens need, particularly when the soil is fertile and the climate is appropriate. This specific business impact may be surprising. Farmers are currently losing money. However, if they become profitable, they will operate and expand. Also, the food currently produced is not up to GFN standards. Finally, another business need is that food is not being purchased by GFN from those countries but should be. Those are the key business measure that must change.

An analysis of what is or is not occurring in the country that is causing the business needs identified three major areas: efficient farming methods are not being used, the equipment is out of date, and the processes and techniques are outdated. As a result, food is not being produced to quality standards, and analysis shows that quality processes need to be in place for this to occur. Available land for farming is not utilized, and crop rotation and crop management are not being employed as a part of the farming process. Also, financing or agriculture loans are not always available for the farmers when they need them.

To address these performance and process needs, farmers must be taught how to be more productive and efficient. They must learn about operations and about farming equipment, finance and accounting methods, and technology. This will require extensive training.

TABLE 5.4 Farmer Production Program: GFN

Level	Needs	Objectives	Evaluation	Level
5	• Country must produce food for citizens.	• Break even (BCR = 1:1).	• Compare program benefits to program costs.	5
4	• Farmer profits must be positive. • Food quality must meet GFN standards. • Food should be purchased by GFN. • Money needs to be available.	• Raise farmer profits to ensure that percent of food meets GFN standards. • Raise GFN purchase to percent of production. • Secure loans for farmers.	• Check farm records. • Check GFN records.	4

3	• Efficient farming methods must be used.
	• Standards must be followed.
	• Land must be properly utilized.
	• Farmers must seek financial assistance.
		• Farmers will:
		  • follow standards
		  • utilize land resources
		  • sell food to GFN
		  • apply for low-interest loans
			• Use interviews.
			• Check action plans.
			• Distribute questionnaires.
			• Examine GFN records.
				3

2	• Need to know:
	  • Operations equipment finance/accounting
	  • Management
	  • Technology
	  • Loan applications
		• Farmers will demonstrate their knowledge of:
		  • operations
		  • equipment utilization
		  • finance/accounting principles
		  • operations management
		  • technology
		  • loan application
			• Prepare a simple quiz.
			• Offer checklists.
			• Provide demonstrations.
			• Promote self-assessment.
				2

1	• Farmers must see program as:
	  • Feasible
	  • Important to their survival
	  • Relevant to their work
	  • Something they will use
		• Program receives favorable rating of 4 out of 5 on feasibility, importance, relevance, and usefulness.
		• Farmers commit to follow processes.
			• Administer reaction questionnaire to farmers.	1

Finally, for this program to be successful, the farmers must see that it is feasible to have a successful program and that it is imperative for the survival of their farms and the country. They must perceive all elements of the program as relevant. Farmers must view what they are taught as immediately useful.

With these needs clearly defined, the specific objectives are developed as outlined in Table 5.4, which represents a simplified version of a complex program that was sponsored by wealthy donors, who requested that the program be evaluated to the ROI level. The important point is that for any project, the multiple levels of analysis are an excellent way to understand the needs so that objectives can be developed and used to drive success in the process. With objectives at Level 3, 4, and 5, and appropriate data collection at Level 3 and 4, the project is not only positioned for ultimate success, but it can easily be evaluated at the impact and ROI level.

Final Thoughts

The alignment of any sustainability initiative with relevant needs and objectives positions the project for success. This level of detail ensures that the green project remains results-focused throughout its implementation. Without upfront analysis, the project runs the risk of failing to deliver the value that it should, or of not being in alignment with one or more business needs. The outputs of the analysis are objectives, which provide a focus for project designers, developers, and implementers, as well as participants and users who must make the project successful. The third and final phase of aligning projects to organization needs and strategies occurs through the evaluation process. By evaluating projects against objectives that are representative of stakeholder needs, project owners can report, with confidence, the contribution their project makes to the organization and the environment.

Part II

The Value of Measuring ROI

The Antidote to "Green-Sky" Thinking

Chapter 6

Measuring Reaction, Perceived Value, and Learning

"This is inconvenient, and I don't understand why it's necessary." Statements like these are green killers, raising a flag that additional steps must be taken to reverse attitudes.

Chapter 6 focuses on the measurement of reaction and learning. These two levels of evaluation provide the first wave of data generated through the ROI Methodology. Participant feedback supplies powerful information to use in making adjustments to a project as it rolls out. Project participants' reactions, value perceptions, and acquired learning with regard to the green initiative provide indications of its potential for success. This chapter outlines the most common approaches to collecting these data and explores ways to use the information for maximum value.

Why Measure Reaction and Perceived Value?

It is difficult to imagine a project being conducted without the collection of feedback from those involved. The collection of reaction and perceived value data represents the first level of outcomes that result from the launch of a green project. Participant feedback is critical to a project's success so that adverse reactions can be identified and corrected before they derail an otherwise successful project. Here are a few specifics to consider as an organization works to measure reaction.

CUSTOMER SATISFACTION

Reaction and perceived value are essentially measures of customer satisfaction with the project. Without sustained, favorable reactions from participants—the employees, volunteers, members, citizens, suppliers, or customers involved in a green project—the project success may be in jeopardy. Individuals who have a direct role in the project are immediately affected; they often must change processes or procedures or make other adjustments in response to the project's initiation. Participant feedback on preferences is necessary to make positive adjustments and changes in the project as it unfolds. The feedback of project supporters is also important because this group will be in a position to influence the project's continuation and development. Sponsors—who approve budgets, allocate resources, and ultimately live with the project's success or failure—must be satisfied with the project, and their overall satisfaction must be verified early and often.

IMMEDIATE ADJUSTMENTS

Projects can go astray quickly, and at times a project can end up being the wrong solution for the specified problem. A project can also be mismatched to the solution from the beginning. Securing feedback early in the process allows for immediate adjustments. This can help prevent misunderstandings, miscommunications, and, more important, misappropriations. Collecting and using reaction data promptly can enable an improperly designed project to be altered before more serious problems arise.

PREDICTIVE CAPABILITY

A relatively recent application of reaction data involves predicting the success of a project using analytical techniques. Project participants are asked about their reaction to the project in terms of its potential utility. The measures of utility are compared to the project's measures of success with application. The reaction data thus become a predictor of application. Figure 6.1 demonstrates the correlation between reaction feedback and application data.

In this analysis, reaction measures are taken as the green project is introduced, and the success of the implementation is later judged using the same scale (e.g., a 1 to 5 rating). When significant positive correlations are present, reaction measures can have predictive capability. Some reaction measures shown to have predictive capability include statements such as these:

- The project is relevant to my work.
- The project is necessary.
- The project is important.
- The project represents a valuable investment.
- I intend to make the project successful.
- I recommend that others pursue similar projects.

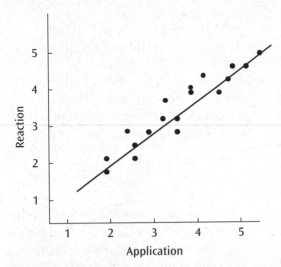

FIGURE 6.1 Correlations Between Reaction and Application

These measures consistently lead to strong positive correlations and consequently represent more powerful feedback than typical measures of overall satisfaction with the project. Some organizations collect these or similar reaction measures for every project.

IMPORTANT BUT NOT EXCLUSIVE

Feedback data are critical to a project's success and should be collected for every project. Unfortunately, in some organizations, feedback alone has been used to measure project success. For example, in one particular trucking firm, the traditional method of measuring the effectiveness of a project is to rely entirely on feedback data from employees by asking them if the green project is appropriate, important, and necessary. Positive feedback is critical to the project's acceptance, but it is no guarantee the project will be successfully executed. Executives become interested in the extent to which employees change their approach or behavior and implement the project in their work (application), and the effectiveness of the project in reducing the impact on the environment (impact). Only when these additional measures are taken can the full scope of success be identified.

Sources of Data for Measuring Reaction

Possible sources of reaction and perceived value data concerning the success of a project can be grouped into six distinct categories. We address each here.

PARTICIPANTS

The most widely used data source for green project evaluation is the participants who are directly involved in the project. "Users" must take the knowledge and skills they acquire during the project and apply them in their work or personal lives, and they may be asked to explain the potential impact of that application. Participants are a rich source of data for almost every aspect of a project. They are the most credible source of reaction and perceived value data.

MANAGERS AND SUPERVISORS

For organizations, another key source of data are the individuals who directly supervise or lead participants. Managers and supervisors have a vested interest in the project and are often in a position to observe the participants as they attempt to apply the knowledge and skills acquired in the project. Consequently, they can report on the successes associated with the project as well as the difficulties and problems.

OTHER TEAM MEMBERS

When entire teams are involved in the implementation of the project, all team members can provide useful information about the perceived changes prompted by the project. It's important to note that input from this group is pertinent only to issues directly related to their work; otherwise, the potential exists for introducing inaccuracies to the feedback process. Data collection should be restricted to those team members who are capable of providing meaningful insight into the value of the project.

CUSTOMERS

Customers are another source of reaction and perceived value data. In some situations, customers provide input on perceived changes linked to the project. This source of data is appropriate only for projects directly affecting the customers. They report on how the green project has influenced (or will influence) their product purchase decisions or their satisfaction. Although this group may be somewhat limited in their knowledge of the scope of a project, their perceptions can be a source of valuable data that may indicate a direction for change in the project.

PROJECT LEADERS AND PROJECT TEAM MEMBERS

The project leader and project team may also provide input on the project's success. This input may be based on observations during the implementation of the project. Data from this source have limited utility because project leaders often have a vested interest in the outcome of the evaluation and thus may lack objectivity.

SPONSORS AND SENIOR MANAGERS

One of the most useful data sources is the sponsor group, usually a senior management team. The perception of the sponsor, whether an individual or a group, is critical to project success. Sponsors can provide input on all types of issues and are usually available and willing to offer feedback. Sponsors and senior managers are a preferred source for reaction data, since these data usually indicate what is necessary to make adjustments and to measure success.

Areas of Feedback

When capturing reaction and perceived value data, it is important to focus on the content of the green project. Too often, feedback data reflect aesthetic issues that may not be relevant to the project's substance. Table 6.1 distinguishes content and non-content issues explored in a reaction questionnaire from an event designed to launch a green project. A traditional way to evaluate activities is to focus on non-content issues (experience) or inputs. The column on the left in the table represents areas important to the activity surrounding the event, but contains nothing indicating results achieved from the event. The column on the right reflects a focus on content. This is not to suggest that the service, the atmosphere of the event, and the quality of the speakers are not important; it is assumed that these issues will be addressed appropriately if there are problems. A more important set of data, focused on results, incorporates detailed information about the perceived value of the green project kickoff event, the importance of the content, and the planned use of material or a forecast of the impact—indicators that successful results were achieved.

Many topics are critical targets for feedback, which is needed in connection with almost every major issue, step, or process to make sure things are advancing properly. Stakeholders will provide reaction input as to the appropriateness of the project planning schedule and objectives, and the progress made with the planning tools. If the project is perceived as irrelevant or unnecessary to the participants, more than likely it will not succeed in the workplace. Support for the project—including resources—represents an important area of feedback.

Participants must be assured that the project has the necessary commitment. Issues important to project management and the organization spon-

TABLE 6.1   Content Versus Non-Content Issues

Non-Content Issues	Content Issues
Demographics	Facilities
Location	Service
Transportation	Relevance of meeting theme
Registration	Importance of topics
Logistics	Timing of meeting
Hotel service	Use of time
Food	Amount of new information
Breaks and refreshments	Quality of speakers
Cocktail reception	Perceived value
Opening keynote	Contacts made
Quality of speakers	Planned use of material
Future needs	Forecast of impact
Overall satisfaction	Overall satisfaction

soring the project include project leadership, staffing, coordination, and communication. Also, it is important to collect feedback on how well the project team is working to address such issues as motivation, cooperation, and capability.

Finally, the perceived value of the project is often a critical parameter. Major funding decisions are made based on perceived value when stronger evidence of value is unavailable.

Data Collection Timing for Measuring Reaction

The timing of data collection centers on particular events connected with the project. As discussed previously, feedback during the early stages of implementation is critical. Ideally, this feedback validates the decision to go forward with the project and confirms the alignment with business needs. Notation of problems in initial feedback means that adjustments can be made early in its implementation. In practice, however, many organizations omit this early feedback, waiting until significant parts of the project have been implemented, at which point feedback may be more meaningful.

For longer projects, concerns related to the timing of feedback may require data collection at multiple points in time. Measures can be taken at the beginning of the project and then at routine intervals once the project is underway.

Data Collection Methods for Measuring Reaction

A variety of methods can be used to collect reaction data. Instruments range from simple surveys to comprehensive interviews. The appropriate measure depends on the type of data needed (quantitative vs. qualitative), the convenience of the method to potential respondents, the culture of the organization, and the cost of a particular instrument.

QUESTIONNAIRES AND SURVEYS

The questionnaire or survey is the most common method of collecting and measuring reaction data. Questionnaires and surveys come in all sizes, ranging from short forms to detailed, multiple-page instruments. They can be used to obtain subjective data about participants' reactions as well as to document responses for future use in a projected ROI analysis. Proper design of questionnaires and surveys is important to ensure versatility.

There are several basic types of questions such as yes-or-no and numerical scale (e.g., 1 to 5). Essentially with numerical scores, the individual is indicating the extent of agreement with a particular statement or is giving an opinion of varying conviction on an issue. When a follow-up evaluation is planned, a wide range of issues will be covered in a detailed questionnaire. Asking for too much detail in either the reaction questionnaire or the follow-up questionnaire can reduce the response rate. The following actions can help maximize response rates:

- Provide advance communication regarding the need for data.
- Identify who will see the data.
- Describe the data integration process.
- Design the instrument for simplicity and ease of response.
- Use local management support, if feasible.
- If applicable, let the participants know they are part of the sample.
- Consider the use of incentives.
- Have an executive sign the introductory letter or memo.
- Issue at least two follow-up reminders.
- Send a copy of the results to the participants.
- Make sure the survey or questionnaire looks professional.
- Introduce the questionnaire or survey in the early stages of the project.
- Collect the data anonymously or confidentially.

INTERVIEWS

Interviews, although not used as frequently as questionnaires to capture reaction data, may be conducted by the project team or a third party to secure data that are difficult to obtain through written responses. Interviews can uncover success stories that may help to communicate early achievements of the project. The interview is versatile and is appropriate for soliciting reaction data as well as application data. A major disadvantage of the interview is that it consumes time, which increases the cost of data collection. It also requires interviewer preparation to ensure that the process is consistent.

FOCUS GROUPS

Focus groups are particularly useful when in-depth feedback is needed. The focus group format involves a small-group discussion conducted by an experienced facilitator. It is designed to solicit qualitative judgments on a selected topic or issue. All group members are required to provide input, with individual input building on group input.

Compared with questionnaires, surveys, and interviews, the focus group approach has several advantages. The basic premise behind the use of focus groups is that when quality judgments are subjective, several individual judgments are better than one. The group process, in which participants often motivate one another, is an effective method for generating and clarifying ideas and hypotheses. Focus groups are inexpensive and can be quickly planned and conducted. The flexibility of this process allows exploration of a project's unexpected outcomes or applications.

Use of Reaction Data

Unfortunately, reaction and perceived value data are sometimes collected and then disregarded. Too many project leaders use the information to feed their egos and then allow it to quietly disappear into their files, forgetting the original purpose behind its collection. In an effective evaluation, the information collected must be used to make adjustments or verify success; otherwise, the exercise is a waste of time. Because this input is the principal measure supplied by key stakeholders, it provides an indication of their reaction to, and satisfaction with, the project. More important, these data provide evidence relating to the potential success of the project. Data collected at this level (Level 1) should be used to:

• Identify the strengths and weaknesses of the project and make adjustments.
• Evaluate project team members.

- Evaluate the quality and content of planned improvements.
- Develop norms and standards for benchmarking and comparison.
- Link with follow-up data, if feasible.
- Market future projects based on the positive reaction.

Why Measure Learning?

Several key principles illustrate the importance of measuring learning during the course of a project. Collectively, these principles provide an indication of the full range of benefits that result from measuring the changes in knowledge and skills information provided during the project.

COMPLIANCE ISSUES

Organizations face an increasing number of environmental regulations with which they must routinely comply. These regulations involve all aspects of business and are considered essential by governing bodies to protect customers, investors, and the environment. Employees must have a certain amount of knowledge about the regulations to maintain compliance. Consequently, an organization must measure the extent of employee learning and understanding with regard to regulations to ensure that compliance is not a problem.

Some projects are compliance driven. For example, a foundry had to implement a major project to ensure that its employees were all familiar with waste disposal regulation. This project was precipitated by the firm's continuing failure to comply with the regulations. The problem appeared to be a lack of knowledge of the rules. When projects such as this are initiated, learning must be measured.

USE AND DEVELOPMENT OF COMPETENCIES

The use of competencies has dramatically increased in recent years. In the struggle for a competitive advantage, many organizations have focused on people as the key to success. Competency models are used to ensure that employees do the right things, clarifying and articulating what is required for effective performance. These models help organizations align behavior and skills with the strategic direction of the company. A competency model describes a particular combination of knowledge, skills, and characteristics necessary to perform a role in an organization. With the increased focus on competencies, measuring learning is a necessity, particularly when environmental and sustainability issues are a part of the competencies.

ROLE OF LEARNING IN GREEN PROJECTS

Although some green projects involve new equipment, processes, and technology, the human factor remains critical to project success. Employees must understand green issues and learn how to work in the new way, and this requires the development of new knowledge and skills. Simple tasks and procedures do not always come with new processes. Sometimes, complex environments, procedures, and tools must be used in an intelligent way to reap the desired environmental benefits. Employees must learn in different ways—not just in a formal meeting, but through technology-based learning and informal processes. Team leaders and managers may serve as coaches or resource experts in some projects. In a few cases, learning coaches or subject matter experts are used in conjunction with a project to ensure that learning is transferred to the job and is implemented as planned.

Participants do not always fully understand what they must do. Although the chain of impact can be broken at any level, a common place for such a break is at Level 2 (learning), when participants do not know what to do or how to do it properly. When the application and implementation does not go smoothly, project leaders can determine if a learning deficiency is the problem; if so, they may be able to correct it. In other words, learning measurement is necessary to contribute to the leaders' understanding of why employees are, or are not, performing the way they should.

Challenges and Benefits of Measuring Learning

Measuring learning involves major challenges that may inhibit a comprehensive approach to the process. The good news is that a comprehensive approach is not necessary on most green projects and sustainability issues. While measuring learning is an essential part of the ROI Methodology, this measurement provides many benefits that help ensure a project's success.

CHALLENGES

The greatest challenge in measuring learning is to maintain objectivity without crossing ethical or legal lines while keeping an eye on time and costs. A common method of measuring learning is testing, but this approach generates additional challenges.

The first challenge is the "fear" factor. Few people enjoy being tested, and some are offended by it. They may feel that their professional prowess is being questioned. Others are intimidated by tests, which bring back memories of their third-grade math teacher, red pen in hand.

Another challenge with tests is the legal and ethical repercussions of basing decisions involving employee status on test scores. Therefore, organizations use other techniques to measure learning, such as surveys, questionnaires, and simulations. The challenge with these methods, however, is the potential for inaccurate measures and the financial burden they impose. Consequently, there is a constant tradeoff between additional resources and the accuracy of the learning measurement process.

BENEFITS

Learning measurement checks the progress of the project against the learning objectives. Learning objectives are critical to a project in terms of participant readiness to execute the project. Fundamentally, the measurement of learning reveals the extent to which knowledge, skill, and information are acquired during project roll out. This knowledge is necessary to fully understand the project and make it successful. Learning measurements provide data to project leaders so that adjustments can be made. They can identify strengths and weaknesses in the project presentation and may point out flaws in the design or delivery.

Learning measures enhance participant performance. Verification and feedback concerning the knowledge and skills acquired can encourage participants to improve in certain areas. When employees excel, feedback motivates them to enhance their performance even further.

Measuring learning also helps to maintain accountability. Because projects are aimed at making the environment better, learning is an important part of any project and its measurement is vital in confirming that improvement has in fact occurred.

Learning Measurement Issues

Several items affect the nature and scope of measurement at the learning level. These include project objectives, the measures themselves, and timing.

PROJECT OBJECTIVES

The starting point for any level of measurement is the project objectives. The measurement of learning builds on the learning objectives. For green projects, the first step is to ensure that objectives are in place. Typically, the objectives are broad and indicate only major information or general knowledge areas that should be acquired as the project is implemented. These are sometimes called *key project learning objectives.* They can be divided into subcomponents that provide more detail, which is necessary when a tremendous number of tasks, procedures, or new skills must be learned to implement a green project. For other projects, this level of detail may not be needed; identifying the major objectives and indicating what must be accomplished to meet each objective is often sufficient.

TYPICAL MEASURES

Measuring learning focuses on knowledge, skills, and attitudes as well as the individual's confidence in applying or implementing the project or process as desired. Typical measures collected at this level concern the following areas:

- Knowledge
- Awareness
- Understanding
- Information
- Skills
- Capability
- Capacity
- Readiness
- Contacts
- Confidence

Obviously, the more detailed the knowledge area, the greater the number of objectives. The concept of knowledge is quite general and often includes the assimilation of facts, figures, and ideas. Instead of knowledge, terms such as *awareness*, *understanding*, and *information* may be used to denote specific categories. Sometimes skills are improved for comprehensive green projects. In some cases, the issue involves developing a reservoir of knowledge and related skills toward improving capability, capacity, or readiness. Networking is often part of a project, and developing internal or external contacts that may be valuable later is important. For example, a community project may include people to contact at particular times in the future. For projects that involve different organizations, such as a green meeting, new contacts that result from the meeting can be important and ultimately pay off with shared approaches.

Data Collection Timing for Measuring Learning

The measurement of learning can occur at various times. If formal learning sessions connected with the project are offered, the measure is taken at the end of those sessions to ensure that participants are ready to apply their newly acquired knowledge. If a project has no formal learning sessions, measurement may occur at different intervals. For long-term projects, as skills and knowledge grow, routine assessment may be necessary to measure both the acquisition of additional skills and knowledge and the retention of the previously acquired skills. The timing of measurement is balanced with the need to know the new information; this is offset by the cost of obtaining, analyzing, and responding to the data. In an ideal situation, the timing of measurement is part of the data collection plan.

Data Collection Methods for Measuring Learning

One of the most important considerations with regard to measuring learning is the specific way in which data are collected. Learning data can be collected using many different methods. Here are just some of the data collection methods.

QUESTIONNAIRES AND SURVEYS

Questionnaires and surveys, introduced earlier in the chapter with the focus on measuring reaction, are also used to collect learning data. These questionnaires may include similar types of questions used in collecting reaction data including yes-or-no questions; agree-or-disagree questions; and rating scales. Multiple-choice is probably the most common question type, where participants are asked to choose one or more items from a series of alternative answers. Matching exercises are also useful, where participants match particular items. Short-answer questions can be easy to develop, but they are difficult to score. Developing questions in an attempt to measure learning can be fairly simple. The key is to ensure that the questions asked are relevant to the knowledge or information presented.

SIMULATIONS

Another technique for measuring learning is simulation. This method involves the construction and application of a procedure or task that simulates or models the work involved in the project. The simulation is designed to represent, as closely as possible, the actual job situation. Participants attempt the simulated activity and their performance is evaluated based on how well they accomplish the task or understand the process. For example, a simple simulation shows the energy use of light bulbs or small appliances as they are connected to a Watt meter. This vividly shows people who are involved in projects the most energy-saving appliances and bulbs. This simple simulation helps others to understand the effects of making changes or selecting the proper ones.

Although the initial development can be expensive, simulations can be cost-effective in the long run, particularly for large projects or situations where a project may be repeated. For example, Luminant, the Texas-based energy production and distribution company, has developed large simulations of their power plants. These simulations, which are located at Luminant Academy, adjacent to a community college in Texas, provide power plant operators an opportunity to simulate different sequences, schedules, and possibilities. It not only teaches them the correct way to run the power plant, but it also helps them understand the most efficient way to operate the plants. Although this is expensive, it has provided savings over the long run.

CASE STUDIES

A popular technique of measuring learning is the case study. A case study presents a detailed description of a problem and usually contains a list of several questions posed to the participant. The participant is asked to analyze the case and determine the best course of action. The problem should reflect conditions in the real world and in the content of the project. This approach is helpful for green projects.

The difficulty in using a case study lies in objectively evaluating the participant's performance. Many possible courses of action are available, making an objective, measurable performance rating of successful knowledge and understanding difficult.

INFORMAL ASSESSMENTS

Many projects include activities, exercises, or problems that must be explored, developed, or solved. Some of these are constructed in the form of interactive exercises, while others require individual problem-solving skills. When these tools are integrated into the learning activity, they can be effective in gathering learning data.

A commonly used informal method is participant self-assessment. Participants are provided with an opportunity to assess their acquisition of skills and knowledge. In some situations, a project leader or a facilitator provides an assessment of the learning that has taken place. Although this approach is subjective, it may be appropriate when project leaders or facilitators work closely with participants.

Use of Learning Data

Data must be used to add value and improve processes. Among the appropriate uses of learning data are the following:

- Provide individual feedback to build confidence.
- Validate that learning has been acquired.

- Provide additional support to ensure successful implementation.
- Evaluate project leaders and facilitators.
- Build a database for project comparisons.
- Improve the project, program, or process.

Final Thoughts

This chapter discusses data collection at the first two levels of evaluation: reaction and learning. Measuring reaction is a component of every study and is a critical factor in a project's success. Projects fail because of a negative reaction. Learning must be assessed to determine the extent to which the participants in a project learn new information, knowledge, processes, and procedures. By measuring learning, project leaders can ascertain the degree to which participants are capable of successfully executing the green project plan. Measuring learning provides an opportunity to make adjustments quickly so that improvements can be made.

Reaction and learning data are collected using a variety of techniques, although surveys and questionnaires are most often used because of their cost-effectiveness and convenience. The data are important in allowing immediate adjustments to be made to the project. While reaction and learning data are important, value of data to executives increases as the evaluation moves up the chain of impact. Data collection at the next two levels, application and impact, is discussed in the next chapter.

Chapter 7

Measuring Application, Implementation, and Impact

Many projects fail because of breakdowns in implementation. In these cases, green project participants simply do not do what they should do on a timely basis. Measuring application and implementation is critical to understanding the success of project implementation. Without successful implementation, positive impact will not occur—and no positive return will be achieved.

Most sponsors regard business impact data as the most important data type because of its connection to business success. For many projects, the opportunity to improve business measures (the business need) is what has initiated the project. Impact evaluation data closes the loop by showing a project's success in meeting the business needs.

This chapter explores the most common ways to measure two of the most important levels of data: application and implementation data and business impact data. The possibilities vary from using questionnaires to monitoring business performance records. In addition to describing the techniques to evaluate these two levels, this chapter addresses the challenges and benefits of each approach.

Why Measure Application and Implementation?

Measuring application and implementation is absolutely necessary if a project is intended to improve organizational and environmental measures. For some projects, it is the most critical data set because it provides an understanding of the extent to which successful project implementation occurs. It also provides evidence of the barriers and enablers that influence success.

FOCUS OF THE PROJECT

Because many projects focus directly on implementation and application, a project sponsor often speaks in these terms and has concerns about these measures of success. For example, the sponsor of a recycling project will want to know if people are engaged in the process: Is the target audience naturally recycling? By measuring and monitoring the extent to which people are doing what they need to do, a focus remains on the project and its ultimate intent.

IDENTIFY PROBLEMS AND OPPORTUNITIES

If the chain of impact breaks at this level, little or no corresponding impact data will be available. Without improvement in impact measures, there is no ROI. This breakdown most often occurs because participants in the project encounter barriers, inhibitors, and obstacles that deter implementation. A dilemma arises when reactions to the project are favorable and participants learn what is intended, but then they fail to apply necessary tools, knowledge, or skills, thereby, failing to accomplish the objective.

When a project goes astray, the first question usually asked is, "What happened?" More important, when a project appears to add no value, the first question should be, "What can we do to change its direction?" In either scenario, it is important to identify the barriers to success, the problems in implementation, and the obstacles to application. At this level of evaluation, these issues are addressed, identified, and examined. In many cases, the stakeholders directly involved in the process can provide important recommendations for making changes or using a different approach in the future.

When a project is successful, the obvious question is, "How can we repeat this or improve it in the future?" The answer to this question is also found at Level 3. Identifying the factors that contribute directly to the success of the project is critical. Those same items can be used to replicate the process and produce enhanced results in the future. When key stakeholders identify those issues, they make the project successful and provide an important case history of what is necessary for success.

REWARD EFFECTIVENESS

Measuring application and implementation allows the sponsor and project team to reward those who do the best job of applying the processes and implementing the project. Measures taken at this level provide clear evidence of success and achievement, and they provide a basis for performance reviews. Rewards often have a reinforcing value, helping keep participants on track and communicating a strong message for future improvement.

Application Measurement Issues

Collecting application and implementation data brings into focus issues that must be addressed for success at this level. These challenges often inhibit an otherwise successful evaluation.

THE NECESSITY FOR DATA

Whether collecting data by questionnaires, interviews, or focus groups, insufficient response rates are a problem in most organizations. Having individuals participate in the data collection process is a challenge. To ensure that adequate amounts of high-quality data are available, a serious effort is needed to improve response rates.

Because many projects are planned on the basis of the ROI Methodology, it is expected that sponsors will collect impact data, monetary values, and the project's actual ROI. This need to "show the money" sometimes results in less emphasis being placed on measuring application and implementation. In many cases, it may be omitted or slighted in the analysis. But it is through focused effort on process and behavior change that business impact will occur. Therefore, emphasis must be placed on collecting application and implementation data.

CONNECTION TO APPLICATION NEEDS

A needs assessment (detailed in Chapter 5) asks, "What is being done—or not being done—that's inhibiting the business measure?" When this question is answered adequately, a connection is made between the solution and the business measure. When this issue is addressed, the activities or behaviors that need to change are identified, serving as the basis of the data collection. The bottom line is that too many evaluations focus on either impact measures, which define the business measure to collect, or on learning, which uncovers what people need to know. More focus is needed at Level 3, which involves the tasks, processes, procedures, and behaviors that need to be in place for successful implementation on the job.

PROJECT OBJECTIVES

As with the other levels, the starting point for data collection is the objectives set for project application and implementation. Without clear objectives, collecting data would be difficult. Objectives define what activity is expected. Chapter 5 discusses the basic principles for developing these objectives.

COVERAGE AREAS

To a certain extent, the area of coverage for this level focuses on activity or action, not on the ability to act (Level 2) and not on the consequences of acting (Level 4). The sheer number of activities to measure can be mindboggling. Table 7.1 shows examples of coverage areas for application, which will vary from project to project.

TABLE 7.1   Examples of Coverage Areas for Application

Action	Explanation	Example
Increase	Increasing a particular activity or action	Increase the frequency of use of a particular skill
Decrease	Decreasing a particular activity or action	Decrease the number of times a particular process must be checked
Eliminate	Stopping a particular task or activity	Eliminate the formal follow-up meeting, and replace it with a virtual meeting
Maintain	Keeping the same level of activity for a particular process	Continue to monitor the process with the same schedule previously used
Create	Designing or implementing a new procedure, process, or activity	Create a procedure for resolving the differences between two green projects
Use	Using a particular process, procedure, skill, or activity	Use the new skill in situations for which it was designed
Perform	Carrying out a particular task, process, or procedure	Conduct a post-audit review at the end of each activity
Participate	Becoming involved in various activities, projects, or programs	Submit a suggestion for reducing energy costs
Enroll	Signing up for a particular process, program, or project	Enroll in a recycling program
Respond	Reacting to groups, individuals, or systems	Respond to inquiries within fifteen minutes
Network	Facilitating relationships with others who are involved in or have been affected by the project	Continue networking with contacts on (at minimum) a quarterly basis

Sources of Data for Measuring Application

Essentially, all key stakeholders are potential sources of data. Perhaps the most important sources of data are the users of the solutions—those directly involved in the application and implementation of the project. Good sources may also be the project team or team leaders charged with the implementation. In some cases, the source may be the organizational records or system.

Data Collection Timing for Measuring Application

The timing of data collection can vary significantly. Because data collection occurs as a follow-up after the project launch, the key issue is determining the best time for a post-implementation evaluation. The challenge is to analyze the nature and scope of the application and implementation, and to determine the earliest time that a trend and pattern will evolve. This occurs when the application becomes routine and the implementation is making significant progress. Identifying this timing is a judgment call. Going in as early as possible is important so that potential adjustments can still be made. At the same time, leaders must wait long enough so that behavior changes are allowed to occur and so implementation can be observed and measured. In green projects that span a considerable length of time, several measures may be taken at three- to six-month intervals. Using effective measures at well-timed intervals will provide successive input on implementation progress, and clearly show the extent of improvement.

Convenience and constraints also influence the timing of data collection. If the participants are conveniently meeting to observe a milestone or special event, this would be an excellent opportunity to collect data. Sometimes, constraints are placed on data collection. Consider, for example, the time constraint that sponsors may impose. If they are anxious to have the data to make project decisions, they may request that the data collection is moved to an earlier time than would otherwise be ideal.

Data Collection Methods for Measuring Application

Some of the techniques previously mentioned that are available to collect application and implementation data are easy to administer and provide quality data. Other techniques are more robust, providing greater detail about success but raising more challenges in administration.

QUESTIONNAIRES

Questionnaires have become a mainstream data collection tool for measuring application and implementation because of their flexibility, low cost, and ease of administration. One of the most difficult tasks is determining the specific issues to address in a follow-up questionnaire. Figure 7.1 presents content items necessary for capturing application, implementation, and impact information (Level 3 and Level 4 data).

INTERVIEWS, FOCUS GROUPS, AND OBSERVATION

Interviews and focus groups can be used during implementation or on a follow-up basis to collect data on implementation and application. Observing participants and recording any changes in behavior and specific actions taken is also an approach to collect application data. When observation is used, the observer must be invisible or unnoticeable, such as when using a mystery shopper. Technology lends itself as a tool to assist with observations. Recorders, video cameras, and computers play an important role in capturing application data. Call centers are a classic forum for gathering observation data using technology. Supervisors or other observers routinely listen in while call center representatives respond to calls.

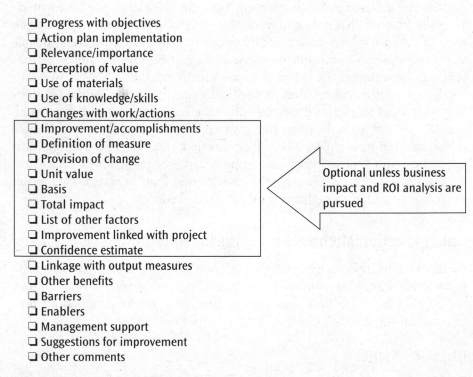

❏ Progress with objectives
❏ Action plan implementation
❏ Relevance/importance
❏ Perception of value
❏ Use of materials
❏ Use of knowledge/skills
❏ Changes with work/actions
❏ Improvement/accomplishments
❏ Definition of measure
❏ Provision of change
❏ Unit value
❏ Basis
❏ Total impact
❏ List of other factors
❏ Improvement linked with project
❏ Confidence estimate
❏ Linkage with output measures
❏ Other benefits
❏ Barriers
❏ Enablers
❏ Management support
❏ Suggestions for improvement
❏ Other comments

Optional unless business impact and ROI analysis are pursued

FIGURE 7.1   Questionnaire Content Checklist

ACTION PLANS

In some cases, follow-up assignments can be used to develop implementation and application data. A typical follow-up assignment requires the participant to meet a goal or complete a task or project by a set date. A summary of results of the completed assignment provides further evidence of the project's success.

Barriers to Application

One of the important reasons for collecting application and implementation data is to uncover barriers and enablers. Although both groups are important, barriers, which are a serious problem that exist in every project, can kill a project. The barriers must be identified in order to become important reference points for change and improvement. Then actions must be taken to minimize, remove, or circumvent them so that the project can be implemented. Typical barriers that will stifle the success of green projects include:

- We have no opportunity to use this knowledge or information.
- The management does not support this for the project.
- Resources are not available to implement the project.
- The project is not appropriate for our work unit.
- Another project or issue has gotten in the way.
- The culture in our group does not support the project.
- We have no time to implement the project.
- We don't see a need to implement the project.

As noted, the important point is to identify any barriers and to use the data in meaningful ways to make the obstacles less of a problem.

Use of Application Data

Data are meaningless if they are not used properly. As we move up the chain of impact, the data become more valuable in the minds of sponsors, key executives, and others who have a strong interest in the project. They also become more useful in ensuring successful project implementation. Although data can be used in dozens of ways. Much like the data collected at the reaction and learning levels, the principal uses of application data are to:

- Report and review results with various stakeholders.
- Adjust project design and implementation.

- Identify and remove barriers.
- Identify and enhance enablers.
- Recognize individuals who have contributed to project success.
- Reinforce in current and future project participants the value of desired actions.
- Improve management support for green projects.
- Market future projects.

The key difference in using reaction and learning data and using application data is that the use of application data reaches beyond the boundaries of the green project implementation team. Application data provide evidence that the system (or organization) is supporting implementation. When it does not, these data can be leveraged to help other departments or functions that may be impeding progress with the project. Following the assumption that higher-level data create more value for key stakeholders, business impact measures often offer the most valuable data for stakeholders.

Why Measure Impact?

For most projects, business impact data represent the initial drivers for the project. The problem of deteriorating performance (e.g., fuel costs) or the opportunity for improvement of a business measure (e.g., material costs) usually leads to a project. If the business needs defined by business measures are the drivers for a project, then the key measure for evaluating the project is the business measure. The extent to which measures have changed is the principal determinant of project success.

"SHOWS THE MONEY" TO SPONSORS

From the sponsor's perspective, business impact data reflect key payoff measures that the sponsor desires or wants to see changed or improved. They often represent hard, indisputable facts that reflect performance that is critical to the business and operating unit level of the organization. Business impact leads to "the money"—to the actual ROI in the project. Without credible business impact data linked directly to the project, it would be difficult, if not impossible, to establish a credible monetary value for the project. This makes this level of data collection one of the most critical.

EASY TO MEASURE

One unique feature of business impact data is that they are often easy to measure. Hard and soft data measures at this level often reflect key measures that are plentiful throughout an organization. It is not unusual for an organization to have hundreds or even thousands of measures reflecting specific business impact measures such as kWh usage, fines due to environmental violations, tons of solid waste, failure rate, cycle time, equipment downtime, safety violations, etc. The challenge is to connect the objectives of the project to the appropriate business measures. This is more easily accomplished at the beginning of a project.

Impact Measurement Issues

Chapter 5 defines impact measures as hard-data, soft data, tangible or intangible. However they are categorized, these measures are plentiful. The key is to identify relevant impact measures specifically linked to the project.

METRIC FUNDAMENTALS

When determining the type of measures to use, reviewing metric fundamentals can be helpful. The first important issue is identifying what makes an effective measure. Table 7.2 shows some of the criteria of an effective measure. These are issues that should be explored when examining any type of measure.

These criteria serve as a screening checklist as measures are considered, developed, and ultimately added to the list of possibilities. In addition to meeting criteria, the factual basis of the measure should be stressed. In essence, the measure should be subjected to a fact-based analysis, a level of analysis never before applied to decisions about many projects, even when these decisions have involved huge sums of money. Distinguishing between the various "types" of facts is beneficial. As the following list shows, the basis for facts ranges from common sense to what employees "say" to actual data:

- *Omits facts.* Common sense tells us that employees will recycle if it is convenient for them.
- *Includes unreliable facts.* Employees say they are more likely to stay with a company if it is environmentally friendly.
- *Offers irrelevant facts.* We have benchmarked three world-class companies for green project measures: a bank, a hotel chain, and a defense contractor. All reported good results.
- *Is fact-based.* Energy waste and inefficiencies are increasing operational costs.

SCORECARDS

In recent years, interest has increased in developing documents that reflect appropriate measures in an organization. Scorecards, like those used in sport-

TABLE 7.2 Criteria for Effective Measures (Kerr, 1995), (Mayo, 2003)

Criteria: Effective Measures Are	Definition: The Extent to Which a Measure ...
Important	Connects to strategically important business objectives rather than to what is easy to measure
Complete	Adequately tracks the entire phenomenon rather than only part of the phenomenon
Timely	Tracks at the right time rather than being held to an arbitrary date
Visible	Is visible, public, openly known, and tracked by those affected by it, rather than being collected privately for management's eyes only
Controllable	Tracks outcomes created by those affected by it who have a clear line of sight from the measure to results
Cost-effective	Is efficient to track using existing data or data that are easy to monitor without requiring new procedures
Interpretable	Creates data that are easy to make sense of and that translate into employee action
Simple	Is simple to understand from each stakeholder's perspective
Specific	Is clearly defined so that people quickly understand and relate to the measure
Collectible	Can be collected with no more effort than is proportional to the usefulness that results
Team-based	Will have value in the judgment of a team of individuals, not in the judgment of just one individual
Credible	Provides information that is valid and credible in the eyes of management

ing events, provide a variety of measures for top executives. In their landmark book, *The Balanced Scorecard* (1996), Robert Kaplan and David Norton explore the concept of the scorecard for use by organizations. They suggest that data can be organized in four categories: finances, customers, learning and growth, and process. Measures driven by green projects exist in all four categories.

The scorecard approach is appealing because it provides a quick comparison of key business impact measures and examines the status of the organization. As a management tool, scorecards can be important in shaping and improving or maintaining the performance of the organization through the implementation of projects. Scorecard measures often link to green projects. In many situations, it was a scorecard deficiency measure that initially prompted the project.

SPECIFIC MEASURES LINKED TO PROJECTS

An important issue that often surfaces when considering ROI applications is the understanding of specific measures that are frequently driven by specific green projects. Although no standard answers are available, most projects are driving business measures. The monetary values are based on what is being changed in the various business units, divisions, regions, and individual workplaces. These are the measures that matter to senior executives. The difficulty often comes in ensuring that the connection to the program exists. This is accomplished through a variety of techniques to isolate the effects of the project on the particular business measures, as discussed in Chapter 8.

BUSINESS PERFORMANCE DATA MONITORING

Data are available in every organization to measure business performance. Monitoring performance data enables management to measure performance in terms of output, quality, costs, time, job satisfaction, customer satisfaction, and other measures. In determining the source of data in the evaluation, the first consideration should be existing databases, reports, and scorecards. In most organizations, performance data will be available that are suitable for measuring improvement resulting from a project. If such data are not available, additional record-keeping systems will have to be developed for measurement and analysis. At this point, the question of economics surfaces. Is it economical to develop the record-keeping systems necessary to evaluate a project? If the costs will be greater than the expected benefits, developing those systems is pointless.

APPROPRIATE MEASURES

Existing performance measures should be thoroughly researched to identify those related to the proposed objectives of the project. Often, several performance measures are related to the same item. For example, the fuel efficiency of a truck fleet can be measured in several ways:

- Miles per gallon
- Total gallons per day
- Fuel cost per hour of service
- Fuel cost per ton delivered
- Fuel cost per ton per mile
- Total fuel cost

Each of these measurements in its own way evaluates the fuel efficiency of the fleet. All related measures should be reviewed to determine those most relevant to the project.

Data Collection Methods for Measuring Impact

For many projects, business data are readily available to be monitored. However, at times, data will not be easily accessible to the project team or to the evaluator. Sometimes data are maintained at the individual, work unit, or department level and may not be known to anyone outside that area. Tracking down all those data sets may be too expensive and time-consuming. When this is the case, other data collection methods may be used to capture data sets and make them available for the evaluator. Three other options described in this book are the use of action plans, performance contracts, and questionnaires.

ACTION PLANS

Action plans can capture application and implementation data, as discussed earlier. They can also be a useful tool for capturing business impact data. For business impact data, the action plan is more focused and credible than using a questionnaire. The basic design principles and the issues involved in developing and administering action plans are the same for business impact data as they are for application and implementation data (Phillips and Phillips, 2007).

For example, a large package delivery company implemented several efforts for green projects and sustainability efforts. To make these efforts work throughout the company, a green implementation program (GIP) was put into place. Volunteers were sought and representatives were appointed to a group that would initiate, organize, and drive various green projects. The program involved two weeks of training to prepare volunteers for this assignment, underscoring and outlining specifically what could be accomplished. As part of the program, an action plan was created, which was used to drive the projects and collect data. Time was allotted to complete the action plan, and the process was overseen by the facilitator. It placed detail on specific projects volunteers were willing to participate in or steps they would take to implement a major project. The specific measures the project was intended to influence were also on the action plan. Not only did this step-by-step process become an application tool for the participants, but it also became an input for the program evaluation. Essentially the program was a collection of the impact for the various projects. This allowed the organization to evaluate dozens of projects at the impact level, minimizing the normal resources that would be needed to evaluate them.

PERFORMANCE CONTRACTS

Another technique for collecting business impact data is the performance contract, which is a slight variation of the action plan. Based on the principle of mutual goal setting, a performance contract is a written agreement between a participant and the participant's manager. It states the goal for the participant to accomplish during the project or after the project's completion and details what is to be accomplished, at what time, and with what results.

Although the steps can vary according to the organization and the specific kind of contract, a common sequence of events usually follows:

- The employee (participant) becomes involved in project implementation.
- The participant and his or her immediate manager agree on a measure or measures for improvement related to the project.
- Specific, measurable goals for improvement are set.
- In the early stages of the project, the contract is discussed and plans are developed to accomplish the goals.
- During project implementation, the participant works to meet the deadline set for contract compliance.
- The participant reports the results of the effort to his or her manager.
- The manager and participant document the results and forward a copy, with appropriate comments, to the project team.

The process of selecting the area for improvement is similar to the process used in an action plan. The topic can cover one or more of the following areas:

- Routine performance related to the project, including specific improvement in measures such as energy savings, efficiency, and material costs
- Problem solving focused on such problems as an unexpected increase in water usage, a decrease in food supplies, or a loss of an energy source
- Innovative or creative applications arising from the project, which could include the initiation of green practices, methods, procedures, techniques, and processes

The topic of the performance contract should be stated in terms of one or more objectives that are:

- Written
- Understandable by all involved
- Challenging (requiring an unusual effort to achieve)
- Achievable (something that can be accomplished)
- Largely under the control of the participant
- Measurable and dated

QUESTIONNAIRES

As described in the previous chapters, the questionnaire is one of the most versatile data collection tools, and it can be appropriate for collecting data at Levels 1 through 4. Essentially, the design principles and content issues for a business impact evaluation are the same as at other levels, except that questionnaires will include additional questions to capture those data specific to business impact.

Using questionnaires for impact data collection has advantages and disadvantages. The good news is that questionnaires are easy to implement and low in cost. Data analysis is efficient, and the time required to provide the data is often minimal, making questionnaires among the least disruptive of data collection methods. The bad news is that the data can be distorted and inaccurate, and are sometimes missing. The challenge is to take all the steps necessary to ensure that questionnaires are complete, accurate, and clear, and that they are returned.

As noted, questionnaires are popular, convenient, and low-cost; for these reasons, they have become a way of life. Unfortunately, questionnaires are among the weakest methods of data collection. Paradoxically, they are the most commonly used because of their advantages. Of the first 300 case studies published on the ROI Methodology, roughly 50 percent used questionnaires as a method of data collection. The philosophy in the ROI Methodology is to take processes that represent the weakest method and make them as credible as possible. Here the challenge is to make questionnaires credible and useful by ensuring that they collect all the data needed, that participants provide accurate and complete data, and that return rates are in at least the 70- to 80-percent range.

The reason return rates must be high is explained in the sixth guiding principle of the ROI Methodology that was outlined in Table 4.4: if an individual provides no improvement data, it is assumed that the person had no improvement to report. This is a conservative principle, but it is necessary to bring the credibility required. Consequently, using questionnaires will require effort, discipline, and personal attention to ensure proper response rates. There are other references that present suggestions for ensuring high response rates for data collection. For example, "Return to Sender: Improving Response Rates for Questionnaires and Surveys" (Phillips and Phillips, 2004) can be found at www.roiinstitute.net/publications/articles/?page=7.

Considerations for Selecting Data Collection Methods

The data collection methods presented in this and earlier chapters offer a wide range of opportunities for collecting data in a variety of situations. Eight aspects of data collection should be considered when deciding on the most appropriate method of collecting any type of data.

TYPE OF DATA

One of the most important issues to consider when selecting the data collection method is the type of data to be collected. Some methods are more appropriate for business impact. Follow-up questionnaires, observations, interviews, focus groups, action planning, and performance contracting are best—sometimes exclusively—suited for application data. Performance monitoring, action planning, and questionnaires can easily capture business impact data.

INVESTMENT OF PARTICIPANTS' TIME

Another important factor when selecting the data collection method is the amount of time participants must spend with data collection and evaluation systems. Time requirements should always be minimized, and the method should be positioned so that it is a value-added activity. Participants must understand that data collection is a valuable undertaking, and not an activity to be resisted. Sampling can be helpful in keeping total participant time to a minimum. Methods such as performance monitoring require no participant time, whereas others, such as conducting interviews and focus groups, require a significant investment in time.

COST OF METHOD

Cost is always a consideration when selecting the method. Some data collection methods are more expensive than others. For example, interviews and observations are expensive, whereas surveys, questionnaires, and performance monitoring are usually inexpensive. The balance between accuracy and cost is always an issue.

DISRUPTION OF NORMAL ACTIVITIES

For organizations the issue that generates perhaps the greatest concern among managers is the degree of work disruption that data collection will create. Routine processes should be disrupted as little as possible. Data collection techniques like performance monitoring require little time and cause little distraction from normal activities. Questionnaires generally do not disrupt the work environment and can often be completed in just a few minutes, perhaps even after normal work hours. At the other extreme, techniques such as the focus group and interviews may disrupt the work unit.

ACCURACY OF METHOD

The accuracy of the technique is another factor to consider when selecting the method. For example, performance monitoring is usually accurate, whereas questionnaires are subject to distortion and may be unreliable. If on-the-job behavior must be captured, observation is clearly one of the most accurate methods. There is often a tradeoff in the accuracy and costs of a method.

UTILITY OF AN ADDITIONAL METHOD (SOURCE OR TIME FRAME)

Because many different methods to collect data exist, using too many methods is tempting. Multiple data collection methods add time and cost to the evaluation, and may result in little added value. Utility refers to the value added by each additional data collection method. When more than one method is used, the utility should always be addressed. Does the value obtained from the additional data warrant the extra time and expense of the method? If the answer is no, the additional method should not be implemented. The same issue must be addressed when considering multiple sources and time frames.

CULTURAL BIAS OF DATA COLLECTION METHOD

The culture or philosophy of the organization can dictate which data collection methods are best to use. For example, questionnaires will work well in an organization or audience that is accustomed to using questionnaires. If, however, an organization tends to overuse questionnaires, this may not be the best choice for collecting project data. Some organizations routinely use focus groups. However, others view the technique as invasive.

Measuring the Hard to Measure

Impact measures are typically easy to collect and easy to measure. They represent the classic definitions of hard data and soft data and tangible and intangible data. For green projects, much attention today is focused on the hard to measure—that is, on some of the classic soft items such as image, reputation, social responsibility, and environmental friendliness. Although this subject is discussed in more detail in Chapter 9, a few brief comments are appropriate here.

EVERYTHING CAN BE MEASURED

Contrary to the views of some professionals, any item, issue, or phenomenon that is important to an organization can be measured. Even image, perception, and ideas can be measured. The thorny issue usually lies in identifying the best way and the available resources to measure. Although the community's image of an organization or the way customers become aware of a brand can be measured accurately, doing so takes time and money.

Organizations collect this type of data in various time frames from different sources. For example, Starbucks has been implementing sustainability projects and green initiatives for years. They make it a point for the customers, the public, and the employees to fully understand their commitment to helping and protecting the environment. Starbucks is interested in feedback on their corporate social responsibility position, sustainability success, and environmental stewardship. They routinely collect data on their website and in customer surveys. They also collect similar data from employees so executives will fully understand the success of these projects, which are aimed at image building.

PERCEPTIONS ARE IMPORTANT

Many measures are based on perceptions. For example, corporate social responsibility is an important component of a company's image. Concepts such as brand awareness are based strictly on perception (i.e., on what a person knows or perceives about an item, product, or service). At one time, perceptions were considered irrelevant and not valuable, but today many decisions are based on perceptions. For instance, customers' perceptions about service quality often drive tremendous organizational changes. Similarly, employees' perceptions of their employer often drive huge investments in projects to improve job satisfaction, organizational commitment, and engagement. Because perceptions are important, they must be part of the measurement plan for the hard to measure.

ALL MEASURES CAN BE CONVERTED TO MONEY, BUT NOT ALL MEASURES SHOULD BE

Just as everything can be measured, so too can every measure be converted to monetary value. The concern involves credibility and resources. As the eleventh guiding principle of Table 4.4 indicates, some measures (intangibles) cannot credibly be converted to money with minimum resources.

Important emphasis must be placed on measuring the hard to measure and valuing the hard to value—the intangibles. Intangible measures are often the principal drivers for green projects. Knowing when to pursue conversion to money and when to avoid it is important. More details on intangibles are presented in Chapter 9 with more examples and techniques to measure the hard to measure and address the issue of converting to money.

Final Thoughts

Measuring application and implementation is critical in determining the success of a project or program. This essential measure not only determines the success achieved but also identifies areas where improvement is needed and where success can be replicated in the future.

Business impact data are critical to addressing an organization's business needs. These data lead the evaluation to the "money." Although perceived as difficult to find, business impact data are readily available and credible. This chapter presents a variety of techniques to collect application and impact data, ranging from questionnaires to monitoring records and systems. The method chosen must match the scope of the project. Understanding success is important to the ability to provide evidence that business needs are being met.

Chapter 8

Isolating the Impact
of Green Projects

Reporting improvement in business impact measures such as energy consumption, waste, and raw material cost is an important step in a green project evaluation. Invariably, however, one essential question arises: How much of this improvement was the result of the green project (or which green project)? Unfortunately, the answer is rarely given with an acceptable degree of accuracy and confidence. Although the change in performance may in fact be linked to the green project, other, non–project-related factors may have contributed to the improvement as well. If this issue is not addressed, the results reported will lack credibility. This chapter explores useful techniques for isolating the effects of the green project.

Why the Concern About Isolating Project Impact?

Multiple factors influence the business measures targeted by almost any project. Isolating the effect of a green project is necessary for accuracy and credibility. Without this isolation, the project's success cannot be confirmed; moreover, the effects of the project may be overstated if the change in the business impact measure is attributed entirely to the project. If this issue is ignored, the impact study may be considered invalid and inconclusive. This places appropriate pressure on green project leaders to take credit only for what their projects have accomplished.

REALITY

Isolating the effects of projects on business measures has led to some important conclusions. First, in almost every situation, multiple factors generate business results. The rest of the world does not stand still while a green proj-ect is being implemented. Other processes and programs are also operating to improve the same metrics targeted by the green project or sustainability initiatives.

Next, if the project effects are not isolated, no business link can be estab-lished. Without steps taken to document the project's contribution, there is no proof that the project actually influenced the measures. Instead, the evi-dence will show that the project *might* have made a difference. Results have improved, but other factors may have influenced the data. Proof is much better than evidence.

Also, the outside factors and influences have their own protective own-ers, who will insist that it was their processes that made the difference. Some of them will probably be certain that the results are due entirely to their efforts. They may present a compelling case to management, stressing their achievements. For example, a green project at a large hospital chain focused on eliminating or minimizing paper, saving millions of dollars and thou-sands of trees. The green project focused on employee attitudes, habits, and practices. At the same time, a lean six-sigma program targeted the same area, using process improvement techniques and technology enhancement. When the savings were tabulated, the lean six-sigma team claimed all of the results in paper reduction, leaving the green team disappointed.

Finally, isolating the effects of the project on impact data is a challeng-ing task. For complex projects in particular, the process is not easy, especially when strong-willed owners of other processes are involved. Fortunately, a va-riety of approaches are available to facilitate the procedure. These approaches are presented in this chapter.

MYTHS

The myths surrounding the isolation of project effects create confusion and frustration with the process. Some researchers, professionals, and consultants go so far as to suggest that such isolation is not necessary. Here are the most common myths:

1. *Our project is complementary to other processes; therefore, we should not attempt to isolate the effects of the project.* A project often complements other factors at work (or other green projects), all of which together drive results, sometimes even the same measure. If the sponsor of a particular project needs to understand its relative contribution, the isolation process is the only way to do it. If accomplished properly, the isolation process will reveal how the complementary factors interact to drive improvements.

2. *Other project leaders do not address this issue.* Some project leaders do not grapple with the isolation problem because they wish to make a con-

vincing case that all of the improvement is directly related to their own processes. However, customer surveys completed after the purchase of a new green product ask why the purchase was made. This is one way organizations try to isolate the results of multiple variables. They want to know which of their processes or systems persuaded the customer to make the purchase.

3. *If we cannot use a research-based control group, we should not attempt this procedure.* Although an experimental research design using randomly assigned control and experimental groups is the most reliable approach to identifying causes and effects, it is not applicable in the majority of situations. Consequently, other methods must be used to isolate the effects of a project. The challenge is to find a method that is effective—with reproducible results—even if it is not as credible as the group comparison method.

4. *The stakeholders will understand the link to business impact measures; therefore, we do not need to attempt to isolate the effects of the project.* Unfortunately, stakeholders try to understand only what is presented to them. The absence of information makes it difficult for them to understand the business linkage, particularly when others are claiming full credit for the improvement.

5. *Estimates of improvement provide no value.* It may be necessary to tackle the isolation process using estimates from those who understand the process best. Although this should be pursued only as a last alternative, the technique can provide value and credibility, particularly when the estimates have been adjusted for error to reduce subjectivity. A tremendous amount of research from the past one hundred years supports the validity of estimates (Surowieki, 2004).

6. *If we ignore the issue, maybe the others will not think about it.* Audiences are becoming more sophisticated on this topic, and they are aware of the presence of multiple influences. If no attempt is made to isolate the effects of the project, the audience will assume that the other factors have had a major effect—perhaps the only effect. A project's credibility can deteriorate quickly.

These myths underscore the importance of addressing the isolation step. The emphasis on isolation is not meant to suggest that a project is implemented independently and exclusively of other processes. Obviously, all groups should be working as a team to produce the desired results. Multiple green projects are often implemented at the same time. However, when funding is parceled among different functions, departments, or project leaders, there is always a struggle to show, and often to understand, the connection between their activities and the results. If you do not undertake this process, others will—leaving your project with reduced budgets, resources, influence, and respect.

Preliminary Issues

The cause-and-effect relationship between a project and performance can be confusing and difficult to prove, but it can be demonstrated with an acceptable degree of accuracy. The challenge is to develop one or more specific techniques to isolate the effects of the project early in the process, usually as part of an evaluation plan conducted before the project begins. Up-front attention ensures that appropriate techniques will be used with minimal cost and time commitments. Two important issues in isolating the effects of a project are covered next, followed by specific methods.

CHAIN OF IMPACT

Before presentation of the methods, reflecting on the chain of impact described in earlier chapters is important. Measurable impact data from a green project (Level 4 data) should be derived from the project's application (Level 3 data). Successful application of the project should stem from the project participants' learning (Level 2 data) of new skills or techniques. Success with learning will usually occur when project participants react favorably to the green project's intent, content, and objectives (Level 1 data). Without this preliminary evidence, isolating the effects of a project is difficult. From a practical standpoint, this requires data collection at four levels for an ROI calculation (the first guiding principle in Table 4.4) as a prerequisite to isolating the project's effects.

IDENTIFY OTHER FACTORS: A FIRST STEP

As a first step to isolate a project's impact on performance, all key factors that may have contributed to the performance improvement should be identified. This step communicates to interested parties that other factors may have influenced the results, underscoring that the project is not the sole source of improvement. Consequently, the credit for improvement is shared among several possible variables and sources—an approach that is likely to garner the sponsor's respect. Several potential sources are available for identifying major influencing variables:

- The sponsor
- Participants in the project (employees, customers, suppliers, citizens, etc.)

- The immediate managers of participants
- The project implementation team
- Subject matter experts
- Other process owners
- Experts on the situation, issue, or project
- Middle and top management

The importance of identifying all of the factors is underscored by an example. A low-cost hotel chain decided to pursue a variety of green projects. While the principal driver was image with customers, much of it was an attempt to save operating costs. Several different functions and departments were involved, including marketing, maintenance, engineering, staff training, procurement, and quality. Although there were several impact measures representing the payoff for the green projects, one important measure was energy consumption, a number that is monitored for each property routinely. A year into the program, the electrical energy savings had been impressive, representing a significant amount of cost savings. To determine what caused the improvement, several factors were identified:

- The marketing department communicated directly with the customers, requesting permission to not change the linens and wash the towels every day, asking them to conserve by keeping the air conditioning thermostat higher and the heating thermostat lower, and reminding them to turn the lights off whenever possible. The maintenance function installed more efficient lighting systems, a system to automatically shut off the lights when a person leaves, and automatic adjustments for the heating and air conditioning during the daytime.
- Engineering reviewed the electrical bill and made consolidations, changed some purchasing arrangements, improved some efficiency on connections to the property, and upgraded some of the generators and pumps for more energy-efficient ones.
- Procurement purchased materials that were friendly to the environment, and some of these also caused less energy consumption. For example, the housekeeping department purchased laundry detergent that used cold water only, thus saving energy when washing the linens and towels.
- The quality function worked on several projects, including ways to cut down on waste. The waste reduction meant less use of the trash compactor, which saved some electrical energy.
- Staff training had a brief one-day session on the entire green issue and taught all employees to take specific steps to conserve wherever possible.

The challenge was to determine how much electrical energy savings is connected to each factor.

A method is available to sort out the cause-and-effect relationship. Project team leaders should go beyond assuming the contribution of their efforts.
They should use one or more of the following techniques to isolate the impact of their project.

Methods to Isolate the Impact of Projects

Just as there are many data collection methods available for collecting data at
different levels, a variety of methods are also available to isolate the effects of
a project. Some are more credible than others. The most credible approaches
are presented first.

CONTROL GROUPS

The most accurate approach for isolating the project's impact is an experimental design with control groups. This approach involves the use of an experimental group that experiences the implementation of the green project
and a control group that does not. The two groups should be as similar in
composition as possible and, if feasible, participants for each group should be
randomly assigned. When this is achievable and the groups are subjected to
the same environmental influences, any difference in performance between
the two groups can be attributed to the project.

As illustrated in Figure 8.1, the control group and experimental group
do not necessarily require pre-project measurements. Measurements can
be taken during the project and after the project has been implemented,
with the difference in performance between the two groups indicating the
amount of improvement that is directly related to the project.

For green initiatives and sustainability projects, the use of a comparison
group analysis should be feasible. It is a matter of comparing one situation to
another, such as a green project in one building compared to another similar building with no project. Natural sets occur when considering the vast
opportunities for green projects. For example, stores, buildings, branches,
houses, subdivisions, employees, customers, plants, neighborhoods, cities—
there are often many natural comparisons that can be possible because the
green projects and initiatives should be, can be, and are being implemented
everywhere.

One caution should be observed: the use of control groups may create
the impression that the project leaders are reproducing a laboratory setting,
which can cause a problem for some executives and administrators. To avoid
this perception, some organizations conduct a pilot project as the experi-

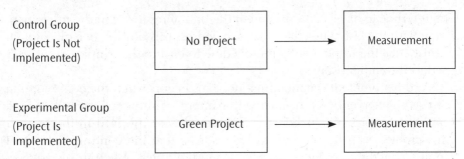

| Control Group (Project Is Not Implemented) | No Project | ⟶ | Measurement |
| Experimental Group (Project Is Implemented) | Green Project | ⟶ | Measurement |

FIGURE 8.1 Use of Control Groups

mental group. A similarly constituted comparison group is selected but is not involved in the project. The terms *pilot project* and *comparison group* are less threatening to executives than *experimental group* and *control group*.

It's also important to recognize that the control group approach has some inherent problems that can make it difficult to apply in practice. The first involves the selection of the groups. From a theoretical perspective, having identical control and experimental groups is next to impossible. Dozens of individual and contextual factors can affect performance, so on a practical basis, it is best to select the four to six variables that will have the greatest influence on performance. Essentially, this involves the 80/20 rule (the Pareto principle). This rule is aimed at selecting the 20 percent of variables that might account for 80 percent of the difference. It requires working from the most important variable and moving to the next to cover four to six issues that have the greatest influence on the improvement in the impact measure in question.

Another major problem is that the control group process is not suited to many situations. For some types of green projects, withholding the initiative from one particular group while implementing it with another may not be appropriate. This is particularly true where critical solutions are needed immediately; management is usually not willing to withhold a solution from one area to see how it works in another. This limitation keeps control group analyses from being implemented in many instances. However, in practice, many opportunities arise for a natural control group to develop in situations where a solution is implemented throughout an organization. If it takes several months for the solution to be implemented in the organization, enough time may be available for a parallel comparison between the first group and the last group for implementation. In these cases, ensuring that the groups are matched as closely as possible is critical. These naturally occurring control groups can often be identified in the case of major enterprise-wide project implementations. Let's say a restaurant chain is "greening" all of the restaurants, one at a time. The project will take one year to complete, which offers enough time to have a comparison of the first stores to begin the implementation with the last. The challenge is to address this possibility early enough to influence the implementation schedule to ensure that similar groups are used in the comparison.

Another problem is contamination. This occurs when the control group realizes an intervention is occurring that improves important measures—and that their performance is being compared to those involved in the project. This problem can be minimized by ensuring that the control and project groups are at different locations or different buildings. When this is not possible, it should be explained to participants in both groups that one group will be involved in the project now and the other will be involved at a later date. Appealing to participants' sense of responsibility and asking them not to share information with others may help prevent contamination.

A closely related problem involves the passage of time. The longer a control versus experimental group comparison operates, the greater the likelihood that other influences will affect the results; more variables will enter into the situation, contaminating the results. On the other end of the scale, enough time must pass to allow a clear pattern of success to emerge, distinguishing the two groups. Thus, the timing of control group comparisons must strike a delicate balance between waiting long enough for performance differences to show and not waiting so long that the results become contaminated.

Still another problem occurs when the different groups are subject to different environmental influences during the experiment. This is usually the case when groups are at dissimilar locations. Sometimes the selection of the groups can prevent this problem from occurring. Another tactic is to use more groups than necessary and discard those groups that show some environmental differences.

A final problem is that the use of control and experimental groups may appear too research-oriented for most business organizations. For example, management may not want to take the time to experiment before proceeding with a project, in addition to the selective withholding problem discussed earlier. Because of these concerns, some project managers will not entertain the idea of using control groups.

Because the use of control groups is an effective approach for isolating impact, it should be considered when an ROI study is planned. In these situations, isolating the project impact with a high level of accuracy is essential, and the primary advantage of the control group process is accuracy.

TREND-LINE ANALYSIS

Another useful technique for approximating the project's impact is trend-line analysis. In this approach, a trend line is drawn to project the future, using previous performance as a base. When the project is fully implemented, actual performance is compared with the trend-line projection. Any improvement in performance beyond what the trend line predicted can be reasonably attributed to project implementation when certain conditions are met. While this is not a precise process, it can provide a reasonable estimate of the project's impact.

Figure 8.2 shows a trend-line analysis from the delivery fleet of a food distribution company. The vertical axis reflects the level of fuel consumption per day, per truck. The horizontal axis represents time. Data reflect conditions before and after a fuel savings scheduling project was implemented in October. As shown in the figure, an upward trend for the data began prior to project implementation. However, the project apparently had a dramatic effect on fuel consumption as the trend line is much greater than the return. Project leaders may have been tempted to measure the improvement by comparing the one-year average for consumption prior to the project (55) to the one-year average after the project (35), which would yield a twenty-gallon difference. However, this approach understates the improvement because the measure in question is moving in the wrong direction and the project turns it in the right direction.

A more accurate comparison is actual value after the project (the last two months) versus the trend-line value for the same period, a difference of 54 (75 – 21). Using this measure increases the accuracy and credibility of the process in terms of isolating the project's impact. To use this technique, two conditions must be met:

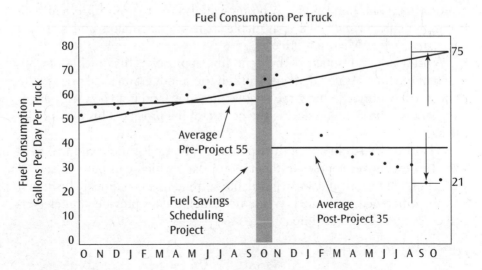

FIGURE 8.2 Trend-Line Analysis for Fuel Savings Project

1. It can be assumed that the trend that developed prior to the project would have continued if the project had not been implemented to alter it (i.e., had the project not been implemented, this trend would have continued on the same path). The experts who understand the situation best should be able to provide input to confirm this assumption. If the assumption does not hold, trend-line analysis cannot be used. If the assumption is valid, the second condition is considered.

2. No other new variables or influences entered the process during project implementation. The key word here is *new*; the understanding is that the trend has been established from the influences already in place, and no additional influences have entered the process beyond the green project. If this is not the case, another method will have to be used. Otherwise, the trend-line analysis presents a reasonable estimate of the impact of this project.

In the example, the fleet operators indicated that the trend prior to the project implementation was caused by the growth in customers and was still there in the post-project period. Also, this group stated that no other new influence entered the process during the post-project period. Nothing else had caused this improvement. Thus, the improvement of 54 gallons per day, per truck, was attributed to the fuel-savings project.

Pre-project data must be available in order for this technique to be used, and the data should show a reasonable degree of stability. If the variance of the data is high, the stability of the trend line will be an issue. If the stability cannot be assessed from a direct plot of the data, more detailed statistical analyses can be used to determine if the data are stable enough to allow a projection. The trend line can be projected directly from historical data using a simple formula that is available in many calculators and software packages, such as Microsoft Excel.

A primary disadvantage of the trend-line approach is that it will not work much of the time. As noted, it only works if the trends established prior to the project will continue in the same relative direction, and if no new influences have entered the situation during the course of the project. This may not be the case.

The primary advantage of this approach is that it is simple and inexpensive. Top executives appreciate this type of data, which can be represented with charts. If historical data are available, a trend line can quickly be drawn and the differences estimated. While not exact, it does provide a quick general assessment of project impact.

FORECASTING METHODS

A more analytical approach to isolation is the use of forecasting methods that predict a change in performance variables. This approach represents a mathematical interpretation of the trend-line analysis when other variables enter the situation at the time of implementation. With this approach, the output measure targeted by the project is forecast based on the influence of variables that have changed during the implementation or evaluation period for the project. The actual value of the measure is compared with the forecast value, and the difference reflects the contribution of the project.

A major disadvantage to this approach emerges when several variables enter the process. The complexity multiplies, and the use of sophisticated statistical packages designed for multiple variable analyses is necessary. Even with this assistance, however, a good fit of the data to the model may not be possible. This technique may be appropriate for large, expensive projects when it is essential to know more precisely the impact of the green project. Still, some organizations have not developed mathematical relationships for output variables as a function of one or more inputs, and without them the forecasting method is difficult to use.

ESTIMATES

The most common method of isolating the effects of a project is to use estimates from a group of individuals. Although this is a weak method, it is feasible in all situations and its credibility can be enhanced if adequate precautions are taken. The beginning point in using this method is ensuring that the estimates are provided by the most credible source, which is often the participants in the project or other experts (i.e., the third guiding principle in Table 4.4). The individuals who provide this information must understand the different factors and, particularly, the influence of the project on those factors. Essentially, there are four common groups for input:

1. The participants directly involved in the project are the first source considered.
2. Managers are another possible source.
3. Customers provide credible estimates in particular situations.
4. Technical experts may provide insight into causes for improvement.

These sources are described in more detail next.

Participants' Estimate of Impact

An easily implemented method of isolating the project's impact is to obtain information directly from participants involved in project implementation. The participants are the employees, suppliers, volunteers, citizens, or other individuals who should be able to make the project successful. The usefulness of this approach rests on the assumption that participants are capable of determining or estimating how much of the performance improvement is related to the project implementation. Because their actions have led to the improvement, participants may provide accurate data. Although an estimate, the value they provide is likely to be acceptable with management because they know that the participants are at the center of the change or improvement. The estimate is obtained by defining the improvement and then asking participants the series of questions shown in Table 8.1.

Participants who do not provide answers to the questions in Table 8.1 are excluded from the analysis. Erroneous, incomplete, and extreme information should also be discarded before the analysis. To obtain a conservative estimate, the confidence percentage, which is a reflection of the error in the estimate, can be factored into each of the values. Thus, an 80-percent confidence level equates to a potential error range of plus or minus 20 percent. In this approach, the estimate is multiplied by the level of confidence to adjust for (remove) the error.

An example will help describe the situation. In an effort to increase recycling in the community, three actions were taken. Recycling had been available but because of the apathy of the community, the inconvenience of the location, and a lack of incentive to do it, the results were not acceptable. The community implemented three new approaches. One approach was to conduct awareness sessions in the schools, neighborhoods, community groups, and churches to make people aware of the recycling program and what it means to them and the environment. In addition, recycling was made more convenient so it was easier for residents to conserve. Essentially, they could place three different containers on the street and have them picked up. In addition, when citizens participated in recycling, a discount was applied to their regular waste management bill. With these three services implemented, it was important to understand the effects of each of the processes. On a questionnaire, a sample of participants were asked to allocate the percentage that each of these services led to their increased participation.

As well, the participants were told the amount of increase in recycling volume (a fact), and they were asked to indicate if other factors could have

---

TABLE 8.1   Questions for Participant Estimation

- What is the link between these factors and the improvement?
- What other factors have contributed to this improvement in performance?
- What percentage of this improvement can be attributed to the implementation of this project?
- How much confidence do you have in this estimate, expressed as a percentage? (0 percent equals no confidence; 100 percent equals complete confidence.)
- What other individuals or groups could provide a reliable estimate of this percentage to determine the amount of improvement contributed by this project?

TABLE 8.2 Example of a Participant's Estimation			
Fact: Recycling volume has increased by 50 percent			
Factor That Influenced Improvement	Percentage of Improvement Caused by Project	Confidence Expressed as a %	Adjusted % of Improvement Caused by Project
Green awareness	60%	80%	48%
Convenience of participation	15%	70%	10.5%
Discounts for participating	20%	80%	16%
Other	5%	60%	3%
Total	**100%**		

caused this increase in addition to the three processes. Residents mentioned only a few other processes. Table 8.2 shows one participant's response. In the example, the participant allocates 60 percent of the improvement to the awareness program and has a level of confidence in the estimate of 80 percent.

The confidence percentage is multiplied by the estimate to produce a usable project value of 48 percent. This adjusted percentage is then multiplied by the actual amount of the improvement in recycling volume (post-project minus pre-project value) to isolate the portion attributed to the project. For example, if volume increased by 50 percent, 24 percent would be attributed to the awareness program. The adjusted improvement is now ready for conversion to monetary value and, ultimately, use in the ROI calculation. Although the reported contribution is an estimate, this approach offers accuracy and credibility. Five adjustments are effectively applied to the participant estimate to produce a conservative value:

1. Participants who do not provide usable data are assumed to have observed no improvements.
2. Extreme data values and incomplete, unrealistic, or unsupported claims are omitted from the analysis, although they may be included in the "other benefits" category.
3. For short-term projects, it is assumed that no benefits are realized from the project after the first year of full implementation. For long-term projects, several years may pass after project implementation before benefits are realized.

4. The amount of improvement is adjusted by the portion directly related to the project, expressed as a percentage.

5. The improvement value is multiplied by the confidence level, expressed as a percentage, to reduce the amount of the improvement in order to reflect the potential error.

As an enhancement of this method, the level of management above the participants may be asked to review and concur with each participant's estimate if this is an employment (versus community) situation.

In using participants' estimates to measure impact, several assumptions are made:

1. The project encompasses a variety of different activities, practices, and tasks all focused on improving the performance of one or more business measures.

2. One or more business measures were identified prior to the project and have been monitored since the implementation process. Data monitoring has revealed an improvement in the business measure.

3. There is a need to associate the project with a specific amount of performance improvement and determine the monetary impact of the improvement. This information forms the basis for calculating the actual ROI.

Given these assumptions, the participants can specify the results linked to the project and provide data necessary to develop the ROI. This can be accomplished using a focus group, an interview, or a questionnaire.

Manager's Estimate of Impact

In lieu of, or in addition to, participant estimates, the participants' manager may be asked to provide input concerning the project's role in improving performance if the project participant is an employee of an organization. In some settings in organizations, the managers may be more familiar with the other factors influencing performance and therefore may be better equipped to provide estimates of impact. The questions to ask managers, after identifying the improvement ascribed to the project, are similar to those asked of the participants.

Managers' estimates should be analyzed in the same manner as the participant estimates, and they may also be adjusted by the confidence percentage. When participants' and managers' estimates have both been collected, the decision of which estimate to use becomes an issue. Each estimate source provides a unique perspective. If there is a compelling reason to believe that one estimate is more credible than the other, then that estimate should be used. If both are equally credible, the most conservative approach is to use the lowest value and include an appropriate explanation. This is in the fourth guiding principle shown in Table 4.4.

In some cases, higher levels of management may provide an estimate of the percentage of improvement attributable to a project. After considering other factors that could contribute to the improvement—such as technology, procedures, and process changes—they apply a subjective factor to represent the portion of the results that should be attributed to the project. Note that a word of caution may be in order. Since higher levels of management are further from the action, their input may be subjective, yet it may still be accepted by those who provide or approve funding for the project. Sometimes, their comfort level with the process becomes the most important consideration.

Customers' Input on Project Impact

An approach that is useful in some situations is to solicit input on the project's impact directly from customers. In this scenario, customers are asked how a green project has influenced them to make improvements or buy a product. This technique focuses directly on what the project is designed to improve. For example, an electric utility company implemented an educational program for customers to help them lower their electric utility bills. Market research data showed that the customers attributed a 5.1 percent of the reduction of their bills to the project, with an average confidence of 83 percent. Consequently, a 4.23-percent savings (5.1 × .83) is attributed to the green project.

Routine customer feedback provides an excellent opportunity to collect input directly from customers concerning their reactions to new or improved green products and services and their success. Pre- and post-project data can pinpoint the improvements spurred by a new project.

Customer input should be secured using existing data collection methods; the creation of new surveys or feedback instruments should be minimized. Ideally, this measurement process should not add to the data collection systems in use. Customer input may constitute the most powerful and convincing data if it is convenient, complete, accurate, and valid.

Technical Experts' Input

External or internal experts are usually available to estimate the portion of results that can be attributed to a green project. With this technique, experts must be carefully selected based on their knowledge of the process, project, and situation. For example, an expert in green lighting may be able to provide estimates of how much electricity is saved with a change in bulbs. Other experts may know how much can be attributed to other factors. Also, this industry has many experts who have documented this type of information (MacKay, 2009).

This approach has its drawbacks, however. It can yield inaccurate data unless the project and the setting where the estimate is made are familiar to the expert. Also, this approach may lack credibility if the estimates come from sources that do not have credibility.

This process has the advantage that its reliability is often a reflection of the reputation of the expert or independent consultant. It is a quick and easy form of input from a reputable expert or consultant, and as noted, many experts are often available. Sometimes top management has more confidence in external experts than in members of its own staff.

ESTIMATE CREDIBILITY: THE WISDOM OF CROWDS

The following story is a sample of the variety of research showing the power of input from average individuals. It is taken from James Surowieki's bestselling book *The Wisdom of Crowds* (2004).

In the fall of 1906, British scientist Francis Galton left his home in the town of Plymouth and headed for a country fair. Galton was eighty-five years old. While he was beginning to feel his age, he was still brimming with the curiosity that had won him renown—and notoriety—for his work on statistics and the science of heredity.

Galton's destination was the annual West of England Fat Stock and Poultry Exhibition, a regional fair where the local farmers and townspeople gathered to appraise the quality of each other's cattle, sheep, chickens, horses, and pigs. Wandering through rows of stalls examining workhorses and prize hogs may seem like a strange way for a scientist to spend an afternoon, but there was certain logic to it. Galton was obsessed with the measurement of physical and mental qualities and breeding. The livestock show was no more than a large showcase for the effects of good and bad breeding?

Galton was interested in breeding because he believed that only a few people had the characteristics necessary to keep societies healthy. He had devoted much of his career to measuring those characteristics, in fact, in an effort to prove that the vast majority of people did not possess them. His experiments left him with little confidence in the intelligence of the average person, "the stupidity and wrong-headedness of many men and women being so great as to be scarcely credible." Galton believed, "Only if power and control stayed in the hands of the select, well-bred few, could a society remain healthy and strong."

As he walked through the exhibition that day, Galton came across a weight-judging competition. A fat ox had been selected and put on display, and many people were lining up to place wagers on what the weight of the ox would be after it was slaughtered and dressed. For sixpence, an individual could buy a stamped and numbered ticket and fill in his or her name, occupation, address, and estimate. The best guesses would earn prizes.

Eight hundred people tried their luck. They were a diverse group. Many of them were butchers and farmers, who were presumably experts at judging the weight of livestock, but there were also quite a few people who had no insider knowledge of cattle. "Many non-experts competed," Galton wrote later in the scientific journal *Nature*. "The average competitor was probably as well fitted for making a just estimate of the dressed weight of the ox, as an average voter is of judging the merits of most political issues on which he votes."

Galton was interested in figuring out what the "average voter" was capable of because he wanted to prove that the average voter was capable of very little. So he turned the competition into an impromptu experiment. When the contest was over and the prizes had been awarded, Galton borrowed the tickets from the organizers and ran a series of statistical tests on them. Galton arranged the 787 legible guesses in order from highest to lowest and plotted them to see if they would form a bell curve. Then, among other things, he added up all of the contestants' estimates and calculated the mean. That number represented, you could say, the collective wisdom of the Plymouth crowd. If the crowd were viewed as a single person, that would be the person's guess as to the ox's weight.

Galton had no doubt that the average guess of the group would be way off the mark. After all, mix a few smart people with some mediocre people and a lot of dumb people, and it seems likely that you would end up with a dumb answer. But Galton was wrong. The crowd had guessed that the slaughtered and dressed ox would weigh 1,197 pounds. In fact, after it was slaughtered and dressed, the ox weighed 1,198 pounds. In other words, the crowd's judgment was essentially perfect. The "experts" were not even close. Perhaps breeding did not mean so much after all. Galton wrote later: "The result seems more creditable to the trustworthiness of a democratic judgment than it might have been expected."

On that fateful day in Plymouth, Francis Galton discovered a simple but powerful truth: under the right circumstances, groups, of even the most average of people, are remarkably intelligent and are often smarter than the smartest people in them.

Groups do not need to be dominated by exceptionally intelligent people in order to be smart. Even if most of the people within a group are not especially informed or rational, collectively they can reach a wise decision. Although estimates are based on input from average individuals, the combined effort of those people often leads to an accurate assumption of a condition.

CALCULATE THE IMPACT OF OTHER FACTORS

It is often possible to calculate the impact of factors (other than the green project in question) that account for part of the improvement and then credit the project with the remaining part. The project assumes credit for improvement that cannot be attributed to other factors.

Another example taken from the low-cost hotel chain's situation will help explain this approach. As noted, the hotel had implemented several different types of green projects and initiatives, which were owned by different parts of the organizations (see Table 8.3).

Green initiatives such as these can drive several different measures in the organization. In this particular example, the improvement measure was electricity use. When considering the impact of the various factors on the reduction of electricity, some can be calculated based on a variety of studies and previous analyses. For example, in the maintenance project, many—if not all—of the items could be estimated or could be developed. For engineering, changes in purchase, distribution, and equipment could be easily translated into electricity cost reductions. Procurement could estimate how the new materials are affecting electricity based on previous analysis examples. The same is true for quality, but this may not be as accurate. What is not possible is to show the impact of the customers' efforts and the green training—these will have to be estimated.

The important point is that whenever a factor's contribution can be calculated, it is developed and taken out of the total pie. The total electricity savings is the complete pie; only part of it goes to each of these different green initiatives.

TABLE 8.3   The Contributing Factors

Green Initiatives Contributing to the Improvement	Is the Impact a Known Factor?
Customer Green Project (e.g., requesting guests' permission not to wash towels)	No
Maintenance Green Project (e.g., changing systems to turn off lights)	Yes, part of it
Engineering Green Project (e.g., replacing low-efficiency pumps)	Yes
Procurement Green Project (e.g., purchasing environmentally friendly detergents)	Yes
Quality Green Project (e.g., focusing on waste reduction)	Yes, maybe
Green Training Project (e.g., teaching employees conservation techniques)	No

This method is appropriate when the other factors can be easily identified and the appropriate mechanisms or experts are in place to calculate their impact on the improvement. In some cases, estimating the impact of outside factors is just as difficult as estimating the impact of the project, limiting this approach's applicability. However, the results can be reliable if the procedure used to isolate the impact of other factors is sound.

Considerations When Selecting Isolation Methods

With all of these techniques available to isolate the project's impact, selecting the most appropriate ones for a specific project can be difficult. Some techniques are simple and inexpensive; others are time-consuming and costly. In choosing among them, the following factors should be considered:

- Feasibility of the technique
- Accuracy associated with the technique, compared to the necessary need
- Credibility of the technique with the sponsor audience
- Specific cost to implement or use the technique
- Amount of disruption in normal work activities resulting from the technique's implementation
- Participant, staff, and management time required to use the technique

The use of multiple techniques or multiple sources of data input should be considered since two sources are usually better than one.

When multiple sources are used, a conservative method should be used to combine the inputs. This means using the technique that provides the lowest ROI (as noted in the fourth guiding principle of Table 4.4), because a conservative approach builds acceptance. The client should always be provided with an explanation of the process and the subjective factors involved.

Multiple sources allow an organization to experiment with different strategies and build confidence in the use of a particular technique. For example, if management is concerned about the accuracy of participants' estimates, the combination of a control group arrangement and participant estimates could be useful for checking the accuracy of the estimation process.

It is not unusual for the ROI of a project to be extremely large. Even when a portion of the improvement is allocated to other factors, the magnitude can still be impressive in many situations. The audience should understand that even though every effort has been made to isolate the project's impact, it remains an imprecise figure that is subject to error, although every attempt has been made to adjust for the error. The result is the most accurate amount of the contribution given the constraints, conditions, and resources available.

Chances are it is more accurate than other types of analysis regularly used in other functions within the organization. More information on how to isolate the results are found in other sources (Phillips and Aaron, 2008).

Final Thoughts

Isolating the effects of a green project is an important step in answering the question of how much of the improvement in a business measure was caused by the project. The techniques presented in this chapter are the most effective approaches available to answer this question and are used by some of the most progressive organizations. Too often, results are reported and linked to a project with no attempt to isolate the specific portion of the outcome associated with the project. This leads to a suspicious report about project success. If managers and professionals in the field wish to improve the success of green projects and are committed to obtaining results, the need for isolation must be addressed early in the process for all major projects. When this important step is completed, the impact data must be converted to monetary values to prepare for the ROI calculation. The process for converting data to monetary values is detailed in the next chapter.

Chapter 9

Converting Impact
Data to Money

To show the economic contribution of a green project, the improvement in business measures that is attributable to the project (after the effects of the project have been isolated from other influences) must be converted to monetary values, which are then compared with project costs. This represents the ultimate level of project success in the five-level evaluation framework presented in Chapter 2. This chapter explains how business leaders and project owners develop the monetary values of impact measures used to calculate ROI.

In addition to showing stakeholders the money, it is important to also account for the intangible benefits of the project. Sometimes these benefits are just as powerful as the monetary benefits derived from sustainability initiatives. As mentioned earlier, intangible measures are those measures not converted to money. In addition to describing how to convert measures to money, this chapter explores the role of intangibles, how to measure them, when to measure them, and how to report them.

Why the Concern About Converting Data to Monetary Values?

Placing monetary values on measures is not new. Monetary values have been placed on some of the most difficult measures, such as human life, for centuries. But why do it? Because money is the ultimate normalizer. It places different types of measures in a similar unit, thereby allowing for comparison among multiple measures, including project costs.

A project can be shown to be a success just by providing business impact data, showing the amount of change directly attributable to the project. For example, a change in quality, cycle time, market share, or customer satisfaction can represent a significant improvement linked directly to a new project. For some green projects, this may be sufficient. However, many sponsors want to relate that improvement to tangible value. There are five fundamental reasons why this is important. Converting improvement in impact measures to money:

1. Normalizes the definition of value
2. Makes impact more meaningful
3. Aligns the evaluation process to the budgeting process
4. Aligns project implementation to operations
5. Clarifies the magnitude of an issue

Each of these reasons is discussed in more detail in the following sections.

NORMALIZE THE DEFINITION OF VALUE

As described earlier, there are many different types of value. However, monetary value is becoming one of the primary criteria of success for all types of projects. Executives, sponsors, administrators, and other leaders are concerned in particular with the allocation of funds. Unless the value of processes is represented by a common measure, resource allocation is much more difficult. Value is ultimately an indicator of financial gains. Rather than leaving that financial gain to guesswork, converting a measure to money defines value in meaningful terms.

MAKE IMPACT MORE MEANINGFUL

For some projects, the impact is more understandable when it is stated in terms of monetary value. Consider for example the impact of a major project to improve the creativity of an organization's employees and thereby enhance the organization's innovation. Suppose this project involved all employees and had an impact on all parts of the organization. The only way to understand the value of such a project would be to convert the individual efforts and their consequences to monetary values. Totaling the monetary values of all the innovations would provide some sense of the project's value. Then the project's impact could be compared to the project's costs to show the actual return on investment.

ALIGN BUDGETING PROCESS

Professionals and administrators are typically occupied with budgets, and they are expected to develop budgets for projects with an acceptable degree of accuracy. They are also comfortable with handling costs. When it comes to benefits, however, many are not comfortable, even though some of the same techniques used in developing budgets are used to determine benefits. Some of the project's benefits will take the form of cost savings or cost reductions, and this can make identification of the costs or value easier. The monetary benefit resulting from a project is a natural extension of the budget.

ALIGN OPERATIONS

With global competitiveness, the drive to improve the efficiency of operations, and the drive to sustain Mother Earth, awareness of the costs related to particular processes and activities is essential. In the 1990s this emphasis gave rise to activity-based costing (ABC) and activity-based management (ABM), processes used to identify and cost business activities. ABC is used to assign overhead costs to activities so these costs are more precisely allocated to products and services. ABM focuses on managing activities to reduce costs and increase customer value. ABC is not a replacement for traditional, general ledger accounting. Rather, it is a translator or medium between cost accumulations, or the specific expenditure account balances in the general ledger, and the end users who must apply cost data in decision making. In typical cost statements, the actual cost of a process or problem is not readily discernible. ABC converts inert cost data to relevant, actionable information. ABC has become increasingly useful for identifying improvement opportunities and measuring the benefits realized from performance initiatives on an after-the-fact basis (Cokins, 1996). Most green projects and sustainability initiatives contribute to cost savings for the organization. For example, U.S. Bank, the fifth-largest commercial bank in the United States, changed their direct-mail campaign by eliminating mailings to customers who would have purchased anyway. In addition to increasing sales from the new target audience, they reduced mailings on campaigns for direct deposits by 32 percent. In monetary terms, this is a $400,000 per campaign cost savings (Tsai, 2010). Consequently, understanding the cost of a problem and the payoff of the corresponding solution is essential to proper management of the business.

CLARIFY THE MAGNITUDE OF AN ISSUE

In any business, costs are essential to understanding the magnitude of a problem. Consider, for example, the cost of green house gas (GHG) emissions. Traditional records, and even those available through activity-based costing, will not indicate its full value or cost. A variety of estimates and expert inputs may be necessary to supplement immediately available data to arrive at a definite value. The good news is that organizations have developed a number of standard procedures for identifying costs of such magnitude. For example,

Walmart has calculated the cost of one truck sitting idle at a store for one minute, waiting to be unloaded. When this cost is multiplied by the hundreds of deliveries per store and the result then multiplied by five thousand stores, the cost becomes huge, not to mention the environmental impact of these idling trucks.

Five Steps to Convert Data to Money

Converting measures to monetary value involves five steps for each data item:

1. Focus on the unit of measure.
2. Determine the value of each unit.
3. Calculate the change in performance.
4. Determine the annual change in performance.
5. Calculate the annual value of improvement.

FOCUS ON THE UNIT OF MEASURE

First, a unit of measure must be defined. For output data, the unit of measure is the item produced (e.g., one item assembled), service provided (e.g., one package shipped), or sale completed. Time measures could include the time to complete a project, cycle time, or customer response time, and the unit here is usually expressed in terms of minutes, hours, or days. Quality is another common measure, with a unit defined as one error, reject, defect, or reworked item; one ton of waste; one ton of carbon emissions; or one kilowatt-hour. Soft data measures vary, with a unit of improvement expressed in terms of absences, turnover, or a change in the customer satisfaction index. Specific examples of units of measure are:

- One project
- One full-time equivalent (FTE) employee
- One hour of commute time
- One grievance
- One reworked item
- One ton of fuel
- One hour of downtime
- One hour of employee time
- One hour of cycle time
- One gallon of water
- One pound of solid waste

- One customer complaint
- One point increase in customer satisfaction
- One kilowatt-hour of electricity

DETERMINE THE VALUE OF EACH UNIT

The second step is to place a monetary value (V) on the unit identified in the first step. For measures of productivity, quality, cost, and time, the process is relatively easy. Most organizations maintain records or reports that can pinpoint the cost of one unit of production or one defect. Soft data are more difficult to convert to money. For example, the monetary value of one customer complaint or a one point change in an employee attitude may be difficult to determine. The techniques described in this chapter provide an array of approaches for making this conversion. When more than one value is available, the most credible or conservative is generally used in the calculation.

CALCULATE THE CHANGE IN PERFORMANCE DATA

The change in impact data is calculated after the effects of the project have been isolated from other influences. This change (Δ) is the performance improvement that is directly attributable to the project, represented as the Level 4 impact measure. The value may represent the performance improvement for an individual, a team, a group of participants, or several groups of participants.

DETERMINE THE ANNUAL AMOUNT OF CHANGE

The Δ value is annualized to develop a value for the total change in the performance data for one year (ΔP). Using annual figures is a standard approach for organizations seeking to capture the benefits of a particular project, even though the benefits may not remain constant throughout the year. For a short-term project, first-year benefits are used even when the project produces benefits beyond one year. This approach is considered conservative; therefore, it presents a more credible (and likely) outcome.

CALCULATE THE ANNUAL VALUE OF THE IMPROVEMENT

The total value of improvement is calculated by multiplying the annual performance change (ΔP) by the unit value (V) for the complete group in question. For example, if one group of participants is involved in the project that is being evaluated, the total value will include the total improvement for all participants who are providing data in the group. This value for annual project benefits is then compared with the costs of the project to calculate the BCR, ROI, or payback period.

Five Steps to Convert Data in Practice

A simple example will demonstrate these five steps described in the previous section. Suppose a large retail store chain pilots an effort to replace all traditional lighting with energy-efficient LED bulbs. Prior to project implementation, the 90,000-square-foot store in which the pilot program occurs uses approximately 14 kilowatt-hours (kWh) per square foot annually for a total of 1,260,000 kWh per year. On average this is 105,000 kWh per month. After implementing the project, the store monitors electricity usage for six months, showing a new average monthly usage of 73,500 kWh. This is a decrease of 31,500 kWh per month. By comparing this store's usage to that of another store with comparable characteristics, the 31,500 reduction is attributed to the change in bulbs. Given a monthly change in performance, the annual change is 378,000 kWh. The value of a kWh is approximately 10 cents per kWh. The total annual savings to the store is $37,800. Table 9.1 shows the example using the five steps.

TABLE 9.1 Converting Kilowatt-Hours to Monetary Values
Setting: Retail store piloting replacement of traditional lighting to LED lighting.
Step 1: Define the unit of measure. The unit of measure is defined as one kWh.
Step 2: Determine the value (V) of each unit. According to historical data (i.e., the cost per kWh paid per month), the cost is 10 cents per kWh ($V = 10$ cents).
Step 3: Calculate the change (Δ) in performance data. Six months after the project was completed, electricity usage decreased an average of 31,500 kWh per month. The isolation technique used was a control group (see Chapter 8).
Step 4: Determine an annual amount of the change (ΔP). Using the six-month average of 31,500 kWh per month yields an annual improvement of 378,000 ($\Delta P = 31,500 \times 12 = 378,000$).
Step 5: Calculate the annual monetary value of the improvement. ($\Delta P \times V$) = 378,000 $\times$ .10 = $37,800 cost savings

Methods to Convert Impact Measures to Money

The steps to convert a measure to money are straightforward. The challenge, however, is determining the value (Step 2) of a particular measure. A variety of techniques are available that run the gamut from standard values to the use of conservative estimates.

STANDARD VALUES

A standard value is a monetary value assigned to a unit of measurement that is accepted by key stakeholders. Most hard data items (output, quality, cost, and time) have standard values. Standard values have been developed because these are often the measures that matter to the organization. They reflect problems, and their conversion to monetary values shows their impact on the organization's operational and financial well-being. Standard values are used to convert measures of output, quality, and time to money. Virtually every major function within an organization has standard monetary values, particularly for measures they monitor on a routine basis. Standard values can typically be found in:

- Finance and Accounting
- Production
- Operations
- Engineering
- IT
- Administration
- Sales and Marketing
- Customer Service
- Procurement
- Logistics
- Compliance
- Research and Development
- HR
- Risk Management

The following discussion describes how measures of output, quality, and time can be converted to standard values.

Converting Output Data to Money

When a project results in a change in output, the value of the increased output can usually be determined from the organization's accounting or operating records. For projects intended to drive profit, this value is typically the marginal profit contribution of an additional unit of production or service provided. For projects that are performance driven rather than profit driven, this value is usually reflected in the savings realized when an additional unit of output is realized for the same input. For example, United Parcel Service (UPS) implemented a new mapping system that enabled a "no left turn" rule, which enabled drivers to deliver the same number of packages in less time and with less fuel costs by avoiding left-hand turns (Myrow, 2007). One of the more important measures of output is productivity, particularly in a competitive organization. Today, most organizations competing in the global economy do an excellent job of monitoring productivity and placing a value on it.

Calculating the Cost of Quality

Quality and the cost of quality are important issues in manufacturing and service organizations. Because many projects are designed to increase quality, the project team may have to place a value on the improvement of certain quality measures. For some quality measures, the task is easy. For example, if quality is measured in terms of the defect rate, the value of the improvement is the cost to repair or replace the product. The most obvious cost of poor quality is the amount of scrap or waste generated by mistakes. Defective products, spoiled raw materials, and discarded paperwork, rework, and repair are all the result of poor quality and represent monetary costs to the organization.

Quality costs can be grouped into six major categories (Campanella, 1999):

1. *Internal failure* represents costs such as those related to reworking and retesting.
2. *Penalty costs* are fines or penalties incurred as a result of unacceptable quality.
3. *External failure* refers to problems detected after product shipment or service delivery, such as technical support, complaint investigation, remedial upgrades, and fixes.
4. *Appraisal costs*, such as product quality audits, assess the condition of a particular product or service.
5. *Prevention costs* include service quality administration, inspections, process studies, and improvement costs.
6. *Customer dissatisfaction*, which is perhaps the costliest element of inadequate quality, may be difficult to quantify, and arriving at a monetary value may be impossible using direct methods. More and more quality experts are measuring customer and client dissatisfaction with the use of market surveys (Rust, Zahorik, and Keiningham, 1994).

The good news is that many quality measures have been converted to standard values. Some of these measures are:

- Defects
- Rework
- Processing errors
- Complaints
- Equipment downtime
- System downtime
- Solid waste

Converting Employee Time Using Compensation

A third type of standard value is the value of time. Reducing the workforce or saving employee time is a common objective for projects. In a team environment and on an individual basis, a project may enable an organization to reduce time in completing tasks. The value of the time saved is an important measure, and determining a monetary value for it is relatively easy.

The most obvious time savings stem from reduced labor costs for performing a given amount of work. The monetary savings are found by multiplying the hours saved by the labor cost per hour. For example, Tecmotiv's lean and energy environment initiatives (LE2), which include value stream mapping, help the team identify cost savings opportunities in their processes. One such cost savings opportunity was over-processing. By addressing this unnecessary effort in their process inhibitor labor hours were reduced (Chapman and Green, 2010).

The average wage, with a percentage added for employee benefits, will suffice for most calculations of the cost of time. However, employee time may be worth more. For example, additional costs for maintaining an employee (office space, furniture, telephones, utilities, computers, administrative support, and other overhead expenses) could be included in calculating the average labor cost. However, for most projects, the conservative approach of using salary plus employee benefits is recommended.

A word of caution is needed concerning time savings. Savings are realized only when the amount of time saved translates into a cost reduction or a profit contribution. Even if a project produces savings in time, monetary value is not realized unless the time saved is put to productive use. Having individuals estimate the percentage of time saved that is devoted to productive work may be helpful, if it is followed up with a request for examples of how the extra time was used. An important preliminary step in figuring time savings is determining whether the expected savings will be genuine. FedEx is a primary example of assigning value to time (Hurd and Nyberg, 2004).

HISTORICAL COSTS

Sometimes standard values are unavailable. When this occurs, the next best measure of monetary value is the use of historical costs. This classic approach to placing monetary value on measures considers how much performance a measure has cost in the past.

Take the earlier example of converting kilowatt-hours to money. Because this is not standard, the next best technique is to consider how much has been paid for kWh usage in the past.

The challenges with using historical cost include the time to sort through databases, cost statements, financial records, and activity reports to calculate the cost of performance in a measure; the accuracy of the cost, accounting for all related costs; accessing the data, particularly those that are somewhat sensitive; and accuracy in the analysis of the data that result in historical cost of a measure. Because of these issues it is important that two conditions exist:

1. The sponsor approves the use of additional time, effort, and money to develop cost.
2. The measure is simple and can be formed by searching only a few records.

EXPERT INPUT

When it is necessary to convert data items for which historical cost data are not available, input from experts might be a consideration. Internal experts can provide the cost (or value) of one unit of improvement in a measure. Individuals with knowledge of the situation and the confidence of management must be willing to provide estimates—as well as the assumptions behind the estimates. Internal experts may be found in the department in which the data originated—sales, marketing, procurement, engineering, labor relations, or any number of other functions. Most experts have their own methodologies for developing these values. So when their input is required, it is important to explain the full scope of what is needed and to provide as many specifics as possible.

If internal experts have a strong bias regarding the measure or are not available, external experts are sought. External experts should be selected based on their experience with the unit of measure. Fortunately, many experts are available who work directly with important measures, such as employee attitude and customer satisfaction. They are often willing to provide estimates of the cost (or value) of these.

The credibility of the expert, whether internal or external, is a critical issue if the monetary value placed on a measure is to be reliable. Foremost among the factors behind an expert's credibility is the individual's experience with the process or measure at hand. Ideally, he or she should work with this measure routinely. Also, the person must be unbiased. Experts should be neutral in connection with the measure's value and should have no personal or professional interest in it.

In addition, the credentials of external experts—published works, degrees, and other honors or awards—are important in validating their expertise. Many of these people are tapped often, and their track records can and should be checked. If their estimate has been validated in more detailed studies and was found to be consistent, this can serve as a confirmation of their qualifications in providing such data.

EXTERNAL DATABASES

If standard values and historical costs are unavailable and if obtaining expert input is not feasible, it may be appropriate to use values developed through the research of others. This technique makes use of external databases that contain studies and research projects focusing on the cost of data items. Fortunately, many databases include cost studies of data items related to projects, and most are accessible on the Internet. Data are available on the costs of complaints, safety, hazardous and nonhazardous waste, customer satisfaction, and more. The difficulty lies in finding a database with studies or research germane to the particular project. Ideally, the data should originate from a similar setting in the same industry, but that is not always possible. Sometimes, data on industries or organizations in general are sufficient, with adjustments possibly required to suit the project at hand.

LINKAGE WITH OTHER MEASURES

When standard values, records, experts, and external studies are not available, a feasible alternative may be to find a relationship between the measure in question and some other measure that can be easily converted to a monetary value. This involves identifying existing relationships that show a strong correlation between one measure and another with a standard value.

A classic relationship is the correlation between job satisfaction and employee turnover. Studies repeatedly show that job satisfaction and employee loyalty have a strong correlation with reduction in employee turnover. Using standard data or external studies, the cost of turnover can be determined. Therefore, a change in job satisfaction can be immediately converted to a monetary value, or at least an approximate value.

Finding a correlation between a customer satisfaction measure and another measure that can easily be converted to a monetary value is sometimes possible. A strong correlation often exists between customer satisfaction and revenue. Connecting these two variables allows the monetary value of customer satisfaction to be estimated. For example, Toyota Motor Sales in the U.S. conducted a survey of its dealerships over the 1986–1993 time period (Bailey and Dandrade, 1995). A comparison of the differences between top performing dealerships versus bottom performing dealerships in terms of customer satisfaction showed that top performers recorded:

- 43 percent less sales person turnover
- 30 percent less advertising costs
- 46 percent higher profits
- 10 percent less selling expense

Each of these measures can be converted to money and all are linked to customer satisfaction.

In some situations, a chain of relationships may establish a connection between two or more variables. A measure that may be difficult to convert to a monetary value is linked to other measures that, in turn, are linked to measures to which values can be assigned. Ultimately, these measures are traced to a monetary value typically based on profits. Figure 9.1 shows the model used by Sears (Ulrich, 1998). The model connects job attitudes (collected directly from the employees) to customer service, which is directly related to revenue growth. The rectangles in the figure represent survey information, and the ovals represent hard data. The shaded measurements are collected and distributed in the form of Sears' total-performance indicators.

As the model shows, a 5-point improvement in employee attitudes leads to a 1.3-point improvement in customer satisfaction. This, in turn, drives a 0.5 percent increase in revenue growth. If an employee's attitude at a local store improved by 5 points and the previous rate of revenue growth was 5 percent, the new rate of revenue growth would then be 5.5 percent.

ESTIMATES

In some cases, estimating the value of improvement in a measure is the best choice. This estimate may come from participants involved in the project, the management team, or the staff charged with project implementation.

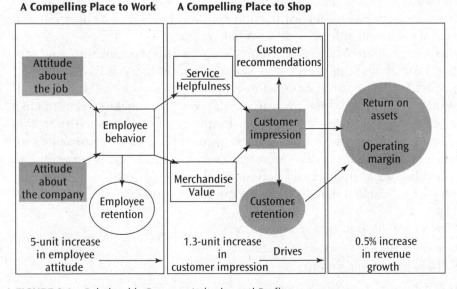

FIGURE 9.1   Relationship Between Attitudes and Profits

The key is selecting from whom to get the estimate, which depends on who has the most knowledge about the measure and who can provide the most credible estimate. The advantage of participant estimates is that the individuals who are most closely connected to the improvement are often able to provide the most reliable estimates of its value. As with isolating project effects, when estimates are used to convert measures to monetary values, adjustments are made to reduce the error in those estimates.

In some situations, participants in a project may be incapable of placing a value on the improvement. Their work may be so far removed from the ultimate value of the process that they cannot provide reliable estimates. In these cases, the team leaders, supervisors, or managers of participants may be able to provide estimates. Thus, they may be asked to provide a value for a unit of improvement linked to the project. In other situations, managers are asked to review and approve participants' estimates and confirm, adjust, or reject those values.

Senior management can often provide estimates of the value of data. In this approach, senior managers concerned with the project are asked to place a value on the improvement based on their perception of its worth. This approach is used when calculating the value is difficult or when other sources of estimation are unavailable or unreliable.

The final source of estimates is the project staff. Using all available information and experience, the staff members most familiar with the situation provide estimates of the value. Although the project staff may be qualified to provide accurate estimates, this approach is sometimes perceived as biased. It should therefore be used only when other approaches are unavailable or inappropriate.

Considerations When Selecting Data Conversion Methods

With so many techniques available, the challenge is selecting one or more strategies that are appropriate for the situation and available resources. Developing a table or list of values or techniques for the situation may be helpful. The guidelines that follow may aid in selecting a technique and finalizing the values.

TYPE OF DATA

Some strategies are designed specifically for hard data, whereas others are more appropriate for soft data. Thus, the type of data often dictates the strategy. Standard values are developed for most hard data items, and company records and cost statements are used in the process. Soft data often involve the use of external databases, links with other measures, and estimates. Experts are used to convert both types of data to monetary values.

ACCURACY OF METHOD

The techniques in this chapter are presented in order of accuracy. Standard values are always most accurate and, therefore, the most credible. But, as mentioned earlier, they are not always readily available. When standard values are not available, the following sequence of operational techniques should be tried:

- Historical costs from company records
- Internal and external experts
- External databases
- Links with other measures
- Estimates

Each technique should be considered in turn based on its feasibility and applicability to the situation. The technique associated with the highest accuracy is always preferred if the situation allows.

SOURCE AVAILABILITY

Sometimes the availability of a particular source of data determines the method selection. For example, experts may be readily accessible. In other situations, the convenience of a technique is a major factor in the selection. The Internet, for example, has made external database searches more convenient.

As with other processes, keeping the time investment for this phase to a minimum is important so that the total effort directed to the ROI study does not become excessive. Devoting too much time to the conversion process may dampen otherwise enthusiastic attitudes about the use of the methodology, plus drive up the costs of the evaluation.

PERSPECTIVE

As noted in the third guiding principle in Table 4.4, the most credible data source must be used. The individual providing estimates must be knowledgeable of the processes and the issues surrounding the valuation of the data. For example, consider the estimation of a quality complaint in a manufacturing plant. Although a supervisor may have insight into what caused a particular quality issue, he or she may have a limited perspective. A high-level manager may be able to grasp the overall impact of the complaint and how it will affect other areas. Thus, a high-level manager would be a more credible source in this situation.

NEED FOR MULTIPLE TECHNIQUES

The availability of more than one technique for obtaining values for the data is often beneficial. When appropriate, multiple sources should be used to provide a basis for comparison or for additional perspectives. The data must be integrated using a convenient decision rule, such as the lowest value. The conservative approach of using the lowest value is presented in the fourth guiding principle in Chapter 4, but this applies only when the sources have equal or similar credibility.

CREDIBILITY

The discussion of techniques in this chapter assumes that each data item collected and linked to a project can be converted to a monetary value. Highly subjective data, however, such as changes in employee attitudes or a reduction in the number of customer complaints, are sometimes difficult to convert. Although estimates can be developed using one or more strategies, such estimates may lack credibility with the target audience, which can render their use in analysis questionable.

The issue of credibility in combination with resources is illustrated in Figure 9.2. This is a logical way to decide whether to convert data to monetary values or leave them intangible. Essentially, in the absence of standard values, many other ways are available to capture the data or convert them to monetary values. However, there is a question to be answered: Can it be done with minimal resources? Some of the techniques mentioned in this chapter—such as linking measures to others that have been converted to money—cannot be performed with minimal use of resources. However, an estimate obtained from a group or from a few individuals is available with minimal use of resources. Then we move to the next question: Will the executive who is interested in the project buy into the monetary value assigned to the measure with minimum explanation? If so, then it is credible enough to be included in the analysis; if not, then move it to the intangibles. The intangible benefits of a project are also important; they just happen not to be included in the ROI equation. The last section of this chapter discusses the topic of intangibles.

MANAGEMENT ADJUSTMENT

In organizations where soft data are common and values are derived using imprecise methods, senior managers and administrators are sometimes offered the opportunity to review and approve the data. Because of the subjective nature of this process, management may factor (reduce) the data to make

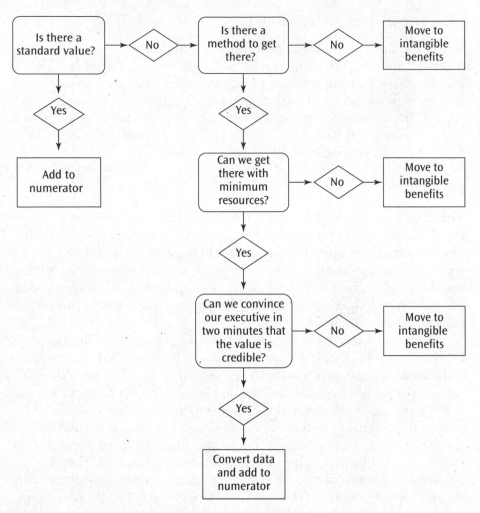

FIGURE 9.2 Four-Part Test: To Convert or Not to Convert?

the final results more credible. In one example, senior managers at Litton Industries adjusted the value for the benefits derived from implementing self-directed teams (Graham et al., 1994).

SHORT-TERM VERSUS LONG-TERM ISSUE

When data are converted to monetary values, usually one year's worth of data is included in the analysis. This follows the ninth guiding principle in Table 4.4, which states that for short-term solutions, only the first year's benefits are used. The issue of whether a project is short-term or long-term depends on the time it takes to complete or implement the project. If one group participating in the project and working through the process takes months to complete it, then it is probably not short-term. Some projects take years to implement even for one particular group.

In general, it is appropriate to consider a project short-term when one individual takes one month or less to learn what needs to be done to make the project successful. When the lag between project implementation and the consequences is relatively brief, a short-term solution is appropriate.

When a project is long-term, no time limit for data inclusion is used, but the time value should be set before the project evaluation is undertaken. Input on the time value should be secured from all stakeholders, including the sponsor, champion, implementer, designer, and evaluator. After some discussion, the estimates of the time factor should be conservative and perhaps reviewed by finance and accounting. When a project involves a long-term solution, forecasting will need to be used to estimate multiple years of value. No sponsor will wait several years to see how a project turns out.

TIME VALUE OF MONEY

Since investment in a project is made in one time period and the return is realized at a later time, some organizations adjust project benefits and costs to reflect the time value of money using discounted-cash-flow techniques.

Although this may not be an issue for every project, it should be considered for each project, and some standard discount rate should be used. Consider the following example of how this is calculated. Assume that a project costs $100,000, and it is expected to take two years for the full value of the investment to be realized. In other words, this is a long-term solution spanning two years. Using a discount rate of 6 percent, the cost for the project for the first year would be $100,000 × 106 percent = $106,000. For the second year it is $106,000 × 106 percent, or $112,360. Thus, the project cost has been adjusted for a two-year value with a 6 percent discount rate. This assumes that the project sponsor could have invested the money in some other project and obtained at least a 6 percent return on that investment.

Intangible Benefits of Green Projects

A variety of techniques are available to convert impact measures to money. But what happens when the technique costs too much or the value is not deemed credible? In these cases, as noted earlier, the improvement in the measure is reported as an intangible benefit.

THE IMPORTANCE OF INTANGIBLES

Although intangible measures are not new, they are becoming increasingly important. Intangibles secure funding and drive the economy, and organizations are built on them. In every direction we look, intangibles are becoming not only increasingly important, but also critical to organizations.

The success behind many well-known organizations often includes intangibles. A highly innovative company continues to develop new and improved products; a government agency reinvents itself. An organization shares knowledge with employees, providing a competitive advantage. A different organization is able to develop strategic partners and alliances. These intangibles do not often appear in cost statements and other record keeping, but they are there, and they make a huge difference. Table 9.2 lists intangible measures often measured and monitored in a variety of types of organizations.

From the 1950s forward, the world has moved from the Industrial Age into the Technology and Knowledge Age, which has translated into intangibles. During this time, a natural evolution of technology has occurred. During the Industrial Age, companies and individuals invested in tangible assets like plants and equipment. In the Technology and Knowledge Age, companies invest in intangible assets, like brands or systems. The future holds more of the same, as intangibles continue to evolve into an important part of the overall economic system (Boulton, Libert, and Samek, 2000).

The good news is that more data once regarded as intangible are now being converted into monetary values. Because of this, classic intangibles are now accepted as tangible measures, and their value is more easily understood. Consider, for example, customer satisfaction. Just a decade ago,

TABLE 9.2 Common Intangibles	
• Accountability	• Environmental consciousness
• Alliances	• Intellectual capital
• Attention	• Innovation and creativity
• Awards	• Job satisfaction
• Branding	• Leadership
• Capability	• Loyalty
• Capacity	• Networking
• Clarity	• Organizational commitment
• Communication	• Partnering
• Corporate social responsibility	• Poverty
• Customer service (customer satisfaction)	• Reputation
• Employee attitudes	• Team effectiveness
• Engagement	• Timeliness
• Human life	• Sustainability
• Image	• Work/life balance

few organizations had a clue as to the monetary value of customer satisfaction. Now more firms have taken the extra step to link customer satisfaction directly to revenues, profits, and other measures. Companies are seeing the tremendous value that can be derived from intangibles. More data are being accumulated to show monetary values, moving some intangible measures into the tangible category.

Some green projects are implemented because of the intangibles or intrinsic benefits. For example, the need to engage communities, to increase social consciousness, or to have greater collaboration, partnering, communication, teamwork, or customer service will drive projects. From the outset, the intangibles are the important drivers and become the most important measures. Consequently, more executives include a string of intangibles on their scorecards, key operating reports, key performance indicators, dashboards, and other routine reporting systems. In some cases, the intangibles represent nearly half of all measures that are monitored.

The Federal Reserve Bank of Philadelphia recently estimated that investment in intangible assets amounts to at least $1 trillion (Frangos, 2004). Only 15 percent of the value of a contemporary organization can be tied to such tangible assets as buildings and equipment. Intangible assets have become the dominant investments in businesses. They are a growing economic force that can no longer be ignored, and measuring their values poses challenges to managers and investors. Intangibles must be properly identified, selected, measured, reported, and in some cases, converted to monetary values.

MEASURING INTANGIBLE BENEFITS

In some projects, intangibles are more important than monetary measures. Consequently, these measures should be monitored and reported as part of the project evaluation. In practice, every project, regardless of its nature, scope, and content, will produce intangible measures. The challenge is to identify them effectively and report them appropriately.

Positions taken on intangibles usually come in the form of statements such as "You can't measure it." While it is true that intangibles are not things that can be counted, examined, or seen in quantities, like items produced on an assembly line, they can in fact be measured, or they would not be a concern. A quantitative value can be assigned to or developed for any intangible. Consider human intelligence for example. Although human intelligence is vastly complex and abstract, with myriad facets and qualities, IQ scores are assigned to most people and most people seem to accept them as an accurate measurement. The software engineering institute of Carnegie Mellon University assigns software organizations a score of 1 to 5 to represent their maturity in software engineering. This score has enormous implications for the organizations' business development capabilities, yet the measure goes practically unchallenged (Alden, 2006).

Several approaches are available for measuring intangibles. Intangibles that can be counted include customer complaints, employee complaints, and conflicts. These can be recorded easily, and they constitute one of the most acceptable types of measures. Unfortunately, many intangibles are based on attitudes and perceptions that must be measured. The key is in the development of the instrument. Measurement instruments are usually developed around scales of three, five, and even ten points to represent levels of perception. The instruments to measure intangibles consist of three basic varieties.

Five- or Ten-Point Scales

The first instrument lists the intangible items and asks respondents to agree or disagree on a five-point scale (where the midpoint represents a neutral opinion). A five-point scale can easily be developed to describe degrees of reputation, ranging from the worst rating—a horrible reputation—to the best rating—an excellent reputation. Still other ratings are expressed as an assessment on a scale of one to ten, after respondents review a description of the intangible.

Soft Measures Connected to Hard Measures

Another instrument to measure intangibles connects them, when possible, to an item that is easier to measure or easier to value. As shown in Figure 9.3, most hard-to-measure items are linked to an easy-to-measure item. In the classic situation, a soft measure (typically the intangible) is connected to a hard measure (typically the tangible). Although this link can be developed

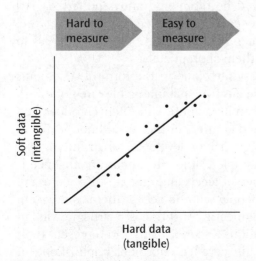

FIGURE 9.3   The Link between Hard-to-Measure and Easy-to-Measure Items

through logical deductions and conclusions, having some empirical evidence through a correlation analysis (as shown in the figure) and developing a significant correlation between the items is the best approach. However, a detailed analysis would have to be conducted to ensure that a causal relationship exists. In other words, just because a correlation is apparent, it does not mean that one caused the other. Consequently, additional analysis, other empirical evidence, and supporting data could pinpoint the actual causal effect.

Indexes of Different Values

A final instrument for measuring the intangible is the development of an index of different values. An index is a single score representing some complex factor that is constructed by aggregating the values of several different measures. Measures making up the index are sometimes weighted based on their importance to the abstract factor being measured. Index measures may be based strictly on hard data items; may combine hard and soft data items to reflect the performance of a business unit, function, or project; or may be completely intangible, such as a customer satisfaction index.

IDENTIFYING AND COLLECTING INTANGIBLES

Intangible measures can be taken from different sources and at different times during the project life cycle, as depicted in Figure 9.4. They can be uncovered early in the process, during the needs assessment, and their collection can be planned for as part of the overall data collection strategy.

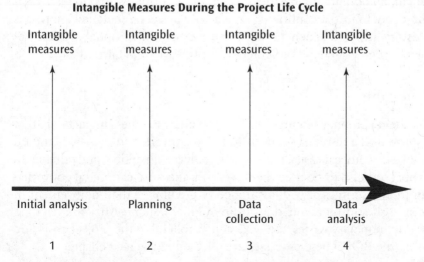

FIGURE 9.4   Identifying Intangible Measures During the Project Life Cycle

A second opportunity to identify intangible benefits occurs during the planning process, when sponsors of the project agree on an evaluation plan. Key stakeholders can usually identify the intangible measures they expect to be influenced by the project.

A third opportunity to collect intangible measures presents itself during data collection. Although the measure may not be anticipated in the initial project design, it may surface on a questionnaire, in an interview, or during a focus group. Questions are often asked about other improvements linked to a project, and participants usually provide several intangible measures for which no plans are available to assign a value.

The fourth opportunity to identify intangible measures is during data analysis and reporting, while attempting to convert data to monetary values. If the conversion loses credibility, the measure is reported as an intangible benefit.

ANALYZING INTANGIBLES

For each intangible measure identified, some evidence of its connection to the project must be shown. However, in many cases, no specific analysis is planned beyond tabulation of responses. Early attempts to quantify intangible data sometimes result in aborting the entire process, with no further data analysis being conducted. In some cases, isolating the effects of the project may be undertaken using one or more of the methods outlined in Chapter 8. This step is necessary when project leaders need to know the specific amount of change in the intangible measure that is linked to the project.

Intangible data often reflect improvement. However, neither the precise amount of improvement nor the amount of improvement directly related to a project is always identified. Because the value of these data is not included in the ROI calculation, intangible measures are not normally used to justify another project or to justify continuing an existing project. A detailed analysis is not necessary. Intangible benefits are often viewed as additional evidence of the project's success and are presented as supportive qualitative data.

Final Thoughts

Showing the real money requires just that—money. Business impact data that have improved as a result of a project must be converted to money. Standard values make this process easier, but easy is not always an option, and other techniques must sometimes be used. However, if a measure cannot be converted with minimal resources or with assurance of credibility, the improvement in the measure should be reported as an intangible benefit. After the data are converted to monetary values, the next step is collecting the project costs and calculating the ROI. These processes are covered in the next chapter.

Chapter 10

Calculating the ROI: Comparing Costs and Monetary Benefits

Chapter 9 described how to convert business impact measures to money. These monetary benefits represent the financial output of a green project. However, until that output is compared to the project costs, the absolute contribution of investing in green is still unknown. This chapter explores the development of project costs. Often confused with the budget allocated to a project, project costs represent all that an organization has invested in a project. Once the fully loaded costs are identified, then a comparison is made to the benefits, resulting in the ROI calculation. This calculation is reported using a variety of metrics, including the benefit-cost ratio, ROI percentage, and payback period.

Why the Concern About Project Costs?

One of the main reasons for monitoring costs is to create budgets for projects. The initial costs of most projects are usually estimated during the proposal process and are often based on previous projects. The only way to have a clear understanding of costs so that they can be used to determine future projects and future budgets is to track them using different categories, as explained later in this chapter.

Costs should be monitored in an ongoing effort to control expenditures and keep the project within budget. Monitoring cost activities not only reveals the status of expenditures but also gives visibility to expenditures and encourages the entire project team to spend wisely. And, of course, monitoring costs on an ongoing basis is much easier, more accurate, and more efficient than trying to reconstruct events to capture costs retrospectively.

Developing accurate costs by category builds a database for understanding and predicting future costs.

Monitoring project costs is an essential step in developing the ROI calculation because it represents the denominator in the ROI formula. ROI has become a critical measure demanded by many stakeholders, including sponsors and senior executives. It is the ultimate level of evaluation, showing the actual payoff of the project expressed as a percentage and based on the same formula as the evaluation for other types of capital investment.

A brief example will highlight the importance of costs and ROI. A new suggestion system was implemented in a large electric utility company. This new plan provided cash awards for employees when they submitted a suggestion that was implemented and resulted in cost savings associated with reduction in solid waste (e.g., recyclable materials, trash, etc.). This project was undertaken to help lower the costs of this publicly owned utility as well as to engage employees in environmentally conscious activities. As the project was rolled out, project leaders captured the employees' reaction to ensure that the employees perceived the suggestion system as fair, equitable, motivating, and challenging. At Level 2, they measured learning to make sure that the employees understood what types of waste to look for, how to document their suggestions, and how and when the awards would be made. Application data (Level 3) considered the actual submission of the awards, indicating that employees were making appropriate and realistic suggestions. The company had the goal of a 10 percent participation rate in the process. Level 4 data corresponded to the actual monetary value of cost savings due to implementation of suggestions. In this case, $1.5 million in cost savings was achieved over a two-year period.

In many organizations, the evaluation would have stopped there. The project appeared to be a success, since the goals were met at each of the four levels. However, the costs of the project for the same two-year period totaled $2 million. Costs included information sessions, motivational rallies, guest speakers, travel and lodging for field personnel, and so forth. Thus, the utility company spent $2 million to save $1.5 million. This negative ROI would not have been recognized if the ultimate measure, the ROI, had not been developed. Incidentally, a negative ROI might be acceptable to some executives. After all, the intangible benefits reflected increased commitment, engagement in environmental activities, teamwork, and cooperation. However, if the objective was a positive ROI, this system failed to achieve it, primarily because of excessive administrative costs.

Fundamental Cost Issues

The first step in monitoring costs is to define and address issues relating to cost control. Several rules apply to tabulating costs. Consistency and standardization are necessary. In addition, all costs must be monitored, even if they are not needed. They must be realistic and reasonable; however, precision can be costly in and of itself, so estimates are okay to use. Finally, all costs should be disclosed. Consideration of these guidelines as well as the issues described in this section will help project owners define, monitor, and manage all costs associated with their green projects.

FULLY-LOADED COSTS

Because a conservative approach is used to calculate the ROI in a green project, costs should be fully loaded, which is the tenth guiding principle covered in Chapter 4. With this approach, all costs (direct and indirect) that can be identified and linked to a particular project are included. The philosophy is simple: for the denominator, "when in doubt, put it in" (i.e., if there is any question as to whether a cost should be included, include it, even if the cost guidelines for the organization do not require it). When an ROI is calculated and reported to target audiences, the process should withstand even the closest scrutiny, when necessary, to ensure its credibility. The only way to meet this test is to include all costs. Of course, from a realistic viewpoint, if the controller or chief financial officer insists on not using certain costs, then leaving them out or reporting them in an alternative way is suggested, but always be certain as to why a cost is being omitted and ensure that you are consistent in your approach.

COSTS WITHOUT BENEFITS

Because costs can easily be collected, they are presented to management in many ingenious ways, such as in terms of the total cost of the project, cost per day, and cost per participant. While these may be helpful for efficiency comparisons, presenting them without identifying the corresponding benefits may be problematic. When most executives review project costs, a logical question is raised: What benefit was received from the project? This is a typical management reaction, particularly when costs are perceived to be high.

Unfortunately, many organizations have fallen into the trap of reporting costs without benefits. For example, in one organization, all costs associated with a major transformation project were tabulated and reported to the senior management team. From an executive perspective, the total figure exceeded the perceived value of the project, and the executive group's immediate reaction was to request a summary of monetary and nonmonetary benefits derived from the overall transformation. The conclusion was that few, if any, economic benefits were achieved from the project. Consequently, budgets for similar projects were drastically reduced in the future. While this may be an extreme example, it shows the danger of presenting only half the equation. Because of this, some organizations have developed a policy of not communicating cost data unless the benefits can be captured and presented along with the costs, even if the benefits are subjective and intangible. This helps maintain a balance between the two components.

COST GUIDELINES

When multiple projects are being evaluated, it may be helpful to develop a philosophy and policy on costs in the form of guidelines for evaluators or others who monitor and report costs. Cost guidelines detail specifically which cost categories to include with projects and how to capture, analyze, and report data. Guidelines include standards, unit cost guiding principles, and generally accepted values. Cost guidelines can range from a one-page brief to a one-hundred-page document in a large, complex organization. The simpler approach is better.

When fully developed, cost guidelines should be reviewed and approved by the finance and accounting staff. The final document serves as the guiding force in collecting, monitoring, and reporting costs. When the ROI is calculated and reported, costs are included in summary or table form, and the cost guidelines are usually referenced in a footnote or attached as an appendix.

SOURCES OF COSTS

Four of the sources of costs are illustrated in Table 10.1. These sources include the project team expenses; vendor and supplier expenses; sponsor expenses; and equipment, services, and other expenses. The charges and expenses from the project team represent the major segment of costs and are usually transferred directly to the sponsor for payment. These are often placed in subcategories under fees and expenses. A second major cost category relates to the vendors or suppliers who assist with the project. A variety of expenses, such as consulting or advisory fees, may fall in this category. A third major cost category is those expenses borne by the sponsor organization—both direct and indirect. In many projects, these costs are not identified but nevertheless are part of the project costs. The final cost category involves expenses not covered in the other three categories. These include payments for equipment and services needed for the project. Finance and accounting records should track and reflect the costs from these different sources, and the process presented in this chapter can also help track these costs.

PRORATED VERSUS DIRECT COSTS

Usually all costs related to a project are captured and expensed to that project. However, some costs are prorated over a longer period. Equipment

TABLE 10.1   Sources of Project Costs

Source of Costs	Cost Reporting Issues
Project team salaries and expenses	• Costs are usually accurate. • Variable expenses are usually underestimated.
Vendor/supplier fees and expenses	• Costs are usually accurate. • Variable expenses are usually underestimated.
Sponsor expenses, direct and indirect	• Direct expenses are usually not fully loaded. • Indirect expenses are rarely included in costs.
Equipment, services, and other expenses	• Costs are sometimes understated. • Expenses may lack accountability.

purchases, software development and acquisitions, and the construction of facilities are all significant costs with a useful life that may extend beyond the project. Consequently, a portion of these costs should be prorated to the project. Under a conservative approach, the expected life of the project is fixed. Some organizations will assume a period of one year of operation for a simple project. Others may consider three to five years appropriate. If a question is raised about the specific time period to be used in this calculation, the finance and accounting staff should be consulted, or appropriate guidelines should be developed and followed.

EMPLOYEE BENEFITS FACTOR

Employee time is valuable, and when time is required for a project, the costs for that time must be fully loaded, representing total compensation, including employee benefits. This means that the employee benefits factor should be included in the cost of employee time in the profit. This number is usually easily available in the organization and is used in other costing formulas. It represents the cost of all employee benefits expressed as a percentage of payroll. In some organizations, this value is as high as 50 to 60 percent. In others, it may be as low as 25 to 30 percent. The average in the United States is 38 percent ("Annual Employee Benefits Report," 2006).

Fully-Loaded Cost Profile

Table 10.2 shows the recommended cost categories for a fully-loaded, conservative approach to estimating project costs. Consistency in capturing all of these costs is essential, and standardization adds credibility. Each category is described in this section.

TABLE 10.2 Project Cost Categories

Cost Item	Prorated	Expensed
Initial analysis and assessment		✓
Development of solutions		✓
Acquisition of solutions		✓
Implementation and application		
Salaries/benefits for project team time		✓
Salaries/benefits for coordination time		✓
Salaries/benefits for participant time		✓
Project materials		✓
Hardware/software	✓	
Travel/lodging/meals		✓
Use of facilities		✓
Capital expenditures	✓	
Maintenance and monitoring		✓
Administrative support and overhead	✓	
Evaluation and reporting		✓

INITIAL ANALYSIS AND ASSESSMENT

One of the most underestimated items is the cost of conducting the initial analysis and assessment that leads to the need for the project. In a comprehensive project, this involves data collection, problem solving, assessment, and analysis. In some projects, this cost is near zero because the project is implemented without an initial assessment of need. However, as more project sponsors place attention on needs assessment and analysis in the future, this item will become a significant cost.

DEVELOPMENT OF GREEN PROJECTS AND SUSTAINABILITY INITIATIVES

Designing and developing a sustainability initiative has significant costs, particularly for those projects intended to solve an expensive problem or drive substantial improvement in key measures. Development costs include time spent in both the design and development and the purchase of supplies, technology, and other materials directly related to the project. As with needs assessment costs, design and development costs are usually charged to the project. However, if the project or initiative is being rolled in with other projects using the same resources, development costs can be prorated.

ACQUISITION

In lieu of development costs, some project leaders choose to purchase a solution or parts of it. When this is the case, the acquisition cost becomes a line item in the project cost profile. The costs for these solutions include the purchase price, support materials, and licensing agreements. Some projects have both acquisition costs and development costs. Acquisition costs can be prorated if the acquired solutions can be used in other projects.

IMPLEMENTATION

The largest cost segment in a project is associated with implementation and delivery. The time (salaries and benefits), travel, and other expenses of those involved in any way in the project are included. These costs can be estimated using average or midpoint salary values for corresponding job classifications. When a project is targeted for an ROI calculation, participants can provide their salaries directly in a confidential manner. Project materials, such as field journals, instructions, reference guides, case studies, surveys, participant workbooks, guidelines, and job aids, should be included in the implementation costs, along with license fees, user fees, and royalty payments. Supporting hardware, software, DVDs, and remote access support systems should also be included.

The cost for the use of facilities needed for the project should be included. For external meetings, this is the direct charge for the conference center, hotel, or motel. If the meetings are conducted in-house, the conference room represents a cost for the organization, and the cost should be estimated and incorporated—even if it is uncommon to include facilities costs in other cost reporting. If a facility or building is constructed or purchased for the project, it is included as a capital expenditure, but it is prorated. The same is true for the purchase of major hardware and software when they are considered capital expenditures.

MAINTENANCE AND MONITORING

Maintenance and monitoring costs, which may be significant for some projects, involve routine expenses necessary to maintain and operate the project. These are ongoing expenses that allow the new project solution to continue.

SUPPORT AND OVERHEAD

The cost of support and overhead includes the additional costs not directly charged to the project—any project cost not considered in the previous calculations. Typical items are the cost of administrative and clerical support, telecommunication expenses, office expenses, salaries of managers, and other fixed costs. Usually, this is provided in the form of an estimate allocated in some convenient way.

EVALUATION AND REPORTING

Evaluation costs complete the fully-loaded cost profile. Activities under evaluation costs include developing the evaluation strategy, designing instruments, collecting data, analyzing data, preparing a report, and communicating the results. Cost categories include time, materials, purchased instruments, surveys, and any consulting fees.

Cost Classifications

Project costs can be classified in two basic ways. One is with a description of the expenditures, such as labor, materials, supplies, or travel. These are expense account classifications, which are standard with most accounting systems. The other way to classify costs is to use the categories in the project steps, such as initial analysis, development, implementation, maintenance, overhead, and evaluation. An effective system monitors costs by account category according to the description of those accounts, but it also includes a method for accumulating costs for the process steps. Many systems stop short of this second task. Although classifying costs by expenditure description (e.g., labor, materials, supplies, travel) adequately states the total project costs, it does not allow for a useful comparison with other projects to understand which steps may incur excessive costs.

The ROI Calculation

The term *return on investment* is occasionally misused, sometimes intentionally. A broad definition for ROI is often given that includes any benefit from the project. ROI then becomes a vague concept in which even subjective data linked to a program are included. In this book, the term *return on investment* is defined more precisely and represents an actual value determined by comparing project costs to benefits of project implementation. The two most common measures are the benefit-cost ratio (BCR) and the ROI percentage. Both are presented in this section along with other approaches to calculate the return or payback.

Project benefits, making up the numerator of the ROI equation, are annualized. For short-term projects, the assumption is based on first-year only. Using annualized values is becoming an accepted practice for developing the ROI in many organizations. This approach is a conservative way to develop the ROI, since many short-term projects have added value in the second or third year, but to assume those future benefits will inflate the ROI based on highly presumptive values. For long-term projects, however, longer time frames should be used. For example, in an ROI analysis of a project involving major software and technology purchases, a five-year time frame was used because the likely benefits would not surface until the project was implemented to its fullest. However, for short-term projects that take only a few weeks to implement (such as a recycling campaign), first-year values are appropriate.

In selecting the approach to measure ROI, the formula used and the assumptions made in arriving at the decision to use this formula should be communicated to the target audience. This helps prevent misunderstandings and confusion surrounding how the ROI value was developed. Although several approaches are described in this chapter, two stand out as preferred methods: the benefit-cost ratio and the basic ROI formula.

BENEFIT-COST RATIO

One of the original methods for evaluating projects is the benefit-cost ratio. This method compares the monetary benefits of the project with the costs, using a simple ratio. In formula form:

$$BCR = \frac{\text{Project benefits}}{\text{Project costs}}$$

In simple terms, the BCR compares the annual economic benefits of the project with the costs of the project. A BCR of 1 means that the benefits equal the costs or that the project breaks even. This is usually written as 1:1. A BCR of 2, usually written as 2:1, indicates that for each dollar spent on the project, two dollars are returned in benefits.

The following example illustrates the use of the BCR. A communication campaign focusing on the benefits of going green was implemented at a large advertising agency. Employees were challenged to implement green initiatives that both contributed to reduction in carbon emissions, solid waste, and to a reduction in costs to the company. The initiatives that achieved the greatest impact for the environment and the company would be recognized at the annual meeting at the end of the year. In a follow-up evaluation, a questionnaire was used to access employee implication of the green projects. To capture success from a business impact standpoint, performance monitoring was used. Each individual or team working on an initiative had to identify the specific measures they intended to improve (e.g., kWh). Then, during post-program evaluation, the improvement in the measures were analyzed, converted to money, and compared to the cost of implementing the idea. Many of the ideas were simple and inexpensive. The first-year payoff for the company's combined efforts was $1,678,450. The total cost of implementing the green projects was $875,650. Thus the BCR was:

$$\text{BCR} = \frac{\$1,678,450}{\$875,650} = 1.92{:}1$$

For every dollar invested in the project, the company recovered $1.92 in benefits, and it had a significant environmental impact.

ROI

Perhaps the most appropriate formula for evaluating project investments is net project benefits divided by costs. This is the traditional financial ROI expressed as a percentage. This metric is related to the BCR, but expresses the return in terms of net gain. In formula form, ROI is:

$$\text{ROI} = \frac{\text{Net project benefits}}{\text{Project costs}} \times 100$$

Net project benefits are project benefits minus costs. Another way to calculate ROI is to subtract 1 from the BCR and multiply by 100 to get the ROI percentage. For example, a BCR of 2.45 translates to an ROI of 145 percent (1.45×100). This formula is essentially the same as the ROI for capital investments. For example, when a firm builds a new plant, the ROI is developed by dividing annual earnings by the investment. The annual earnings are comparable to net benefits (annual benefits minus the cost). The investment is comparable to the fully loaded project costs.

An ROI of 50 percent (BCR = 1.50) means that the costs were recovered and an additional 50 percent ($.50) of the costs were returned. A project ROI of 150 percent indicates that the costs have been recovered and an additional 1.5 ($1.50) times the costs are returned. Using the ROI formula to calculate the return on project investments essentially places these investments on a level playing field with other investments whose evaluation uses the same formula and similar concepts. The ROI calculation is easily understood by key management and financial executives who regularly work with investments and their ROIs.

The following example illustrates the ROI calculation and its application to an environmentally friendly initiative.

TABLE 10.3 Materials Not Requiring Printing	
	Pages
Training Manuals	54,023
Work Instruction/Memos	4,895,397

ROI IN GREEN PROJECTS: THE OPPORTUNITY

One of the important tasks within CVS Caremark Pharmacy Operations is to determine how to best deliver content and information to employees. During an initial assessment it was noted that pharmacy employees primarily used paper manuals and reference materials. Additionally, most communication of process changes within pharmacies was distributed by way of paper memos that each employee would then store in three-ring binders. The creation of an electronic repository and communication system (RxSource) held promise to increase speed and accuracy of information dissemination as well as cut down on paper use, which was expensive. It also promised to provide a more reliable means of ensuring employees were referencing current and relevant information, thereby reducing errors and improving the quality and productivity of their work. So, as is typical of many green projects, while the project was initiated to distribute information more efficiently through the reduction of paper use, leaders recognized the importance of other benefits as well (Faylor, Maisse, and Neal, 2008).

This particular project collected all six types of data as a part of the ROI Methodology; reaction, learning, and application data were collected as well as intangibles, but it is the impact data that served as the basis for the ROI calculations. After the program was implemented, there was a significant reduction in the number of documents that required printing. Table 10.3 shows the materials that did not require printing.

When converted to monetary benefits, a significant cost savings was apparent, as shown in Table 10.4.

In addition to noting a reduction in printing costs, employees estimated the contribution of this new process to their overall job performance. Employees suggested an additional monetary contribution of $1,868,567. This results in a total monetary contribution of $2,168,910, as shown in Table 10.5.

Notice that while there are substantial savings on paper costs, there is a greater savings on performance improvement for employees, although this was not necessarily the goal of the project. To get to the real contribution of

TABLE 10.4   Project Benefits—Paper Reduction

Materials Printing (cost avoidance)	Unit/Value	Value
Training manuals for various classes	3,538 employees trained (costs include paper and binders)	$6,559
Work instructions/memos published via RxSource	3,671,548 pages ($0.08/page)	$293,784
Total printing cost reduction		**$300,343**

TABLE 10.5   Project Benefits—All Measures

Paper Costs Reduction		$300,343
Twelve-Month Performance Improvement Employee Estimate (3.00%)	1,012 employees using RxSource $61,547 avg/yr (salary + benefits)	$1,868,567
Total Monetary Benefit		**$2,168,910**

TABLE 10.6   Project Costs

	Unit/Value	Cost
System Development		
Consultant charges	Invoiced fee for system development	$56,000
Employee time and benefits	1919.5 hours @ $41.32/hr	$79,314
Implementation		
Project salaries and benefits (1.25-hr training and preparation)	50 classes @ $32.52/hr	$2,032
Participant salary and benefits (1-hr training)	1012 @ $29.59/hr	$29,945
Total Project Costs		**$167,291**

the project, costs must be considered then compared to project benefits. The cost for the project is illustrated in Table 10.6.

When the ROI calculation is based on the paper savings alone, you have the following:

$$\text{ROI} = \frac{\$300{,}343 - \$167{,}291}{\$167{,}291} = 0.795 \times 100 = 79.5\%$$

So, roughly an 80 percent ROI is achieved, which certainly would be acceptable with any executive. This makes the project a win—not only because of the number of trees saved, but the direct cost to the company. When the additional performance improvement is considered, there is an overwhelming number, as shown here:

$$\text{ROI} = \frac{\$2{,}168{,}910 - \$167{,}291}{\$167{,}291} = 11.96 \times 100 = 1196\%$$

This is essentially a 1,200 percent ROI. However, there is no need to show this value if the objective is primarily for the reduction in paper and print costs. Taking the additional performance improvement into account demonstrates that there is additional economic benefit beyond what was expected.

In addition to reducing paper costs and improving performance contribution, implementation of the electronic depository and communication systems had an important environmental benefit. Consider that CVS Caremark reduced paper usage by 4,949,420 pages. This is approximately 9,898.84 reams of paper, which weigh about 5 pounds each for a total of 49,494.2 pounds of paper. Assume the paper is post-consumer and that the CO_2 release is 6.1 pounds per pound of paper. Not only did CVS Caremark contribute to bottom-line savings, enough to outweigh the cost of the new system, but they also reduced CO_2 emissions by 301,914.62 pounds.

ROI Misuse

The ROI formula described here should be used consistently throughout an organization. Deviations from or misuse of the formula can create confusion, not only among users but also among finance and accounting staff. The CFO and the finance and accounting staff should become partners in the implementation of the ROI Methodology, using the same financial terms. Without the support, involvement, and commitment of these individuals, the wide-scale use of ROI will be unlikely.

Table 10.7 shows some financial terms that are often misused in literature. Terms such as *return on intelligence* (or *information*), abbreviated as ROI, do nothing but confuse most CFOs, who assume that ROI refers to the return on investment described here. Sometimes *return on expectations* (ROE), *return on anticipation* (ROA), and *return on client expectations* (ROCE) are used, which can also confuse CFOs who assume the abbreviations refer to return on equity, return on assets, and return on capital employed, respec-

TABLE 10.7	Misused Financial Terms	
Term	**Misuse**	**CFO Definition**
ROI	Return of information Return of intelligence	Return on investment
ROE	Return on expectation	Return on equity
ROA	Return on anticipation	Return on assets
ROCE	Return on client expectation	Return on capital employed
ROP	Return on people	?
ROR	Return on resources	?
ROT	Return on technology	?
ROW	Return on web	?
ROM	Return on marketing	?
ROO	Return on objectives	?
ROQ	Return on quality	?

tively. The use of these terms in the payback calculation of a project will also confuse and perhaps lose the support of the finance and accounting staff. Other terms, such as *return on people, return on resources, return on technology*, and *return on web*, are often used with almost no consistency regarding financial calculations. The bottom line: don't confuse the CFO. Consider this person an ally, and use the same terminology, processes, and concepts when applying financial returns for projects.

ROI Targets

Specific expectations for ROI should be developed before an evaluation study is undertaken. Although no generally accepted standards exist, four strategies have been used to establish a minimum expected requirement, or hurdle rate, for the ROI of a project or program. The first approach is to set the ROI using the same values used for investing in capital expenditures, such as equipment, facilities, and new companies. For North America, Western Europe, and most of the Asian Pacific area, including Australia and New Zealand, the cost of capital is low, and the internal hurdle rate for ROI is usually in the 15 to 20 percent range. Thus, using this strategy, organizations would set the expected ROI for a project at the same value expected from other investments.

A second strategy is to use an ROI minimum target value that is above the percentage expected for other types of investments. The rationale is that the ROI process for projects and programs is still relatively new and often involves subjective input, including estimations. Because of this, a higher standard is required or suggested.

A third strategy is to set the ROI value at a break-even point. A 0 percent ROI represents breaking even; this is equivalent to a BCR of 1:1. This approach is used when the goal is to recapture the cost of the project only. This is the ROI objective for many public-sector organizations, where the primary value and benefit from the program come through the intangible measures, which are not converted to monetary values. Thus, an organization will use a break-even point for the ROI based on the reasoning that it is not attempting to make a profit from a particular project.

A fourth, and often the recommended, strategy is to let the program sponsor set the minimum acceptable ROI value. In this scenario, the individual who initiates, approves, sponsors, or supports the project establishes the acceptable ROI. Almost every project has a major sponsor, and that person may be willing to specify an acceptable value. This links the expectations for financial return directly to the expectations of the sponsor.

Intangibles Revisited

Chapter 9 describes the importance of developing and reporting intangible benefits. These benefits deserve mentioning here as well. Although they are not converted to money, their importance cannot be ignored. When reporting the ROI in a profit, it is essential to balance that financial metric with other nonfinancial measures to tell the true story of the project's impact. So, when reporting ROI, report it in the context of other measures of performance. This includes the intangible benefits linked directly to the project as well as the lower levels of data that represent the chain of impact. More detail on how best to report results is presented in Chapter 11.

Other ROI Measures

In addition to the traditional ROI formula, several other measures are occasionally used under the general heading of return on investment. These measures are designed primarily for evaluating other financial measures but sometimes work their way into project evaluation.

PAYBACK PERIOD (BREAK-EVEN ANALYSIS)

The payback period is commonly used for evaluating capital expenditures. With this approach, the annual cash proceeds (savings) produced by an investment are compared against the original cash outlay for the investment to determine the point at which cash proceeds equal the original investment. Measurement is usually in terms of years and months. For example, if the cost savings generated from a project are constant each year, the payback period is determined by dividing the original cash investment (including development costs, expenses, etc.) by the expected or actual annual savings.

To illustrate this calculation, assume that the initial cost of a project is $100,000 and the project has a three-year useful life. Annual savings from the project are expected to be $40,000. Thus, the payback period is:

$$\text{Payback period} = \frac{\text{Total investment}}{\text{Annual savings}} = \frac{\$100,000}{\$40,000} = 2.5 \text{ years}$$

The project will "pay back" the original investment in 2.5 years. Since the projected life-span is three years, one can assume a benefit over and beyond the cost at the end of the three years.

The payback period method is simple to use but has the limitation of ignoring the time value of money. It has not enjoyed widespread use in the evaluation of project investments.

DISCOUNTED CASH FLOW

Discounted cash flow is a method of evaluating investment opportunities in which certain values are assigned to the timing of the proceeds from the investment. The assumption behind this approach is that a dollar earned today is more valuable than a dollar earned a year from now, based on the accrued interest possible from investing the dollar.

There are several ways of using the discounted cash flow concept to evaluate a project investment. The most common approach uses the net present value of an investment. The savings each year are compared with the outflow of cash required by the investment. The expected annual savings are discounted based on a selected interest rate, and the outflow of cash is adjusted by the same interest rate. If the present value of the savings exceeds the present value of the outlays, after the two have been adjusted by the common interest rate, the investment is usually considered acceptable by management. The discounted cash flow method has the advantage of ranking investments, but it requires calculations that can become difficult. Also, for the most part, it is subjective in terms of assumed future benefits as well as assumed future value of the dollar.

INTERNAL RATE OF RETURN

The internal rate of return (IRR) method determines the interest rate necessary to make the present value of the cash flow equal zero. This represents the maximum rate of interest that could be paid if all project funds were borrowed and the organization was required to break even on the project. The IRR considers the time value of money and is unaffected by the scale of the project. It can be used to rank alternatives and to accept or reject decisions when a minimum rate of return is specified. A major weakness of the IRR method is that it assumes all returns are reinvested at the same internal rate of return. This can make an investment alternative with a high rate of return look even better than it really is and make a project with a low rate of return look even worse. In practice, the IRR is rarely used to evaluate project investments.

Final Thoughts

ROI, the final evaluation level, compares project benefits to project costs. From a practical standpoint, some costs may be optional and depend on the organization's guidelines and philosophy, but all costs should be included in some way, even if this goes beyond the requirements of the organization's policy. After the benefits are collected and converted to monetary values and the project costs are tabulated, the ROI calculation itself is easy. Plugging the values into the appropriate formula for the ROI or the benefit-cost ratio is the final step.

Of course, the ROI calculation and results at all other levels are useless data unless they are communicated in terms that resonate with all stakeholders. The next chapter addresses this issue.

Part III

The Green Scorecard at Work

Chapter 11

Reporting Results

Applying a comprehensive evaluation process to your green projects is important to show how the investment in such projects benefits the organization and the environment. But the presentation of that data is just as essential, since decisions are made based on the communication of results. A first step in the communications process is to understand how the data will be used. Should the results be used to modify the project, change the process, demonstrate the contribution, justify new projects, gain additional support, or build goodwill? Your answers will help you determine how best to present the data. Remember, though, the worst course of action is to do nothing. Achieving results without communicating them is like planting seeds and failing to fertilize and cultivate the seedlings—the yield will be less than optimal. This chapter describes how to present the results of your green project evaluations to various audiences in the form of both oral and written reports.

Why the Concern About Communicating Results?

Communicating results is critical to project success. The results achieved must be conveyed to stakeholders not just at project completion but throughout the project implementation. Continuous communication maintains the flow of information so that adjustments can be made and all stakeholders are kept up to date on the status of the project.

Mark Twain once said, "Collecting data is like collecting garbage—pretty soon we will have to do something with it." Measuring project success and gathering evaluation data mean nothing unless the findings are communicated promptly to the appropriate audiences so that they are apprised of the results and can take action in response if necessary. Communication is a critical need that should never be overlooked, even with underfunded projects. Following are just a few of the important reasons for communicating results.

MAKE IMPROVEMENTS

Information is collected at different points during project implementation, and providing feedback to involved groups enables them to take action and make adjustments if necessary. Thus, the quality and timeliness of communication are critical to making improvements. Even after the project is completed, communication is necessary to make sure the target audience fully understands the results achieved, and how the results may be enhanced in future projects or in the current project, if it is still operational. Communication is the key to making important adjustments at all phases of the project.

EXPLAIN THE CONTRIBUTION

The overall contribution of the project, as determined from the six major types of measures, is often unclear at best. The different target audiences will each need a thorough explanation of the results showing a clear connection between the project and the results. The communication strategy— including techniques, media, and the overall process—will determine the extent to which each group understands the contribution. Communicating results, particularly in terms of business impact and ROI, can quickly overwhelm even the most sophisticated target audiences. Communication must be planned and implemented with the goal of making sure the respective audiences understand the full contribution.

MANAGE SENSITIVE ISSUES

Communication is one of those issues that can cause major problems. Because the results of a project may be closely linked to political issues within an organization, communicating the results can upset some individuals while it pleases others. If certain individuals do not receive the information, or if it is delivered inconsistently between groups, problems can quickly surface. Not only must the information be understood, but issues relating to fairness, quality, and political correctness make it crucial that the communication be constructed and delivered effectively to all key individuals.

ADDRESS DIVERSE AUDIENCE NEEDS

With so many potential target audiences requiring communication on the success of a green project, the communication must be tailored to each audience. A varied audience has varied needs. Planning and effort are necessary to ensure that each audience receives all the information it needs, in the proper format, at the proper time. A single report for presentation to all audiences is usually inappropriate. The scope, the format, and even the content of the information will usually vary from one group to another. Thus, the target audience is the key to determining the appropriate method of communication.

Principles of Communicating Results

The skills one must possess to communicate results effectively are almost as sophisticated as those necessary for obtaining results. The style of the communication is as important as the substance. Regardless of the message, audience, or medium, a few general principles apply. These are vital to the overall success of the communication effort and should serve as a checklist for the project team planning the dissemination of project results.

TIME COMMUNICATION STRATEGICALLY

In general, project results should be communicated as soon as they become known. From a practical standpoint, however, it is sometimes best to delay the communication until a convenient time, such as the publication of the next company newsletter or the next general management meeting. Several questions are relevant to the timing decision. Is the audience ready for the results in view of other issues that may have developed? Is the audience expecting results? When will the delivery have the maximum impact on the audience? Do circumstances dictate a change in the timing of the communication?

TARGET COMMUNICATION TO SPECIFIC AUDIENCES

As stated earlier, communication is usually more effective if it is designed for the specific group being addressed. The message should be tailored to the interests, needs, and expectations of the target audience. The results of the project should reflect outcomes at all levels, including the six types of data presented in this book. Some of the data are developed earlier in the project and communicated during project implementation. Other data are collected after project implementation and communicated in a follow-up repost. The results, in their broadest sense, may incorporate early feedback in qualitative form all the way to ROI values expressed in varying quantitative terms.

SELECT MEDIA CAREFULLY

Certain media may be more appropriate for a particular group than others. For instance, face-to-face meetings may be preferable to special bulletins. A memo distributed exclusively to top executives may be a more effective outlet than the company newsletter. The proper format of communication can determine the effectiveness of the process.

KEEP COMMUNICATION OBJECTIVE

For communication to be effective, fact must be separated from fiction and accurate statements distinguished from opinions. Some audiences may approach the communication with skepticism, anticipating the presence of biased opinions. Boastful statements can turn off recipients, and most of the content will be lost. Observable phenomena and credible statements carry much more weight than extreme or sensational claims, which may get an audience's attention but often detract from the importance of the results.

USE COMMUNICATION CONSISTENTLY

The timing and content of the communication should be consistent with past practices. A special presentation at an unusual time during the course of the project may provoke suspicion. Also, if a particular group, such as top management, regularly receives communication on outcomes, it should continue receiving communication even if the results are not positive. Omitting unfavorable results leaves the impression that only positive results will be reported.

INCLUDE TESTIMONIALS FROM RESPECTED SOURCES

Opinions are strongly influenced by other people, particularly those who are respected and trusted. This respect may be related to leadership ability, position, special skills, or knowledge. Testimonials about project results, when solicited from individuals who are respected within the organization, can influence the effectiveness of the message. A testimonial from an individual who commands little respect and is regarded as a substandard performer can have a negative impact on the message.

ACCOUNT FOR AUDIENCE OPINION

Opinions are difficult to change, and a negative opinion toward a project or project team may not change with the mere presentation of facts. However, the presentation of facts alone may strengthen the opinions held by those who already support the project. The presentation of the results reinforces their position and provides them with a defense in discussions with others. A project team with a high level of credibility and respect may have a relatively easy time communicating results. Low credibility can create problems for teams that are trying to be persuasive.

The Process for Communicating Results

The communication of project results must be systematic, timely, and well planned. A seven-step approach will help ensure your communication plan reaps the desired rewards. The seven steps are:

1. Analyze the need for communication
2. Plan the communication strategy
3. Select the target audience
4. Develop the report
5. Select the media
6. Present the results
7. Analyze reactions

By following these seven steps, which are described in more detail in this section, you will ensure that your communication strategy is methodical and consistent.

ANALYZE THE NEED FOR COMMUNICATION

Because there may be various reasons for communicating results, depending on the specific project, the setting, and the unique needs of each party, a list of needs should be tailored to the organization and adjusted as necessary. Some of the most common reasons are:

- Securing approval for the project and the allocation of time and money
- Gaining support for the project and its objectives
- Securing agreement on the issues, solutions, and resources
- Enhancing the credibility of the project leader
- Reinforcing the processes used in the project
- Driving action for improvement in the project
- Preparing participants for the project
- Optimizing results throughout the project and the quality of future feedback
- Showing the complete results of the project
- Underscoring the importance of measuring results
- Explaining techniques used to measure results
- Motivating participants to become involved in the project
- Demonstrating accountability for expenditures
- Marketing future projects

There may be other reasons for communicating results. Just as you analyze the needs of the organization to ensure that the sustainability initiative is in alignment, you must make the needs for the communication clear so the presentation of results is positioned for success.

PLAN THE COMMUNICATION STRATEGY

Any activity must be carefully planned to achieve maximum results. This is a critical part of communicating the results of the project to ensure that each audience receives the proper information at the right time and that necessary actions are taken. Several issues are crucial in planning the communication of results:

- What will be communicated?
- When will the data be communicated?
- How will the information be communicated?
- Where will the information be communicated?
- Who will communicate the information?
- Who is the target audience?
- What are the specific actions required or desired?

The communication plan is usually developed as the project plan is developed. This plan details how specific information is to be developed and communicated to various groups and the expected actions. In addition, the communication strategy details how the overall results will be communicated, the time frame for communication, and the appropriate groups to receive the information. The project leader, key managers, and stakeholders need to agree on the detail of the strategy. If you don't know where you are going, you won't know if you get there–so plan your communication of results.

SELECT THE TARGET AUDIENCE

Audiences range from top management to past participants, and each audience has its own reasons for hearing about project success. The following questions should be asked about each potential audience:

- Are they interested in the project?
- Do they really want to receive the information?
- Has a commitment been made to include them in the communications?
- Is the timing right for this audience?
- Are they familiar with the project?

- How do they prefer to have results communicated?
- Do they know the project leader? The project team?
- Are they likely to find the results threatening?
- Which medium will be most convincing to this group?

For each target audience, three steps are necessary. First, to the greatest extent possible, the project leader should get to know and understand the target audience. Next, the project leader should find out what information is needed and why. Each group will have its own required amount of information; some will want detailed information while others will prefer a brief overview. Rely on the input from others to determine the audience's needs. Finally, the project leader should take into account audience bias. Some audiences will immediately support the results, others may oppose them, and still others will be neutral. The staff should be empathetic and try to understand the basis for the differing views. Given this understanding, communications can be tailored to each group. This is critical when the potential exists for the audience to react negatively to the results.

Determining which groups will receive a particular item of communication requires careful thought, because problems can arise when a group receives inappropriate information or is overlooked altogether. A sound basis for audience selection is to analyze the reason for the communication, as discussed earlier. Table 11.1 identifies common target audiences and the basis for audience selection. Several audiences stand out as critical. Perhaps the most important audience is the project's sponsor. This group (or individual) initiates the project, reviews data, usually selects the project leader, and weighs the final assessment of the effectiveness of the project. Another important target audience is top management. This group is responsible for allocating resources to the project and needs information to help them justify expenditures and gauge the effectiveness of the efforts.

Communication of results to project participants is often overlooked, with the assumption that once the project is completed, they do not need to be informed of its success. However, participants need feedback on the overall success of the effort. Some individuals may not have been as successful as others in achieving the desired results. Communicating the results creates additional pressure to implement the project effectively and improve results in the future. For those achieving excellent results, the communication will serve as reinforcement.

Communicating with the participants' immediate managers is also essential. In many cases, these managers must encourage participants to implement the project. Also, they are keys in supporting and reinforcing the objectives of the project. An appropriate ROI strengthens the commitment to projects and enhances the credibility of the project team.

TABLE 11.1 Common Target Audiences

Primary Target Audience	Reason for Communication
Sponsor, top executives	To secure approval for the project
Immediate managers, team leaders	To gain support for the project
Participants, team leaders	To secure agreement with the issues
Top executives	To enhance the credibility of the project leader
Immediate managers	To reinforce the processes
Project team	To drive action for improvement
Team leaders	To prepare participants for the project
Participants	To improve the results and quality of future feedback
Stakeholders	To show the complete results of the project
Sponsor, project team	To underscore the importance of measuring results
Sponsor, project support staff	To explain the techniques used to measure results
Team leaders	To create the desire for a participant to be involved
All employees	To demonstrate accountability for expenditures
Prospective sponsors	To market future projects

The project team must receive information about project results. Whether for small projects in which team members receive a project update, or for larger projects in which a complete team is involved, those who design, develop, facilitate, and implement the project require information on the project's effectiveness. Evaluation data are necessary so that adjustments can be made if the project is not as effective as it was projected to be.

DEVELOP THE REPORT

The impact study report details the purpose of the program and evaluation. It describes the methodology used and reports results at each level in detail. The report closes out with recommendations about the project as well as lessons learned through the process. The type of formal evaluation report to be issued to the various audiences depends on the degree of detail needed to achieve the purpose of the communication. Brief summaries of project results with appropriate charts may be sufficient for some communication efforts. In other situations, particularly those involving major projects that require extensive funding, a detailed evaluation report is crucial. A complete and comprehensive impact study report is always necessary at least for the project team. This report can then be used as the basis for more streamlined information aimed at specific audiences and using various media. One possible format for an impact study report is presented in Table 11.2.

While the impact study report is an effective, professional way to present ROI data, several cautions are in order. Since this report documents the success of a project involving a large group of employees, credit for the success must go completely to the participants and their immediate leaders. Their performance generated the success. Also, it is important to avoid boasting about results. Grand claims of overwhelming success can quickly turn off an audience and interfere with the delivery of the desired message.

TABLE 11.2   Format of an Impact Study Report

- General information
  - Background
  - Objectives of study
- Methodology for impact study
  - Levels of evaluation
  - ROI Methodology
  - Data collection procedures
    - Data collection methods
    - Data sources
    - Data collection timing
  - Data analysis procedures
    - Techniques to isolate effects of projects
    - Techniques to convert data to money
    - Cost categories
- Results: General information
  - Response profile
  - Success with objectives
- Results: Reaction and perceived value
  - Data sources
  - Data summary
  - Key issues
- Results: Learning and awareness
  - Data sources
  - Data summary
  - Key issues
- Results: Application and implementation
  - Data sources
  - Data summary
  - Barriers and enablers to application
- Results: Impact
  - General comments
  - Linkage with business measures
  - Key issues
- Results: ROI
  - Monetary value of impact measure
  - Project costs
  - ROI
- Results: Intangible measures
- Conclusions and recommendations
  - Conclusions
  - Recommendations
- Exhibits

The evaluation methodology should be clearly explained, along with the assumptions made in the analysis. The reader should easily see how the values were developed and how specific steps were followed to make the process more conservative, credible, and accurate. Detailed statistical analyses should be placed in an appendix.

SELECT THE MEDIA

Many options are available for the dissemination of project results. In addition to the impact study report, commonly used media are meetings, interim and progress reports, organization publications, and case studies. Table 11.3 lists a variety of options to develop the content and the message.

Meetings

If used properly, meetings are fertile ground for the communication of project results. All organizations hold a variety of meetings, and some may provide the proper context to convey project results. Staff meetings are held to review progress, discuss current problems, and distribute information. These meetings can be an excellent forum for discussing the results achieved in a project that relate to the group's activities. Project results can be sent to executives for use in a staff meeting, or a member of the project team can attend the meeting to make the presentation.

Regular meetings with management groups are a common practice. Typically, discussions will focus on items that might be of help to work units. The discussion of a project and its results can be integrated into the regular meeting format. A few organizations have initiated the use of periodic meetings for all key stakeholders, in which the project leader reviews progress and discusses next steps. A few highlights from interim project results can be helpful in building interest, commitment, and support for the project.

TABLE 11.3 Options for Communicating Results

Detailed Reports	Brief Reports	Electronic Reporting	Mass Publications
Impact study	Executive summary	Website	Announcements
Case study (internal)	Slide overview	E-mail	Bulletins
Case study (external)	One-page summary	Blog	Newsletters
Major articles	Brochure	Video	Brief articles

Interim and Progress Reports

A highly visible way to communicate results, although usually limited to large projects, is the use of interim and routine memos and reports. Published or disseminated by e-mail on a periodic basis, they are designed to inform management about the status of the project, to communicate interim results of the project, and to spur needed changes and improvements.

A second reason for the interim report is to enlist additional support and commitment from the management group and to keep the project intact. This report is produced by the project team and distributed to a select group of stakeholders in the organization. The report may vary considerably in format and scope and may include a schedule of planned steps or activities, a brief summary of reaction evaluations, initial results achieved from the project, and various spotlights recognizing team members or participants. Other topics may also be appropriate. When produced in a professional manner, the interim report can boost management support and commitment.

Routine Communication Channels

To reach a wide audience, the project leader can use internal, routine publications. Whether a newsletter, magazine, newspaper, or electronic file, these media usually reach all employees or stakeholders. The content can have a significant impact if communicated appropriately. The scope should be limited to general-interest articles, announcements, and interviews. Project results communicated must be important enough to arouse general interest.

E-mail and Electronic Media

Internal and external Internet pages, company-wide intranets, and e-mails are excellent vehicles for releasing results, promoting ideas, and informing employees and other target groups of project results. E-mail, in particular, provides a virtually instantaneous means of communicating results to and soliciting responses from large groups of people. For major projects, some organizations create blogs to present results and solicit reactions, feedback, and suggestions.

Project Brochures and Pamphlets

A brochure might be appropriate for a project conducted on a continuing basis or for which the audience is large and continuously changing. The brochure should be attractive and present a complete description of the project, with a major section devoted to results obtained with previous participants, if available. Measurable results and reactions from participants, or even direct quotes from individuals, can add spice to what may otherwise be perceived as a dull brochure.

Case Studies

Case studies represent an effective way to communicate the results of a project. A typical case study describes the situation, provides appropriate background information (including the events that led to the project), presents the techniques and strategies used to develop the study, and highlights the key issues in the project. Case studies tell an interesting story of how the project was implemented and the evaluation was developed, including the problems and concerns identified along the way.

PRESENT THE RESULTS

With a plan in place and appropriate media at hand, it is now time to deliver the results. Through the development of content appropriate for the media, the purpose of the communication can be achieved. Perhaps one of the most challenging and stressful types of communication involves presenting an impact study to the senior management team, which also serves as the client for a project, to convince this highly skeptical and critical group that outstanding results have been achieved (assuming they have) in a reasonable time frame, addressing the salient points, and making sure the managers understand the process. Two potential reactions can create problems. First, if the results are impressive, making the managers accept the data may be difficult. On the other extreme, if the data are negative, making sure that managers do not overreact to the results and look for someone to blame is important.

Arrange a face-to-face meeting with senior team members to review the results. If they are unfamiliar with the ROI Methodology, this meeting is necessary to make sure they understand the process. The good news is that they will probably attend the meeting because they have never seen ROI data developed for this type of project. The bad news is that it takes precious executive time, usually about an hour, for this presentation. After the meeting, an executive summary may suffice. At this point, the senior members will understand the process, so a shortened version may be appropriate. When a particular audience is familiar with the process, a brief version may be developed, including a one- to two-page summary with charts and graphs showing the six types of measures.

The results should not be disseminated before the initial presentation or even during the session, but should be saved until the end of the session. This will allow enough time to present the process and collect reactions to it before the target audience sees the ROI calculation. Present the ROI Methodology step by step, showing how the data were collected, when they were collected, who provided them, how the effect of the project was isolated from other influences, and how data were converted to monetary values. Present the various assumptions, adjustments, and conservative approaches along with the total cost of the project, so that the target audience will begin to buy into the process of developing the ROI.

When the data are actually presented, give the results one level at a time, starting with Level 1, moving through Level 5, and ending with the intangibles. This allows the audience to observe the reaction, learning, application and implementation, impact, and ROI procedures. After some discussion of the meaning of the ROI, present the intangible measures. Allocate time for each level as appropriate for the audience. This helps to defuse potential emotional reactions to a positive or negative ROI.

Show the consequences of additional accuracy if this is an issue. The tradeoff for more accuracy and validity often is more expense. Address this issue when necessary, agreeing to add more data if they are required. Collect concerns, reactions, and issues involving the process and make adjustments accordingly for the next presentation.

Collectively, these steps will help in the preparation and presentation of one of the most important meetings in the ROI Methodology. Figure 11.1 shows the recommended approach to an important meeting with the sponsor.

ANALYZE REACTIONS

The best indicator of how effectively the results of a project have been communicated is the level of commitment and support from the managers, executives, and sponsors. The allocation of requested resources and voiced commitment from top management are strong evidence of the management's positive perception of the results. In addition to this macro-level reaction, a few techniques can also be helpful in measuring the effectiveness of the communication effort.

Monitor Reactions

When results are communicated, monitor the reactions of the target audiences. These reactions may include nonverbal gestures, oral remarks, written comments, or indirect actions that reveal how the communication was received. Usually, when results are presented in a meeting, the presenter will have some indication of how they were received by the group, and the interest and attitudes of the audience can be quickly evaluated. Comments about the results—formal or informal—should be noted and tabulated.

Discuss Reactions

Project team meetings provide an excellent arena for discussing the reaction to communicated results. Comments can come from many sources depending on the particular target audience. When major project results are

Purpose of the Meeting	Meeting Ground Rules
• Create awareness and understanding of ROI. • Build support for the ROI Methodology. • Communicate results of study. • Drive improvement from results. • Cultivate effective use of the ROI Methodology.	• Do not distribute the impact study until the end of the meeting. • Be precise and to the point. • Avoid jargon and unfamiliar terms. • Spend less time on the lower levels of evaluation data. • Present the data with a strategy in mind.

Presentation Sequence

1. Describe the project and explain why it is being evaluated.
2. Present the evaluation process.
3. Present the reaction and learning data.
4. Present the application data.
5. List the barriers and enablers to success.
6. Address the business impact.
7. Show the costs.
8. Present the ROI.
9. Show the intangibles.
10. Review the credibility of the data.
11. Summarize the conclusions.
12. Present the recommendations.

FIGURE 11.1 Presenting the Impact Study to Executive Sponsors

communicated, a feedback questionnaire may be administered to the entire audience or a sample of the audience to determine the extent to which the audience understood and believed the information presented. This is practical only when the effectiveness of the communication will have a significant impact on future actions by the project team.

The Green Scorecard

Reporting the results of a green project or sustainability initiative requires a strategy. A detailed report provides a historical look at the project along with the evaluation results. This history serves as backup for questions that arise as well as the basis for future evaluations. Executive summaries, human interest stories, and presentations around key measures are important types of reports that engage audiences at all levels of the organization. Sometimes, however, it is important to communicate project success in a simple format that includes only the critical data. This format—often referred to as a *scorecard*—summarizes the key measures and shows how the project fared in achieving objectives beyond the activity surrounding it.

THE IMPORTANCE OF A SCORECARD

As mentioned throughout this book, organizations are moving away from a focus on activity to one on results, which are defined using a five-level framework. Progressive organizations and communities place great emphasis on results-focused initiatives, including those initiatives that support a greater good, yet if the projects appear to be more costly than beneficial, they are often scrapped and either a new approach is taken or nothing is done at all.

A scorecard provides clear evidence of the contribution made by a green project. While all projects require resource inputs, contribution is defined in terms of:

- The reaction employees have to the project
- The knowledge, skill, and attitude changes as a result of implementing the project
- The new behaviors and actions being taken since project implementation
- The business, community, and environmental impact resulting as a consequence of the project
- The financial return on investment
- The intangible benefits, which are not converted to money

The green scorecard primarily provides information to the sponsor group, including top executives. However, it also provides useful measures for the project team. The scorecard provides a direct linkage between the investment in green initiatives and the organization strategy.

MACRO-LEVEL SCORECARDS

Most evaluation processes concentrate on micro-level activities, evaluating one project at a time. The ROI Methodology presented in this book does the same. The final output of any one of these evaluations is a detailed report with all the peripheral summary reports and presentations, including a micro-level summary or scorecard for that specific project. But for most entities, multiple green initiatives are under way, ranging from the very simple to the very complex. As mentioned earlier and discussed in more detail in the next chapter, not every green project should be evaluated up to ROI, which

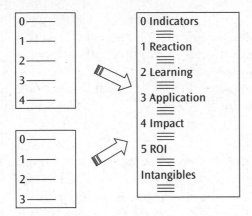

FIGURE 11.2   Micro-Level Versus Macro-Level Scorecard

is intended for the expensive, high-profile projects. Yet there is a need to connect projects not evaluated to ROI to strategy as well. This is accomplished by integrating the data from all evaluations in a meaningful way to show the overall contribution of green investments. In essence, this process takes a micro-level activity (evaluation of a specific green initiative) and presents a macro-level view (evaluation of all green initiatives).

Figure 11.2 illustrates the concept. Though each program is evaluated on the micro-level, only a few selected measures in each of the micro-evaluations are captured for the macro-level evaluation. It takes the most critical, important, and executive-friendly measures to go on the green scorecard.

MEASURES TO INCLUDE IN THE SCORECARD

Figure 11.3 shows an outline of a comprehensive green scorecard. As shown, eight categories of data are included.

Inputs and Indicators

The traditional approach to measuring project success is to report the inputs or activities. These measures are important in that they represent the organization's commitment to green and sustainability projects, efficiencies, and trends in processes. They do not, however, represent results of the project. The number of inputs is vast, so it is important to include in the scorecard measures important to top managers. Ideally, the management group should approve the indicators, and the inputs reported should stimulate interest with executives. A few possible measures to report in this category include:

- The number of employees participating in green projects
- The number of hours employees engage in green projects

0.   Indicators

1. Number of Employees Involved in Green Projects
2. Total Hours of Involvement
3. Hours Per Employee
4. Project Investment as a Percent of Payroll
5. Cost Per Participant

I.   Reaction and Perceived Value

1. Percent of Projects Evaluated at This Level
2. Ratings on 5 Items vs. Target
3. Percent with Action Plans
4. Percent with ROI Forecast

II.   Learning

1. Percent of Projects Evaluated at This Level
2. Types of Measurements
3. Self-Assessment Ratings on 3 Items vs. Targets

III.   Application and Implementation

1. Percent of Projects Evaluated at This Level
2. Ratings on 3 Items vs. Targets
3. Percent of Action Plans Complete
4. Barriers (List of Top 10)
5. Enablers (List of Top 10)
6. Management Support Profile

IV.   Impact

1. Percentage of Projects Evaluated at This Level
2. Linkage with Measures (List of Top 10)
3. Linkage with Sustainability Measures
4. Types of Measurement Techniques
5. Types of Methods to Isolate the Effects of Projects
6. Investment Perception

V.   ROI

1. Percent of Projects Evaluated at This Level
2. ROI Summary for Each Study
3. Methods of Converting Data to Monetary Values
4. Fully Loaded Cost per Participant

Intangibles

1. List of Intangibles (Top 10)
2. How Intangibles Were Captured

Awards and Recognition

1. Industry Awards
2. Sustainability Awards

FIGURE 11.3   Sample Scorecard for All Green Projects

- Various statistics, such as demographics and completion rates
- Financial investment in green projects (total costs, cost per employee, etc.)
- Cost recovery, if there is a financial benefit for implementing green projects (tax breaks, grants, etc.)

Reaction and Perceived Value

There are many measures that can be taken at this level of evaluation. The first measure to report is the percentage of projects evaluated at this level. Typically, this will be 100 percent of the projects. This measure provides senior management with a picture of the investment in the evaluation of green projects. When reporting Level 1 results, it is important to capture other measures that provide some indication that success will be achieved through the green project. Measures to consider include:

- Relevance to the job
- Amount of new information
- Recommendation to others
- Importance of the information
- Intention to apply knowledge, skill, or information

These measures have been shown to have a statistical correlation with measures of application (Level 3).

Another potential measure in this category is the percentage of project participants with actions plans. This can become an important measure, since the action plans will drive specific steps participants will take to make the project successful.

Learning

This level of evaluation, as described earlier, indicates the extent to which project participants are able to proceed with the project given the information they have received or the knowledge and skill they have acquired. Every project has a learning component. How and the extent to which that component is measured depends on the level of learning required to make the project successful. Simple projects, like changing from traditional lighting to LED lighting, do not require a lot of new information. But a major process improvement initiative targeting a variety of types of waste will require knowledge, information, and sometimes skill. For these types of projects, evaluation at Level 2 (learning) will occur. Given these issues, the first measure to report in this category is the percentage of projects evaluated at this level.

Because some learning components will require comprehensive Level 2 evaluation and others will require less formal methods, it is sometimes difficult to compare results at this level across all programs. So, to make it simple to roll up Level 2 measures across projects, it may be useful to develop a set of common measures to determine the extent to which participants acquired the knowledge they need to make the project successful. Measures may include self-reports of learning change, such as:

- Acquisition of knowledge, skill, or information
- Enhanced awareness of need for project
- Change in attitude toward green and sustainability efforts
- Ability to apply knowledge, skill, or information
- Confidence to use knowledge, skill, or information

Using this type of measurement scheme, it is important that the same scale (e.g., a 1–5 Likert scale) be used for every Level 2 evaluation.

Application and Implementation

To measure the actual change in behavior and progress with application, measurements must be taken after a project is launched and implemented. The first measure reported on the scorecard at Level 3 is percentage of projects evaluated at this level. Again, by reporting this measure, leaders will have an indication of the investment being made in evaluation. Follow-up measures for all projects may include these measures:

- The extent of use of knowledge, skill, or information
- The frequency of use of knowledge, skill, or information
- The effectiveness of use of knowledge, skill, or information

Because application and implementation of green projects vary based on the focus of the project, it is important to capture measures that can be summarized and integrated across all projects. These three measures make that possible. Essentially, these items can be collected for every project to show the success in changing behaviors or applying concepts associated with the green project.

Another important set of measures to report in the macro-level green scorecard identifies barriers and enablers. Recognizing and reporting these inhibitors to and supporters of project success are important because they explain why progress is or is not being made. Adding them to the macro-level scorecard is an easy way to show senior managers how the system is supporting green projects and sustainability initiatives.

Impact

Success at this level is reported for only a few projects. So again, the first measure to report here is the percentage of projects evaluated at this level. In addition, any linkage of the project to organization, community, and environmental measures is also reported. Typically, for macro-level scorecard reporting, this linkage is measured through the use of questionnaires, with the top two high scores reported as a composite score. By listing the top ten measures that improved due to a project, it is easy to show how closely aligned projects are to strategy.

Another important measure reported at this level is the method used to isolate the effects of the project. As presented in Chapter 8, a variety of methods are available. Some organizations are moving to more research and analytical methods, while others are using subjective estimations to save time and costs. Either way, reporting the techniques employed in the evaluation of green projects shows senior managers that efforts are under way to make the clearest possible connection between projects and results.

Return on Investment

The ultimate level of evaluation is the actual return on investment. The first measure to report in this category of results is the percentage of projects evaluated at this level. Because the ROI, BCR, and payback period are self-explanatory to senior leaders and administrators, little additional information is needed on the scorecard. Still, it is sometimes helpful to report data conversion methods used so the audience understands how the monetary value is developed.

Intangible Benefits

It is important to include the intangible benefits on the macro-level scorecard. These measures may also be included in the impact category, but it is important to highlight them here. The top ten intangibles are sometimes reported, providing an opportunity to check alignment with organizational strategy.

Awards and Recognition

The extent to which an organization or community is recognized by professional associations, the community, and other entities is often important to senior leaders. These types of recognitions make employees feel proud of their organization, benefit recruiting, and often help economic development. Include awards on the green scorecard so senior managers can see that the awards being pursued (and won) are in alignment with the strategy of the organization.

GETTING STARTED

Green project success is reported in a variety of ways. Individual project evaluations are described in detailed reports, summaries, newsletters, and human interest stories. Key results of the individual projects are also summarized in micro-level scorecards. But because a vast number of projects are often initiated, it is important to integrate results into a macro-level scorecard, which presents the success of all green initiatives and provides evidence of a link between activity and strategy.

To get started developing a macro-level scorecard, follow these simple guidelines:

1. *Start the scorecard development with the ultimate desired outcomes in mind.* In Chapter 5, we described a process to align green projects with strategy. While implementing the alignment process, focus on the payoff needs, business needs, performance needs, and learning needs. Use these data as a basis for your scorecard measures.

2. *Start simple.* The initial scorecard can be brief, showing results of only the key measures. As the scorecard evolves, additional measures can be incorporated.

3. *Limit the focus on activity.* While you will certainly want to capture some input data, limit the focus on activity and give stakeholders the data they want: results!

Final Thoughts

The final step in the ROI Methodology, reporting results, is a crucial step in the overall evaluation process. If this step is not executed adequately, the full impact of the results will not be recognized, and the study may amount to a waste of time. The principles and steps shown in this chapter for communicating project results can serve as a guide for any significant communication effort. Various target audiences should be identified, with an emphasis on the executive group because of its importance, and the suggested format for a detailed evaluation report can be followed. A green scorecard is an excellent way to present the success of all green projects. The final issue in developing a successful approach to accounting for green investments is developing a strategy for implementing and sustaining the process. This issue is covered in the final chapter, which follows.

Chapter 12

Implementing and Sustaining ROI

To be effective, even the best designed process or model must be integrated into the organization. Often, resistance to the ROI Methodology arises. Some of this resistance is based on fear and misunderstanding; some is based on actual barriers and obstacles. Although the ROI Methodology presented in this book is a step-by-step, methodical, and simplistic procedure, it can fail if it is not integrated properly. This integration includes full acceptance and support by those who must make it work within the organization. This chapter focuses on some of the most effective means of overcoming resistance to implementing the ROI process.

Why the Concern About Implementing and Sustaining ROI?

With any new process or change, there is resistance, which may be especially great when implementing a process as complex as ROI. To implement ROI and sustain it as an important accountability tool, the resistance must be minimized or removed. Four key factors serve as the basis for developing a detailed plan to overcome resistance:

- Resistance
- Implementation
- Consistency
- Efficiency

RESISTANCE IS INEVITABLE

Resistance to change is a constant. Sometimes there are good reasons for resistance, but often it exists for the wrong reasons. The important point is to sort out both kinds of resistance and try to dispel any myths. When legitimate barriers are the basis for resistance, minimizing or removing them altogether is the challenge.

IMPLEMENTATION IS KEY

As with any process, effective implementation is the key to its success. This occurs when the new technique, tool, or process is integrated into the routine framework. Without effective implementation, even the best process will fail. A process that is never removed from the shelf will never be understood, supported, or improved. Clear steps must be in place for designing a comprehensive implementation process that will overcome resistance.

CONSISTENCY IS NECESSARY

Consistency is an important consideration as the ROI Methodology is implemented. With consistency come accuracy and reliability—and accountability. The only way to make sure consistency is achieved is to follow clearly defined processes, procedures, and standards each time the ROI Methodology is used. Proper, effective implementation will ensure that this occurs.

EFFICIENCY IS ESSENTIAL

Cost control and efficiency are important considerations in any major undertaking, and the ROI Methodology is no exception. During implementation, tasks must be completed efficiently and effectively. Doing so will help ensure that process costs are kept to a minimum, that time is used economically, and that the process remains affordable.

Implementing the Process: Overcoming Resistance

Resistance shows up in the form of comments, remarks, actions, or behaviors. Table 12.1 lists representative comments that indicate open resistance to the ROI process. Each comment signals an issue that must be resolved or addressed in some way. A few are based on realistic barriers, whereas others are based on myths that must be dispelled. Sometimes resistance to the process reflects underlying concerns. For example, the individuals involved may fear losing control of their processes, and others may feel vulnerable to whatever action may follow if the process is not successful. Still others may be concerned about any process that brings change or requires the additional effort of learning.

Project team members may resist the ROI process and openly make comments similar to those listed in Table 12.1. It may take heavy persuasion and evidence of tangible benefits to convince team members that it is in their best interest to make the project a success. Although most clients do want to see the results of the project, they may have concerns about the information they are asked to provide and about whether their personal performance is being judged while the project is undergoing evaluation. Participants may express the same fears listed in the table.

The challenge is to implement the process systematically and consistently so that it becomes normal business behavior and a routine and standard process that is built into projects. The implementation necessary to overcome resistance covers a variety of areas. Figure 12.1 shows actions outlined in this chapter that are presented as building blocks to help overcome resistance. They are all necessary to build the proper base or framework to dispel myths and remove or minimize barriers. The remainder of this chapter presents specific strategies and techniques devoted to each of the nine building blocks identified in Figure 12.1. They apply equally to the project team and the client organization. In some situations, a particular strategy will work best with the project team. In certain cases, all strategies may be appropriate for both groups.

TABLE 12.1 Typical Objections to Use of ROI Methodology

Open Resistance

1. It costs too much.
2. It takes too much time.
3. Who is asking for this?
4. This is not my job.
5. I did not have input on this.
6. I do not understand this.
7. What happens when the results are negative?
8. How can we be consistent with this?
9. The ROI looks too subjective.
10. Our managers will not support this.
11. ROI is too narrowly focused.
12. This is not practical.

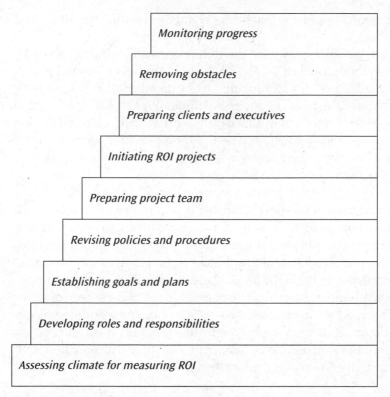

FIGURE 12.1 Building Blocks to Overcome Resistance

Assessing the Climate for Measuring ROI

As a first step toward implementation, some organizations assess the current climate for achieving results. One way to do this is to develop a survey to determine the current perspectives of the management team and other stakeholders (for an example go to *www.thegreenscorecard.com*). Another way is to conduct interviews with key stakeholders to determine their willingness to follow the project through to ROI. With an awareness of the current status, the project leaders can plan for significant changes and pinpoint particular issues that need support as the ROI process is implemented.

Developing Roles and Responsibilities

Defining and detailing specific roles and responsibilities for different groups and individuals addresses many of the resistance factors and helps pave a smooth path for implementation.

IDENTIFYING A CHAMPION

As an early step in the process, one or more individuals should be designated as the internal leader or champion for the ROI Methodology. As in most change efforts, someone must take responsibility for ensuring that the process is implemented successfully. This leader serves as a champion for ROI and is usually the one who understands the process best and sees vast potential for its contribution. More important, this leader is willing to teach others and will work to sustain sponsorship.

DEVELOPING THE ROI LEADER

The ROI leader is usually a member of the project team who has the responsibility for evaluation. This person holds a full-time position in larger project teams or a part-time position in smaller teams. Sponsor organizations may also have an ROI leader who pursues the ROI Methodology from the sponsor's perspective. The typical job title for a full-time ROI leader is Manager of Measurement and Evaluation. Some organizations assign this responsibility to a team and empower it to lead the ROI effort.

In preparation for this assignment, individuals usually receive special training that builds specific skills and knowledge of the ROI process. The role of the implementation leader is broad and serves a variety of specialized duties. In some organizations, the implementation leader can take on many roles, ranging from problem solver to communicator to cheerleader. Leading the ROI process is a difficult and challenging assignment that requires unique skills. Some programs are designed to certify individuals who will be assuming leadership roles in the implementation of the ROI Methodology. (For more detail, see *www.roiinstitute.net*.) This certification is built around ten specific skill sets linked to successful ROI implementation, focusing on the critical areas of collecting data, isolating the effects of the project, converting data to monetary value, presenting evaluation data, and building capability. This process is comprehensive and may be necessary to build the skills needed to take on this challenging assignment.

ESTABLISHING A TASK FORCE

Making the ROI Methodology work well may require the use of a task force, which usually comprises a group of individuals from different parts of the project or client team who are wiling to develop the ROI Methodology and implement it in the organization. The selection of the task force may involve asking for volunteers, or participation may be mandatory depending on specific job responsibilities. The task force should represent the cross section necessary for accomplishing stated goals. Task forces have the additional advantage of bringing more people into the process and developing more ownership of and support for the ROI Methodology. The task force must be large enough to cover the key areas but not so large that it becomes too cumbersome to function. Six to twelve members is a good size.

ASSIGNING RESPONSIBILITIES

Determining specific responsibilities is critical because confusion can arise when individuals are unclear about their specific assignments in the use of the ROI Methodology. Responsibilities apply to two areas. The first is the measurement and evaluation responsibility of the entire project team. Everyone involved in projects must have some responsibility for measurement and evaluation, which includes providing input on designing instruments, planning specific evaluations, analyzing data, and interpreting the results. Typical responsibilities include:

- Ensuring that the initial analysis for the project includes specific business impact measures
- Developing specific application and business impact objectives for the project
- Keeping participants focused on application and impact objectives
- Communicating rationale and reasons for evaluation
- Assisting in follow-up activities to capture application and business impact data
- Providing assistance for data collection, data analysis, and reporting

Although involving each member of the project team in all of these activities may not be appropriate, each individual should have at least one responsibility as part of his or her routine job duties. This assignment of responsibility keeps the ROI Methodology from becoming disjointed and separated during projects. More important, it brings accountability to those directly involved in project implementation.

Another issue involves technical support. Depending on the size of the project team, establishing an individual or a group of technical experts to provide assistance with the ROI Methodology may be helpful. When the group is established, the project team must understand that the experts have been assigned not for the purpose of relieving the team of its evaluation responsibilities, but to supplement its ROI efforts with technical expertise. Technical experts are typically the individuals who participated in the certification and training process to build special skills. Responsibilities of the technical support group include:

1. Designing data collection instruments
2. Providing assistance for developing an evaluation strategy
3. Analyzing data, including specialized statistical analyses
4. Interpreting results and making specific recommendations
5. Developing an evaluation report or case study to communicate overall results
6. Providing technical support in all phases of the ROI Methodology

Although the project team must be assigned specific responsibilities during an evaluation, requiring others to serve in support functions to help with data collection is not unusual. These responsibilities are defined when a particular evaluation strategy plan is developed and approved.

Establishing Goals and Plans

Establishing goals, targets, and objectives is critical to the implementation, particularly when several projects are planned. The establishment of goals can include detailed planning documents for the overall process and for individual ROI projects.

Establishing specific targets for evaluation levels is an important goal-setting strategy. Not every green initiative should be evaluated to ROI. Knowing in advance to which level a project will be evaluated helps in planning which measures will be needed and how detailed the evaluation must be. Table 12.2 presents examples of targets set for evaluation at each level when different types of projects exist.

Another important part is establishing a timetable for the complete integration of the ROI Methodology. This document becomes a master plan for completion of the different elements presented earlier. Beginning with forming a team and concluding with meeting the targets previously described,

TABLE 12.2 Evaluation Targets in a Large Organization with Many Green Projects

Level	Target
Level 1, Reaction and Perceived Value	100%
Level 2, Learning and Awareness	80%
Level 3, Application and Implementation	40%
Level 4, Business Impact	25%
Level 5, ROI	10%

this schedule presents a project plan for transitioning from the current situation to the desired future situation. Items on the schedule include developing specific ROI projects, building staff skills, developing policy, and teaching managers the process. Figure 12.2 is an example of an implementation plan. The more detailed the document, the more useful it becomes. The project plan is a living, long-range document that should be reviewed frequently and adjusted as necessary. More important, those engaged in work on the ROI Methodology should always be familiar with the implementation plan.

Revising or Developing Policies and Guidelines

Another building block to overcoming resistance to the ROI process is revising or developing the organization's policy on project measurement and evaluation. The policy statement contains information developed specifically for the measurement and evaluation process, using input from the project team and key managers or stakeholders. Sometimes, policy issues are addressed during internal workshops designed to build measurement and evaluation skills. The policy statement addresses critical matters that will influence the effectiveness of the measurement and evaluation process. These may include adopting the framework presented in this book, requiring objectives at all levels for some or all projects, and defining responsibilities for the project team.

Policy statements are important because they provide guidance and direction for the staff and others who work closely with the ROI Methodology, keeping the process clearly focused and enabling the group to establish goals for evaluation. Policy statements also provide an opportunity to communicate basic requirements and fundamentals of performance and accountability. More than anything else, they serve as learning tools to teach others, especially when they are developed in a collaborative way. If policy statements are developed in isolation, staff and management will be denied the sense of their ownership, which makes them neither effective nor useful.

Guidelines for measurement and evaluation are important for showing how to use the tools and techniques, guide the design process, provide consistency in the ROI process, ensure that appropriate methods are used, and place the proper emphasis on each of the areas. The guidelines are more technical than policy statements and often include detailed procedures that show how the process is undertaken and developed. They often include specific forms, instruments, and tools necessary to facilitate the process.

Preparing the Project Team

Project team members may resist the ROI Methodology. They often see evaluation as an unnecessary intrusion into their responsibilities that absorbs pre-

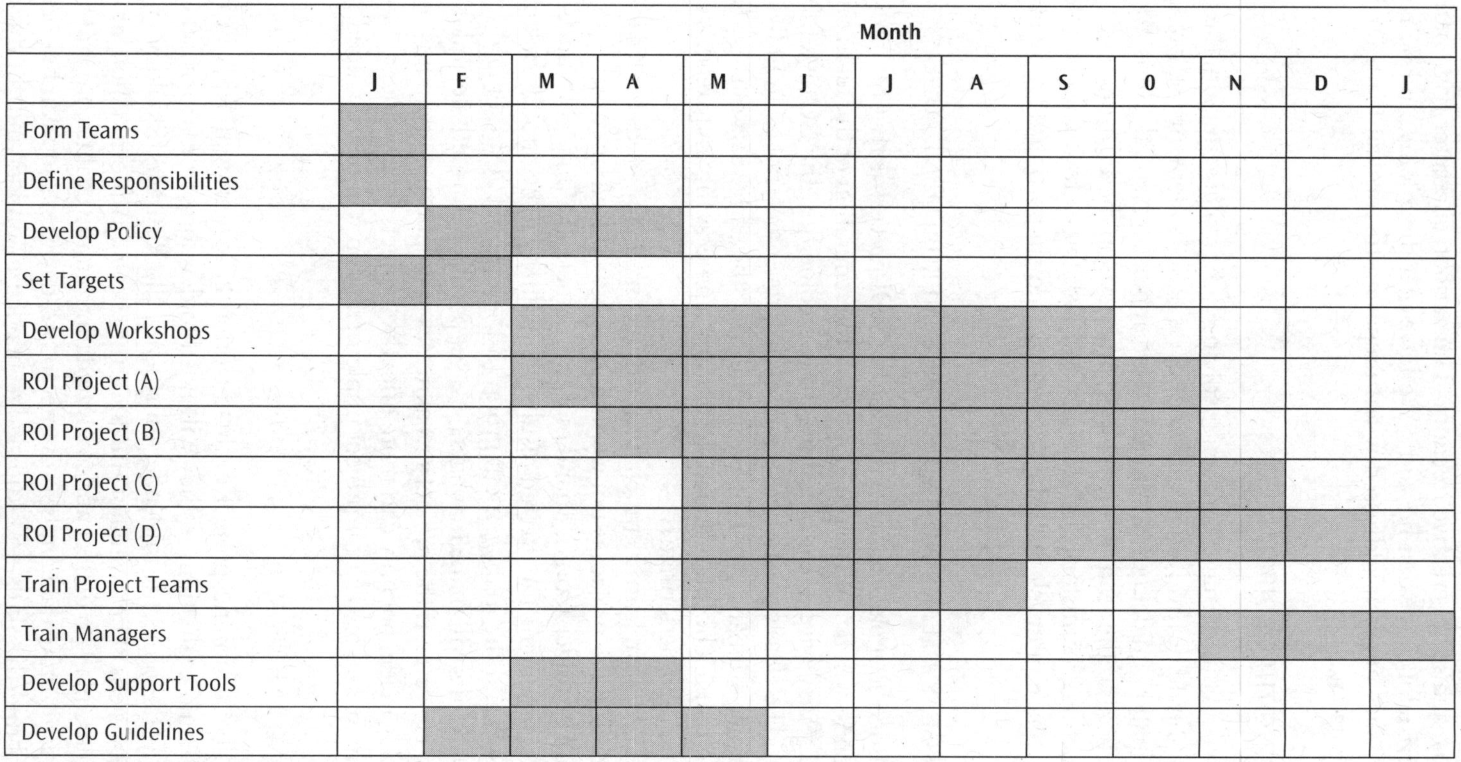

Month

	J	F	M	A	M	J	J	A	S	O	N	D	J
Form Teams	■												
Define Responsibilities	■												
Develop Policy		■	■	■									
Set Targets		■											
Develop Workshops					■	■	■	■	■				
ROI Project (A)					■	■	■	■	■	■			
ROI Project (B)				■	■	■	■	■	■	■	■		
ROI Project (C)						■	■	■	■	■	■	■	
ROI Project (D)						■	■	■	■			■	
Train Project Teams													
Train Managers											■	■	■
Develop Support Tools			■	■									
Develop Guidelines		■	■										

FIGURE 12.2 Implementation Plan for a Large Organization with Many Projects

cious time and stifles creative freedom. The cartoon character Pogo perhaps characterized it best when he said, "We have met the enemy, and he is us." Several issues must be addressed when preparing the project team for ROI implementation.

INVOLVING THE PROJECT TEAM

For each key issue or major decision involving ROI implementation, the project team should be involved in the process. As policy statements are prepared and evaluation guidelines developed, team input is essential. Resistance is more difficult if the team helped design and develop the ROI process. Convene meetings, brainstorming sessions, and task forces to involve the team in every phase of developing the framework and supporting documents for ROI.

USING ROI AS A LEARNING AND PROJECT IMPROVEMENT TOOL

One reason the project team may resist the ROI process is that the project's effectiveness will be fully exposed, putting the reputation of the team on the line. They may have a fear of failure. To overcome this, the ROI Methodology should be clearly positioned as process improvement, not as an individual performance evaluation tool (at least not during the early years of use). Team members will not be interested in developing a process that may reflect unfavorably on their performance.

Evaluators can learn as much from unsuccessful projects as from successful projects. If the project is not working, it is best to find out quickly so that issues can be understood firsthand, not from others. If a project is ineffective and is not producing the desired results, the failure will eventually be known to sponsors and the management group (if they are not aware of it already). A lack of results will make managers less supportive of immediate and future projects. However, if the project's weaknesses are identified and adjustments are quickly made, not only can more effective projects be developed, but the credibility of and respect for project implementation will be enhanced.

TEACHING THE TEAM

The project team and project evaluator often have minimal skills in measurement and evaluation, so they will need to develop some expertise. Consequently, the project team leader must learn the ROI Methodology and its systematic steps. The evaluator must learn to develop an evaluation strategy and specific plan, to collect and analyze data from the evaluation, and to interpret results from data analysis. A one- to two-day workshop can help evaluators to build the skills and knowledge needed to understand the process, and to appreciate what it can do for project success and for the sponsoring organization. Teach-the-team workshops can be valuable tools in ensuring successful implementation of ROI Methodology.

Initiating ROI Projects

The first tangible evidence of the value of using the ROI Methodology arises from the initiation of the first project for which an ROI calculation is planned. Identifying appropriate projects and keeping then on track is critical to successful ROI sustainability.

SELECTING THE INITIAL PROJECT

Projects that qualify for comprehensive, detailed ROI analysis are those that:

1. Are important to strategic objectives
2. Involve large groups of participants
3. Will be linked to major operational problems and opportunities upon completion
4. Are expensive
5. Are time-consuming
6. Have high visibility
7. Have the interest of management in performing their evaluation

Using these or similar criteria, the project leader must select the appropriate projects to consider for ROI evaluation. Ideally, sponsors should agree with or approve the criteria.

DEVELOPING THE PLANNING DOCUMENTS

As described earlier, perhaps the two most useful ROI documents are the data collection plan and the ROI analysis plan. The data collection plan shows what data will be collected, the methods used, the sources, the timing, and the assignment of responsibilities. The ROI analysis plan shows how specific analyses will be conducted, including how to isolate the effects of the project and how to convert data to monetary values. Each evaluator should know how to develop these plans.

REPORTING PROGRESS

As the projects are developed and the ROI implementation gets under way, status meetings should be conducted to report progress and discuss critical issues with appropriate team members. These meetings keep the project team focused on the critical issues, generate the best ideas for addressing problems and barriers, and build a knowledge base for better evaluation of future projects. Sometimes, these meetings are facilitated by an external consultant, perhaps an expert in the ROI process. In other cases, the project leader may facilitate. In essence, the meetings serve three major purposes: reporting progress, learning, and planning.

ESTABLISHING DISCUSSION GROUPS

Because the ROI Methodology is considered difficult to understand and apply, establishing discussion groups to teach the process may be helpful. These groups can supplement formal workshops and other learning activities, and they are often flexible in format. Groups are usually facilitated by an external ROI consultant or the project leader. In each session, a new topic is presented for discussion, which should extend to how the topic applies to the organization. The process can be adjusted for different topics as new group needs arise, driving the issues. Ideally, participants in group discussions will have an opportunity to apply, explore, or research the topics between sessions. Group assignments such as reviewing a case study or reading an article are appropriate between sessions to further the development of knowledge and skills associated with the process.

Preparing the Clients and Executives

Perhaps no group is more important to the use of the ROI Methodology than the management team that must allocate resources for the project and support its implementation. In addition, the management team often provides input to and assistance for the ROI Methodology. The preparation, training, and development of the management team should be carefully planned and executed.

One effective approach for preparing executives and managers for ROI is to conduct a briefing. Varying in duration from one hour to half a day, a practical briefing such as this can provide critical information and enhance support for ROI use. Managers leave these briefings with greater appreciation of the use of ROI and its potential impact on projects, and with a clearer understanding of their role in the ROI process. More important, they often renew their commitment to react to and use the data collected by the ROI Methodology.

A strong, dynamic relationship between the project team and key managers is essential for successful implementation of the ROI Methodology.

A productive partnership is needed that requires each party to understand the concerns, problems, and opportunities of the other. The development of such a beneficial relationship is a long-term process that must be deliberately planned for and initiated by key project team members. The decision to commit resources and support to a project may be based on the effectiveness of this relationship.

Removing Obstacles

As the ROI Methodology is implemented, there will inevitably be obstacles to its progress. The obstacles are usually based on the concerns discussed in this chapter, which may be valid or based on unrealistic fears or misunderstandings.

DISPELLING MYTHS

As part of the implementation, attempts should be made to dispel the myths and remove or minimize the barriers or obstacles. Much of the controversy regarding ROI stems from misunderstandings about what the process can and cannot do and how it can or should be implemented in an organization. After years of experience with ROI, and having noted reactions during hundreds of projects and workshops, we have recognized many misunderstandings about ROI, including:

- ROI is too complex for most users.
- ROI is expensive and consumes too many critical resources.
- If senior management does not require ROI, there is no need to pursue it.
- ROI is a passing fad.
- ROI is only one type of data.
- ROI is not future-oriented; it only reflects past performance.
- ROI is rarely used by organizations.
- The ROI Methodology cannot be easily replicated.
- ROI is not a credible process; it is too subjective.
- ROI cannot be used with soft projects.
- Isolating the influence of other factors is not always possible.
- ROI is appropriate only for large organizations.
- No standards exist for the ROI Methodology.

For more information on these myths see *www.thegreenscorecard.com*.

TABLE 12.3   How to Address Bad News
• Never fail to recognize the power to learn from and improve with a negative study.
• Look for red flags along the way.
• Lower outcome expectations with key stakeholders along the way.
• Look for data everywhere.
• Never alter the standards.
• Remain objective throughout the process.
• Prepare the team for the bad news.
• Consider different scenarios.
• Find out what went wrong.
• Adjust the story line to "Now we have data that show how to make this program more successful," which puts a positive spin on data that are less than positive.
• Drive improvement.

DELIVERING BAD NEWS

One of the obstacles perhaps most difficult to overcome is fear of delivering inadequate, insufficient, or disappointing news. Addressing a bad-news situation is an issue for most project leaders and other stakeholders involved in a project. Table 12.3 presents the guidelines to follow when addressing bad news. As the table makes clear, the time to think about bad news is early in the process, using it to recognize that things need to change and that the situation can improve. The team and others may need to be convinced that good news can be found in a bad-news situation.

USING THE DATA

Too often projects are evaluated and data are collected, but nothing is done with the data. This creates a major obstacle to successful implementation because once the project has concluded, the team has a tendency to move on to the next project or issue and get on with other priorities. Table 12.4 shows how the different levels of data can be used to improve projects.

Failure to use the data may mean that the entire evaluation was a waste of time and resources. As the table illustrates, data can become action items for the team to ensure that changes and adjustments are made.

Monitoring Progress

A final building block to overcoming resistance is monitoring the overall progress made and communicating that progress. Although often overlooked,

TABLE 12.4 How Data Should Be Used

Use of Evaluation Data	Appropriate Level of Data				
	1	2	3	4	5
Adjust project or program design	✓	✓			
Improve implementation			✓	✓	
Influence application and impact			✓	✓	
Improve management support for the project			✓	✓	✓
Improve stakeholder satisfaction			✓	✓	✓
Recognize and reward participants		✓	✓	✓	
Justify or enhance budget				✓	✓
Reduce costs		✓	✓	✓	✓
Market projects or programs in the future	✓		✓	✓	✓

an effective progress report can help keep the implementation on target and let others know what the ROI Methodology is accomplishing for project leaders and the client.

The initial schedule for implementation of ROI is based on key events or milestones, and routine progress reports should be developed to communicate their status. Reports are usually developed at six-month intervals, but they may be more frequent for short-term projects. Two target audiences— the project team and senior managers—are critical for progress reporting. All project team members should be kept informed of the progress, and senior managers should know the extent to which ROI is being implemented and how it is working within the organization.

Final Thoughts

This chapter explored the implementation of the ROI Methodology and ways to sustain its use. If the ROI process is not approached in a systematic, logical, and planned way, it will fail to be integrated as part of the evaluation and accountability of green projects and sustainability initiatives. This chapter presented the different elements that must be considered and issues that must be addressed to ensure that implementation is smooth and uneventful, which is the most effective means of overcoming resistance to ROI. The result provides a complete integration of ROI as a mainstream component of green projects.

References

Alden, Jay. 2006. "Measuring the 'Unmeasurable.'" *Performance Improvement*, May/June.

Alliance to Save Energy, 2009. Industry Leader Interview with Susan Story of Gulf Power. http://ase.org/content/article/detail/5268?tr=y&auid=4340080. Accessed June 10, 2010.

Anderson, M., Bensch, I., and Pigg, S. 2007. "Measuring ROI in the Better Buildings, Better Business Conference Energy Center of Wisconsin." In *Proving the Value of Meetings and Events*, edited by J. Phillips, M. Myhill, and J. McDonough. Dallas: MPI Foundation and Birmingham: ROI Institute, Inc.

Anderson, Ray, with White, Robin. 2009. *Confessions of a Radical Industrialist: Profits, People, Purpose—Doing Business by Respecting the Earth*. New York: St. Martin's Press.

"Annual Employee Benefits Report." 2006. *Nation's Business*, January.

Baliey, B., and Dandrade, R. 1995. "Employee Satisfaction + Customer Satisfaction = Sustained Profitability." *Center for Quality Management Journal* 4, no. 3 (Employee Involvement Special Issue, Fall).

Berns, Maurice; Townend, Andrew; Khayat, Zayna; Balagopal, Balu; Reeves, Martin; Hopkins, Michael; and Kruschwitz, Nina. 2009. "The Business of Sustainability: What it Means to Managers Now." *MIT Sloan Management Review*, Fall.

Boulton, Richard E. S., Libert, Barry D., and Samek, Steve M. 2000. *Cracking the Value Code*. New York: HarperBusiness.

Brewer, Clint. 2009. "Green Business." *Media Planet*, July.

Campanella, Jack, ed. 1999. *Principles of Quality Costs*, 3d ed. Milwaukee: American Society for Quality.

Clinton, Bill. 2009. "Creating Value in an Economic Crisis." *Harvard Business Review*, September.

Cokins, Gary. 1996. *Activity-Based Cost Management: Making it Work—A Manager's Guide to Implementing and Sustaining an Effective ABC System*. New York: McGraw-Hill.

Earth Talk. "Do the Benefits of Recycling Outweigh the Costs? Some Argue Recycling Uses More Energy than It Saves." About.com: Environmental Issues. http://environment.about.com/od/recycling/a/benefit_vs_cost.htm. Accessed July 3, 2010.

Environmental Leader: Energy and Environmental News for Business. November 20, 2007. Study Finds Misleading Green Claims in 99% of Products Surveyed. http://www.environmentalleader.com/2007/11/20/study-finds-misleading-green-claims-in-99-of-products-surveyed/. Accessed July 10, 2010.

Esty, Daniel C., and Winston, Andrew S. 2006. *Green to Gold: How Smart Companies Use Environmental Strategy to Innovate, Create Value, and Build Competitive Advantage*. London: Yale University Press.

Evitts, E. A. July 1, 2004. Sorting Information on Recycling. Urbanite. http://www.urbanitebaltimore.com/baltimore/sorting-information-on-recycling/Content?oid=1245075. Accessed July 1, 2010.

Frangos, Cassandra A. 2004. "Aligning Learning with Strategy." *Chief Learning Officer*, March.

Friedman, Thomas. 2008. *Hot, Flat, and Crowded: Why We Need a Green Revolution—and How It Can Renew America*. New York: Farrar, Straus, and Giroux.

"Getting Warmer: A Special Report on Climate Change and the Carbon Economy." 2009. *The Economist*, December.

Going Green Saves Green: University of South Carolina's Green Efforts Becoming Best Practices. http://www.ulsf.org/pdf/going_green_saves_green.pdf. Accessed July 9, 2010.

Graham, Morris, Bishop, Ken, and Birdsong, Ron. 1994. "Self-Directed Work Teams." In *In Action: Measuring Return on Investment*, vol.1., edited by Jack J. Phillips. Alexandria, VA: American Society for Training and Development.

Hopkins, Michael. 2009. "8 Reasons Sustainability Will Change Management (That You Never Thought of)." *MIT Sloan Management Review*, Fall.

Hurd, Mark, and Nyberg, Lars. 2004. *The Value Factor: How Global Leaders Use Information for Growth and Competitive Advantage*. New York: Bloomberg Press.

Jones, Van. 2008. *The Green-Collar Economy: How One Solution Can Fix Our Two Biggest Problems*. New York: HarperOne.

Kaplan, Robert, and Norton, David. 1996. *The Balanced Scorecard: Translating Strategy into Action*. Boston: Harvard Business Press.

Kerr, Steve, 1995. "On the Folly of Rewarding A, While Hoping for B." *Academy of Management Journal*, 18.

Langdon, Danny G., Whiteside, Kathleen S., and McKenna, Monica M., eds. 1999. *Intervention Resource Guide: 50 Performance Improvement Tools*. San Francisco: Jossey-Bass, Pfeiffer.

Langreth, Robert, and Herper, Matthew. 2010. "The Planet Versus Monsanto." *Forbes,* January.

MacKay, David J. 2009. *Sustainable Energy—Without the Hot Air.* Cambridge, UK: UIT.

Mayo, Andrew. 2003. "Measuring Human Capital." *The Institute of Chartered Accountants,* June.

McKinsey and Company. 2009. Pathways to a Low Carbon Economy, Version 2. http://www.mckinsey.com/clientservice/sustainability/pathways_low_carbon_ economy.asp. Accessed July 9, 2010.

Morse, Gardiner. 2009. "On the Horizon, Six Sources of Limitless Energy." *Harvard Business Review,* September.

Myrow, Rachel. 2007. "UPS Takes Left Turn Out of Deliveries." www.npr.org/templates/story/story.php?storyId=7000908.

Owen, David. 2009. *Green Metropolis: Why Living Smaller, Living Closer, and Driving Less Are the Keys to Sustainability.* New York: Riverhead Books.

Parrs, C., and Weinberg, I. 2009. "Green Marketing: Communicating with the Green Consumer." In *Inside the Minds: Greening Your Company.* Boston: ASPATORE.

Phasing Out Conventional Incandescent Bulbs. September 1, 2008. Europa. Brussels.

Phillips, Jack J. 1997. *Return on Investment in Performance Improvement Programs.* Houston: Gulf Publishing.

Phillips, Jack J., and Aaron, Bruce C. 2008. *Isolation of Results: Defining the Impact of the Program.* San Francisco: Pfeiffer.

Phillips, Jack J., and Phillips, Patricia Pulliam. 2004. "Return to Sender: Improving Response Rates for Questionnaires and Surveys." *Performance Improvement Journal,* August.

———. 2007. *Show Me the Money: How to Determine ROI in People, Places, Projects, and Programs.* San Francisco: Berrett Koehler.

———. 2010. *The Consultant's Guide to Results Driven Proposals: How to Write Proposals that Forecast Impact and ROI.* New York: McGraw-Hill.

Rust, Roland T., Zahorik, Anthony J., and Keiningham, Timothy L. 1994. *Return on Quality: Measuring the Financial Impact of Your Company's Quest for Quality.* Chicago: Probus.

Schendler, Auden. 2009. *Getting Green Done: Hard Truths from the Front Lines of the Sustainability Revolution.* New York: PublicAffairs.

Stringer, Leah. 2009. *The Green Workplace: Sustainable Strategies that Benefit Employees, the Environment, and the Bottom Line.* New York: Palgrave Macmillan.

Surowieki, James. 2004. *The Wisdom of Crowds: Why the Many Are Smarter than the Few and How Collective Wisdom Shapes Business, Economics, Societies, and Nations.* New York: Doubleday.

Tsai, J. 2010. "Mail Model of the Year." *Customer Relationship Management* 14, no. 4.

Ulrich, Dave, ed. 1998. *Delivering Results.* Boston: Harvard Business School Press.

Walmart. 2010. Walmart 2010 Annual Report. Retrieved from http://cdn.walmart-stores.com/sites/AnnualReport/2010/PDF/01_WMT%202010_Financials.pdf

Walsh, B. May 26, 2008. Going Green: What is a Green Collar Job, Exactly. Time.com Health and Science. http://www.time.com/time/health/article/0,8599,1809506,00.html. Accessed June 28, 2010.

Wargo, J. 2010. LEED Certification: Where Energy Efficiency Collides with Human Health, EHHI Report. North Haven, CT: Environment and Human Health, Inc. http://ehhi.org/reports/leed/LEED_report_0510.pdf. Accessed July 9, 2010.

Werbach, Adam. 2009. *Strategy for Sustainability: A Business Manifesto.* Boston: Harvard Business Press.

Winston, Andrew. 2009. *Green Recovery: Get Lean, Get Smart, and Emerge from the Downturn on Top.* Boston: Harvard Business Press.

Index

A

accountability, 31
  focus on, 34
  investment strategy and,
    63–66
  learning measures in, 131
  metrics and, 7
  sustaining, 47
accounting, 200
accuracy, 152, 188
acquisition costs, 202, 203
action plans, 143, 148–149
activity-based costing (ABC),
    177
activity-based management
    (ABM), 177
airline industry, 55–56
air quality, indoor, 12
alignment
  analysis for, 96–98
  of budgeting processes,
    176–177
  creating, 95–98
  of operations, 176, 177
  payoff determination and,
    98–101
  positioning and, 95–98, 118
  purpose of, 96
  results framework and, 74–76
  ROI Methodology and, 91
American Plastics Company
    (APC), 50–51
American Recovery and
    Reinvestment Act (2009),
    4, 20

analysis
  for alignment, 96–98
  avoidance of, 97–98
  break-even, 212
  of business alignment,
    74–76
  cost, 202
  of intangibles, 196
  of performance needs, 107
  of preference needs,
    109–110
  of reactions, 229–230
  trend-line, 162–164
Anderson, Ray, 5–6
Angelides, Phil, 18, 20
apathy, 24, 25
application, 37, 38
  barriers to, 143
  correlation of with reaction,
    122–123
  coverage areas, 140
  on green scorecard, 235
  measurement issues with,
    139–141
  metrics on, 137–144
  objectives on, 111–112
  reasons for measuring,
    137–139
  in results framework, 71, 72
  ROI Methodology, 90
  use of data on, 143–144
appraisal costs, 182
Aspen Skiing Company, 27
attitude, 186, 194
audiences, 218–219

selecting target, 221,
    222–224
audits, 39, 41
automobiles, 4
avoidance strategy, 50–53
awards, 236
awareness, 24–26, 29–30,
    37–38
  measuring, 132
  in results framework, 71, 72

B

Balanced Scorecard, The
    (Kaplan & Norton), 146
barriers to application, 143,
    251–252
behavior, changing, 20–21,
    26–27
benchmarking
  advantages and
    disadvantages of, 60
  concerns in, 58–59
  customized, 59
  in investing with the rest,
    57–60
  limitations of, 36
  measures in, 57–58
  sources for, 57
benefit-cost ratio (BCR),
    87–88, 204, 205–206
benefits, costs without,
    199–200
best practices, defining, 36, 60.
    See also benchmarking